THE HISTORY AND THEORY OF INTERNATIONAL LAW

Formalizing Displacement

THE HISTORY AND THEORY OF INTERNATIONAL LAW

General Editors

NEHAL BHUTA

Professor of Public International Law, European University Institute

ANTHONY PAGDEN

Distinguished Professor of Political Science and History, UCLA

BENJAMIN STRAUMANN

Alberico Gentili Fellow, New York University School of Law

In the past few decades the understanding of the relationship between nations has undergone a radical transformation. The role of the traditional nation-state is diminishing, along with many of the traditional vocabularies which were once used to describe what has been called, ever since Jeremy Bentham coined the phrase in 1780, 'international law'. The older boundaries between states are growing ever more fluid, new conceptions and new languages have emerged which are slowly coming to replace the image of a world of sovereign independent nation states which has dominated the study of international relations since the early nineteenth century. This redefinition of the international arena demands a new understanding of classical and contemporary questions in international and legal theory. It is the editors' conviction that the best way to achieve this is by bridging the traditional divide between international legal theory, intellectual history, and legal and political history. The aim of the series, therefore, is to provide a forum for historical studies, from classical antiquity to the twenty-first century, that are theoretically-informed and for philosophical work that is historically conscious, in the hope that a new vision of the rapidly evolving international world, its past and its possible future, may emerge.

PREVIOUSLY PUBLISHED IN THIS SERIES

The Project of Positivism in International Law
Mónica García-Salmones Rovira

Formalizing Displacement

International Law and Population Transfers

UMUT ÖZSU

OXFORD
UNIVERSITY PRESS

OXFORD
UNIVERSITY PRESS

Great Clarendon Street, Oxford, OX2 6DP,
United Kingdom

Oxford University Press is a department of the University of Oxford. It furthers the University's objective of excellence in research, scholarship, and education by publishing worldwide. Oxford is a registered trade mark of Oxford University Press in the UK and in certain other countries

First Edition published in 2015

Impression: 1

Published in the United States of America by Oxford University Press
198 Madison Avenue, New York, NY 10016, United States of America

British Library Cataloguing in Publication Data
Data available

Library of Congress Control Number: 2014951281

ISBN 978–0–19–871743–0

Printed and bound by
CPI Group (UK) Ltd, Croydon, CR0 4YY

Series Editors' Preface

In 2014, the legacies of 1914 and the Great War are still with us. As this book goes to press, an insurgent armed group in Iraq has declared its intention to revoke the borders drawn up in light of the 1916 Sykes–Picot agreement, and there is much discussion concerning the partition of not one but two states (Iraq and Syria), the boundaries of which were drawn in the 1920s. The collapse and division of multinational empires after 1918 took a diverse population of language groups, religious communities, and ethnicities, and made them states, nations, or minorities. Europe became a continent of over 30 states, few of them ideal-typical 'nation-states'. As Michael Mann reminded us in *The Dark Side of Democracy* (echoing Hannah Arendt's summary judgment some 50 years earlier), the period from 1918 to 1939 was characterized by unprecedented ethnic cleansing and population transfer, as firm foundations for the new state were (vainly) sought in the homogenization of peoples along ethnic and linguistic lines—a commonality of blood and soil understood as the decisive guarantee of the 'state-ness' of a people, and the viability of their political order.

What was the role of international law in this epoch-making transformation? For much of the twentieth century, the history of international law in the 1920s was deeply coloured by the polemical realist critique against pacifist and legalist proponents of 'peace through law'. The 1920s were understood as a decade of optimism about the possibilities of the management of international order through law and legal institutions, an optimism which proved unfounded because it failed to grasp the nature of politics and the political. On this understanding, the place of international law in such nakedly political processes as state-formation and population transfer could at best be that of impotent moral critic, if indeed it was not altogether irrelevant. The 1920s were characterized by a strong criticism of state sovereignty and power politics, it is true, but as Mark Mazower (*Governing the World*) has shown, this was also a period in which there were multiple, competing visions and practices about the nature of international order and the role of law.

In this densely argued and richly empirical historical study, Dr Umut Özsu both cuts against the grain of any simplistic understanding, and recovers a complex picture of the role of law in the Greek–Turkish population exchanges of 1923, in which over 1.5 million persons were compulsorily uprooted and depatriated as a means of 'solving' the problem of Turkish minorities in Greece, and Greek minorities in Turkey. Özsu reconstructs the history of population exchange in Europe as a policy technique for addressing heterogeneity (perceived as dangerously destabilizing to political order) and building states, and shows that it was understood as an alternative means of minority protection, not incompatible with it. International law and lawyers would play a 'pragmatic and technical' role in the Greek–Turkish exchange, formalizing and legally legitimating the displacement, and in an important sense accepting an instrumental role for law in this human catastrophe in the interest of greater political goals. These goals—international peace and national stability—were thought to be served by the transfer in no small part because of the powerful influence of what Özsu calls 'ethno-nationalism', an assemblage of ideas, theories, and practices which he identifies as central to both the nationalist political project in Atatürk's Turkey *and* the internationalists' diagnosis of the sources of international order (and disorder) in the East. In his careful (and to my knowledge, unprecedented) analysis of the negotiating record of the Treaty of Lausanne, Özsu demonstrates vividly how these considerations underlay the national delegations' articulation of the purposes of the exchange, and the League of Nations' representatives' endorsement of these objectives. The 'unmixing' of populations was grasped as a 'technical' and legally manageable solution to the political problem of the 'true pacification' of the East. Law was believed to be a means for the constitution of order, provided it hewed closely to political reality in order to moderate and humanize it.

This study repays careful reading, and narrates a complex story of the ways in which lineages of law, political thought, national and international political projects, and colonial and imperial histories, converged in the making of the Greek–Turkish population transfer and its legal architecture. It also opens a window on the situation of international legal thought, its diverse currents and influences, at a time when it was a key medium for contending and competing visions of the international.

Nehal Bhuta

Florence
July 2014

Acknowledgments

This book is a revised version of a doctoral dissertation written and defended at the University of Toronto. I thank Jutta Brunnée and Karen Knop for supervising the original dissertation. Karen went to great lengths to finesse my argument, while Jutta pressed me to engage with the question of legal form, a question I eventually came to understand as central to the project. Nehal Bhuta, who also served on my supervisory committee, offered astute suggestions on the dissertation's orientation, and encouraged its subsequent revision for publication. Anne Orford, my external examiner, provided an exceptionally thoughtful reading of the dissertation, and has supported my work in too many ways to count.

I was fortunate to benefit from the advice of a number of outstanding scholars during the course of writing this book. Nathaniel Berman, David Kennedy, Martti Koskenniemi, Erez Manela, and Mark Mazower provided comments on an early version of Chapter 3. For conversation and correspondence at various points, I am also grateful to Antony Anghie, Helmut Aust, Tanıl Bora, B. S. Chimni, David Dyzenhaus, Anver Emon, Bardo Fassbender, Will Hanley, Fleur Johns, Alexandra Kemmerer, Hans-Lukas Kieser, Benedict Kingsbury, Nico Krisch, Dino Kritsiotis, Patrick Macklem, Susan Marks, Lauri Mälksoo, Frédéric Mégret, China Miéville, Liliana Obregón, Anne Peters, Kerry Rittich, and Teemu Ruskola. I owe a particularly strong debt to Thomas Skouteris, whose support has been both spirited and unstinting. I am also happy to thank my three anonymous reviewers, whose observations helped to sharpen the book in a number of key respects.

Book projects often require a significant degree of technical and financial assistance. The present work has been no exception in that regard. Ahmet Yüksel helped to obtain sources in Ankara. Jacques Oberson was of assistance at the League of Nations Archives in Geneva. Gail Mackisey and Elena Yakovchuk at the University of Manitoba's E. K. Williams Law Library were patient and resourceful. John Louth, Merel Alstein, Anthony Hinton, and Emma Endean, all of Oxford University Press, were efficient and encouraging while coordinating the book's production. Finally, I must thank the University of Toronto and the Social Sciences and Humanities Research Council of Canada for facilitating work on the original dissertation, as well as the University of Manitoba for making subsequent research and revision possible.

Weighty as these debts are, this book would not have been possible without the grace and wisdom of Allison Glaser, my wife. I would most likely have given up on the project, and much else besides, had it not been for the elegance with which she persevered through years of research and writing. Aklan, our son, joined us while I was finalizing the book. Among other things, his arrival has allowed me to see many of the issues broached here from a radically different perspective. For her part, Emma, our cocker spaniel, has spent the later years of her life putting up with my work on this and other projects. I hope she finds the final result to be worth the wait. My parents, Nuran and Tamer Özsu, deserve a final acknowledgment for having supported this project from the beginning.

Portions of this book have previously appeared in print. Chapter 3 and parts of the Introduction refine and augment material first published in 'Fabricating Fidelity: Nation-Building, International Law, and the Greek–Turkish Population Exchange', *Leiden Journal of International Law* 24 (2011), 823. Chapter 4 is a revised version of '"A thoroughly bad and vicious solution": Humanitarianism, the World Court, and the Modern Origins of Population Transfer', *London Review of International Law* 1 (2013), 99. I thank Cambridge University Press and Oxford University Press, respectively, for permission to draw upon these articles. Certain passages also owe a debt to 'Ottoman Empire', in *The Oxford Handbook of the History of International Law*, ed. Anne Peters and Bardo Fassbender (Oxford: Oxford University Press, 2012), 429, and to 'Politis and the Limits of Legal Form', *European Journal of International Law* 23 (2012), 243. I thank Oxford University Press for permission to rely upon them here.

Contents

Table of Cases

Table of Treaties and Other Instruments

List of Abbreviations

AIDI	*Annuaire de l'Institut de droit international*
AJIL	*American Journal of International Law*
AJIL Sup.	*American Journal of International Law Supplement*
ASIL Pd.	*American Society of International Law Proceedings*
BFSP	British Foreign and State Papers
BYIL	*British Year Book of International Law*
CTS	The Consolidated Treaty Series
EJIL	*European Journal of International Law*
HILJ	*Harvard International Law Journal*
LNOJ	*League of Nations Official Journal*
LNTS	League of Nations Treaty Series
PCIJ Rep.	Permanent Court of International Justice Reports
RCADI	*Recueil des cours de l'Académie de droit international de La Haye*
RDILC	*Revue de droit international et de législation comparée*
RGDIP	*Revue générale de droit international public*
RIAA	Reports of International Arbitral Awards
TGS	*Transactions of the Grotius Society*
UNTS	United Nations Treaty Series
ZaöRV	*Zeitschrift für ausländisches öffentliches Recht und Völkerrecht*

Note on Translations and Terminology

Readers familiar with the history of the Ottoman Empire and its successor states will be accustomed to large doses of diacritics, as they will to inconsistencies in translation and transliteration from one text to another. In the case of Turkish terms, I have aimed for simplicity by favouring usages common to modern Turkish. Thus, I prefer 'paşa' to the more familiar 'pasha'. I have, however, made exceptions in the case of recognizable place names, where I usually follow English-language practice rather than contemporary or contemporaneous usages in other languages, Greek, Turkish, or otherwise. Hence, I write 'Izmir' rather than 'İzmir' or 'Smyrna'.

In keeping with most legal and diplomatic documents prior to and contemporaneous with the Greek–Turkish population exchange, I have not maintained a strict distinction between 'Turkey' and 'Ottoman Empire' unless discussing matters specific to the Ottoman Empire or the Republic of Turkey, or to the former's succession by the latter. It should be noted, though, that the Ottomans referred to their multilingual and multi-confessional state as 'Turkey' relatively infrequently, and even then mostly in the context of diplomatic exchanges with Western states or when writing for Western audiences during the empire's final decades.

My occasional reliance upon the dated and always problematic term 'Near East' also warrants explanation. The term is both orientalistic, having gained wide currency in late nineteenth-century European literature concerning the 'Eastern Question', and notoriously ambiguous, with a range of application that fluctuates radically from one source to another. Yet, as a key instrument of geopolitical demarcation in the early twentieth century, it captures many of the assumptions held by those involved in or commenting upon the exchange. As a result, I have chosen to retain it in certain contexts, using it in roughly the same sense in which it was generally employed at the time of the Greek–Turkish exchange, namely as a geographical term whose centre of gravity lies in Anatolia and the Balkans.

Unless otherwise indicated, all translations from the French, German, and Turkish are mine.

Introduction

In the autumn of 1922, more than three years after the commencement of the Paris Peace Conference, Fridtjof Nansen left for Istanbul. He went as League of Nations High Commissioner for Refugees, having had his mandate extended to include Greeks fleeing war in Asia Minor. Once in the city, then under Allied occupation, he wrote to Eleftherios Venizelos, until recently prime minister of Greece and still a leading figure in European diplomatic circles, to propose measures for the resettlement of Greek refugees. Among these proposals was an exchange of minority populations between Greece and Turkey, which Nansen described as being 'within the scope of the mission with which the League of Nations' had entrusted him.[1] Venizelos replied swiftly, asking the distinguished Norwegian to speak to Turkish officials with a view to laying the groundwork for a formal exchange.[2]

Reluctant though he initially seems to have been to accept his League appointment,[3] Nansen was a natural choice for the job. A seasoned diplomat, he would receive the Nobel Peace Prize later in 1922 for his efforts to resettle, repatriate, and provide aid to refugees and prisoners of war, whose numbers had grown considerably as a result of the First World War and the ensuing Russian Civil War.[4] As the League's first High Commissioner for Refugees, he seemed the ideal person to design and supervise a population exchange of the sort envisioned by Greek, Turkish, and west European authorities alike. But Nansen left for Istanbul not simply as a decorated representative of the 'international community'. Having achieved fame for his expeditions to the Arctic,[5] conducted research in zoology and oceanography as a natural scientist,[6] made a name for himself as something of

[1] Quoted in Roland Huntford, *Nansen: The Explorer as Hero* (London: Duckworth, 1997), 526.

[2] For the correspondence see Bruce Clark, *Twice a Stranger: The Mass Expulsions That Forged Modern Greece and Turkey* (Cambridge: Harvard University Press, 2006), ch. 2.

[3] See André Durand, *From Sarajevo to Hiroshima: History of the International Committee of the Red Cross* (Geneva: Henry Dunant Institute, 1984), 209.

[4] For his acceptance speech see Fridtjof Nansen, 'The Suffering People of Europe', in *Nobel Lectures: Peace*, ed. Frederick W. Haberman, vol. 1 (Amsterdam: Elsevier, 1972), 361.

[5] See Fridtjof Nansen, *Vers le Pôle*, trans. Charles Rabot (Paris: Ernest Flammarion, 1897); J. Arthur Bain, *Life and Adventures of Nansen, the Great Arctic Explorer* (London: The Walter Scott Publishing Co., 1897). Nansen himself would write a history of earlier expeditions to the North: *In Northern Mists: Arctic Exploration in Early Times*, 2 vols., trans. Arthur G. Chater (London: William Heinemann, 1911).

[6] See, e.g., Fridtjof Nansen, ed., *The Norwegian North Polar Expedition, 1893–1896: Scientific Results*, 6 vols. (Christiania: Jacob Dybwad, 1900–5).

a monarchist in his native Norway,[7] and subsequently embarked upon a political career, first as Norwegian envoy to London and then with the League, he was a polymath with formidable organizational talents. He had used these talents to begin assisting Russian and other refugees. In the process, he had facilitated the creation of a new travel document (the 'Nansen passport') for displaced persons,[8] and also organized the first modern, internationally coordinated repatriation scheme for those fleeing civil conflict.[9] Now he would see to it that the League contributed to the peaceful resolution of the 1919–22 Greek–Turkish War, an exceedingly bloody conflict that had exacerbated tensions between the great powers.[10]

Nansen seems not to have been entirely comfortable with the notion of a population exchange. The coercive mechanisms it was bound to call forth ran counter to his identity as a 'Great Humanitarian' and 'Citizen of Mankind'.[11] Although the causes he deemed worthy of support were not always laudable (he had backed the tsar's attempt to counter the influence of the 'yellow race' in eastern Siberia),[12] he generally preferred the 'soft power' of behind-the-scenes bargaining to the 'hard power' of state-sanctioned force. While cutting his political teeth in Christiania, for instance, he had lauded Norway and Sweden for dissolving their union by way of a plebiscite in words that foreshadowed his later involvement in Greece and Turkey: '[t]he most important event in the history of the two countries' had 'been settled without a single drop of blood having been shed', a possible indication that the world was 'gradually advancing in culture and civilisation'.[13] Ultimately, though, Nansen would end up coordinating much of the exchange between Greece and Turkey. What others denounced as immoral, even illegal, he came to see as necessary for a pragmatic solution to a large-scale crisis. Shuttling between

[7] P. J. Noel Baker, 'Nansen and Norway', in *Nansen: A Book of Homage*, ed. J. Howard Whitehouse (London: Hodder and Stoughton, 1930), 83, at 92–3.

[8] See Arrangement with respect to the Issue of Certificates of Identity to Russian Refugees, signed at Geneva, 5 July 1922, 13 LNTS 237. The Nansen International Office for Refugees, authorized by the League in 1930, would receive the Nobel Peace Prize in 1938 for its role in furthering recognition and usage of this passport.

[9] Martyn Housden, 'White Russians Crossing the Black Sea: Fridtjof Nansen, Constantinople and the First Modern Repatriation of Refugees Displaced by Civil Conflict, 1922–23', *Slavonic and East European Review* 88 (2010), 495.

[10] The literature on Nansen's work on behalf of refugees is vast. See in particular Kathleen E. Innes, *The Story of Nansen and the League of Nations* (London: Friends Peace Committee, 1931); Atle Grahl-Madsen, 'The League of Nations and the Refugees', in *The League of Nations in Retrospect: Proceedings of the Symposium Organized by the United Nations Library and the Graduate Institute of International Studies, Geneva, 6–9 November 1980* (Berlin: Walter de Gruyter, 1983), 358; Michael R. Marrus, *The Unwanted: European Refugees in the Twentieth Century* (Philadelphia: Temple University Press, 1985), ch. 2; Claudena M. Skran, *Refugees in Inter-war Europe: The Emergence of a Regime* (Oxford: Clarendon Press, 1995); Bruno Cabanes, *The Great War and the Origins of Humanitarianism 1918–1924* (Cambridge: Cambridge University Press, 2014), ch. 3.

[11] Henry Goddard Leach, 'Fridtjof Nansen', *University of Kansas City Review* 14 (1948), 167, at 167, 173.

[12] Fridtjof Nansen, *Through Siberia, the Land of the Future*, trans. Arthur G. Chater (London: William Heinemann, 1914), ch. 16.

[13] Fridtjof Nansen, *Norway and the Union with Sweden* (London: Macmillan, 1905), 153.

cities for months prior to and during the 1922–3 Conference of Lausanne, at which a peace settlement with Turkey was concluded, he would immerse himself in nearly every facet of the endeavour, from its initial design through to its final implementation.

Nansen's voyage to Istanbul was both symbolically charged and logistically pivotal. But he was no thaumaturge, and what is of interest in his expedition is not its 'heroism', or even the influence it enabled him to wield over the exchange with his personal charisma and professional competence. Rather, it is the fact that it encapsulated, in a kind of précis, a much broader mission to reconstitute Greece and Turkey in accordance with imperatives of order and progress. From Europe's north-westernmost tip to its south-easternmost extremity, Nansen would go to calculate and taxonomize his way into an 'unmixed' Near East. In his train would follow a barrage of others. Humanitarian organizations like Near East Relief, with deep roots in Anglo-American missionary movements, would be involved in many aspects of the process. A number of Western states, most prominently Britain and the United States, would provide financial and logistical support for the enterprise. And a new international civil service, centred in the League of Nations' Geneva headquarters but with tentacles extending to Paris, London, and elsewhere, would be tasked with overseeing important facets of the operation. These and other agents and institutions worked with authorities in Greece, as well as with a Turkish nationalist elite intent on transforming the state apparatuses it had inherited from its Ottoman predecessor into a fully modern Turkish nation-state. Convinced that such a state would be possible only with a much greater degree of ethno-national homogeneity than Ottoman traditions of pluralism had permitted, most Turkish nationalists supported the population exchange as a means of overcoming their country's economic and political 'backwardness'.

Reconstituting nations and states was nothing new. The Ottoman Empire's dismemberment had been long in the making,[14] and even the notion of treaty-based population transfer was not entirely unknown to pre-First World War international lawyers. Long before he would appear before the World Court in a dispute arising from the Greek–Turkish exchange, a young Nicolas Politis would, for instance, observe that during the 1897 Greek–Turkish War, the Ottomans had ordered the mass expulsion of Greeks, a measure which may have 'fallen into disuse' over the years but which was nevertheless 'lawful on the condition of being exercised humanely'.[15] To be sure, no legally formalized compulsory exchange had ever been undertaken on anything approaching the level envisioned here. But experience had been gained with ostensibly voluntary treaty-based transfers in Anatolia and the Balkans, and resettlement programmes remained ubiquitous, from deportations and land reforms in Russia to the continued expulsion

[14] A 1914 compendium detailed no less than one hundred proposals for partition over the centuries; the 'list of contributors' included an Erasmus or Leibniz for every Metternich or Garibaldi. See T. G. Djuvara, *Cent projets de partage de la Turquie (1281–1913)* (Paris: Librairie Félix Alcan, 1914).

[15] Nicolas Politis, *La guerre gréco–turque au point de vue du droit international: contribution à l'étude de la question d'Orient* (Paris: A. Pedone, 1898), 21.

of indigenous peoples in Africa, the Americas, and elsewhere. Indeed, as noted by Carl Schmitt—who saw Turkey's 'radical expulsion of the Greeks' as evidence that 'actual democracy' demands the 'eradication of heterogeneity'[16]—manipulation of territories and populations in accordance with principles like *cujus regio ejus religio* had distinguished the European land order, and the international legal order it threw up, since at least the Reformation.[17]

Yet here, in Greece and Turkey, in the very heart of what nineteenth-century jurists and statesmen had termed the 'Eastern Question', international lawyers would be pushed to new limits. In 1906, as president of a 'Balkan Committee' convened by the British Parliament, John Westlake had already been exasperated with the situation: 'extreme misgovernment in Turkey is a nuisance to the neighbouring European States', he had written, adding that 'if the Sultan cannot keep order in his own dominions, or if to keep order he has recourse not to civilised means of repression but to massacre, he loses all claim to be regarded as a ruler to whom international law can apply'.[18] By the time the terms of the Greek–Turkish population exchange were concluded in early 1923, it had become obvious that minority protection, as developed by the Concert of Europe during the nineteenth century and refined in the hands of the Allies after 1919, was not going to be enough to stabilize a region widely regarded as 'perhaps the most important of the world's arenas of imperial friction'.[19] A new batch of protective mechanisms would, admittedly, be introduced for minorities. But something else, a 'more radical remedy' to 'minority problems',[20] was necessary if the region was to have lasting peace and prosperity. It was no less clear, however, that this 'more radical remedy' could not take the form of a top-to-bottom reconstitution of whole economies, societies, and legal systems—a reconstitution of the type that had been undertaken in many corners of the colonial world and that also drove much of the League's Mandate System. While politically and economically dependent upon the West, the Ottoman Empire had never been colonized

[16] Carl Schmitt, *The Crisis of Parliamentary Democracy*, trans. Ellen Kennedy (Cambridge: The MIT Press, 1988 [1923]), 9. See also Carl Schmitt, *Constitutional Theory*, ed. and trans. Jeffrey Seitzer (Durham: Duke University Press, 2008 [1928]), 262.

[17] Carl Schmitt, *The* Nomos *of the Earth in the International Law of the* Jus Publicum Europaeum, trans. G. L. Ulmen (New York: Telos, 2003 [1950]), 128. Regardless of his politics, Schmitt's observation was not without basis. From a growing literature see especially David Eltis, ed., *Coerced and Free Migration: Global Perspectives* (Stanford: Stanford University Press, 2002); Emma Christopher, Cassandra Pybus, and Marcus Rediker, eds., *Many Middle Passages: Forced Migration and the Making of the Modern World* (Berkeley: University of California Press, 2007); Richard Bessel and Claudia B. Haake, eds., *Removing Peoples: Forced Removal in the Modern World* (Oxford: Oxford University Press, 2009).

[18] John Westlake, 'The Balkan Question and International Law', *The Nineteenth Century and After* 60 (1906), 889, at 892. See also Arthur G. Symonds, 'The Balkan Committee 1905–1913', in *Memories of John Westlake* (London: Smith, Elder, & Co., 1914), 107, at 110 ff.

[19] Edward Mead Earle, 'The Secret Anglo–German Convention of 1914 Regarding Asiatic Turkey', *Political Science Quarterly* 38 (1923), 24, at 24.

[20] A. A. Pallis, 'The Exchange of Populations in the Balkans', *The Nineteenth Century and After* 97 (1925), 376, at 377.

sensu stricto, and Turkish nationalists would not permit a regime that smacked of out-and-out colonialism.

As a *via media* solution, the legal mechanism of population transfer thus steered a course between two extremes. On the one hand, there was the typical European scenario of piecemeal minority protection in an equilibrated state system ostensibly underwritten by *uti possidetis juris*. On the other hand, there was the standard colonial or neo-colonial case of total renovation, the sort of case exemplified most brutally in the sordid history of the 'Congo Free State'. Something between the two is what occurred after the Great War in Greece and Turkey, long an unstable region on the semi-periphery of the international legal system and now wracked by the dissolution of the Ottoman land order.

I. The Argument's Architecture

The interwar exchange of minorities between Greece and Turkey marked the final stage in the Ottoman Empire's protracted disintegration. At its height in the sixteenth and seventeenth centuries, the empire maintained control over south-east Europe, the Middle East, and North Africa, organizing itself as an Islamic power spearheaded by a sultan-caliph and boasting a multilingual and multi-confessional population. The scope and strength of Ottoman power in Europe began to waver in the late eighteenth and early nineteenth centuries, when successive wars with Russia led to territorial losses and the emergence of proto-nationalist modes of socio-economic mobilization. Of particular importance was the successful liberation struggle waged by Greek insurgents during the 1820s and 1830s, resulting in the creation of an independent Greek kingdom. In 1878, following the Russo–Turkish War of 1877–8, Serbia, Montenegro, and Romania were constituted as independent sovereign states, and Bulgaria was extended recognition as a de facto independent state.[21] This transformed political and economic dynamics in the Balkans, feeding rival nationalist programmes, fuelling the growth of opposing bourgeoisies, and encouraging the persecution and forced emigration of groups that now found themselves in the position of minorities. Among Muslims evicted from their homes in the Balkans, the war and its consequences came to be known as the 'unweaving of 93' ('93 sökümü'), the year 1293 corresponding to 1877 in the Ottoman Rumi calendar.[22] The resulting ethnic and religious tensions frequently facilitated competition between European powers, from Britain and

[21] For the treaty formalizing these arrangements see Treaty between Austria–Hungary, France, Germany, Great Britain, Italy, Russia, and Turkey for the Settlement of Affairs in the East, signed at Berlin, 13 July 1878, 153 CTS 171.

[22] See Kemal H. Karpat, 'The Transformation of the Ottoman State, 1789–1908', *International Journal of Middle East Studies* 3 (1972), 243, at 272. For variations on the theme see Donald Bloxham, 'The Great Unweaving: The Removal of Peoples in Europe, 1875–1949', in *Removing Peoples: Forced Removal in the Modern World*, ed. Richard Bessel and Claudia B. Haake (Oxford: Oxford University Press, 2009), 167.

France in the west to Russia and Austria–Hungary in the east. Far from being limited to the Balkans, such developments were mirrored, albeit initially with less intensity, in other parts of what had by then come to be known as the 'Near East', particularly Anatolia.

Relations between Greece and the Ottoman Empire were particularly prone to volatility during the late nineteenth and early twentieth centuries. Political and commercial elites in the Kingdom of Greece often nursed ambitions of irredentist expansion, espousing the *Megali Idea*, or 'Great Idea', of detaching Istanbul and territories with significant Greek Orthodox populations from Ottoman rule. For their part, Ottoman authorities tended to be wary of Greek designs, and many retained hopes that the empire might eventually re-establish its hold over European territories it had been forced to abandon. Although stable relations were generally maintained, a series of local skirmishes in Crete led to full-scale war between the two states in 1897, a conflict from which the Ottomans emerged militarily victorious but diplomatically hobbled (Ottoman troops managed to defeat Greek forces in Thessaly and Epirus but were forced to grant autonomy to Crete itself). The 1912–13 Balkan Wars sounded the death knell to all notions of Greek–Ottoman rapprochement. The Ottomans were roundly defeated in the First Balkan War, a conflict that reshaped the map of south-east Europe, but managed to recover some of their losses during the Second Balkan War.

Led by the Young Turks, a political movement that initially espoused constitutional pluralism but that subsequently came to embrace military authoritarianism, the Ottoman Empire suffered an even more catastrophic defeat in the First World War, which it entered in late 1914 on the side of Germany. Mass migrations marked the war, frequently, as in the Armenian genocide, in the form of organized, state-sponsored displacement. At the 1919 Paris Peace Conference, much of what remained of the empire was partitioned between the European powers, with the Treaty of Sèvres, signed by the Allied Powers and a debilitated Ottoman government in August 1920, formalizing these and related arrangements.[23] But conditions on the ground were by that point already in the process of changing significantly. Having occupied the key port of Izmir, Greek troops were preparing for conflict with Turkish nationalist forces under the command of Mustafa Kemal, a former officer who had broken with the Ottoman government. Kemal's movement rejected the Sèvres settlement, consolidated itself in the Anatolian hinterland, and ultimately defeated the Greek army in a lengthy war that saw countless atrocities committed on both sides. With Turkish forces sweeping westward, and entering Izmir in September 1922, hundreds of thousands of Greeks took flight or were expelled, giving rise to an enormous economic, humanitarian, and security-related crisis. It was largely in response to this crisis, the last in a long series of mass displacements spawned by the Ottoman Empire's incremental disintegration, that the compulsory population exchange between Greece and

[23] For the text see Treaty of Peace between the Allied Powers and Turkey, signed at Sèvres, 10 August 1920, *AJIL Sup.* 15 (1921), 179.

Turkey was undertaken. Expelling Muslims from Macedonia, western Thrace, and other regions in Greece would have the effect of 'clearing space' for the settlement of Greeks who had recently been expelled from Turkey. Likewise, removing remaining Greeks from Asia Minor and eastern Thrace would allow the 'new Turkey' to strengthen its claim to national statehood. Most important of all, the enterprise would, it was thought, stabilize a region that had not known stability for some time.

The aim of this book is to demonstrate that the Greek–Turkish population exchange was the principal galvanizing force behind the cultivation of a distinct mode of legally formalized nation-building in the early twentieth century.[24] As the first legally structured compulsory endeavour of its scale and sophistication, the sheer ambition of the exchange was staggering: over 1 million Greeks (or those identified as such) were uprooted from Asia Minor and eastern Thrace immediately before and during the formal exchange, which began in 1923 and continued for years to come, and something in the vicinity of 350,000 Muslims (or those so classified) were expelled from Greece's mainland and islands over the same stretch of time. The formal exchange concluded at Lausanne in January 1923 followed the expulsion of large numbers of Greeks and others from Asia Minor and eastern Thrace in 1922, particularly after the partial destruction of Izmir, and has therefore sometimes been presented as an endorsement of an already existing reality. This ignores the fact that the formal exchange called for a variety of fresh movements (nearly all 350,000 Muslims and roughly 200,000 of the concerned Greeks). It also misses the crucial point that the formal procedure lent legal legitimacy to a set of movements that redistributed land and capital across enormous swathes of territory, establishing a comprehensive legal regime to manage relief, resettlement, and indemnification efforts. More than two months of tough negotiations were needed before Turkey and the Allied Powers were able to agree on the terms of the exchange, and all parties invested heavily in the talks. This was an exercise both in producing new facts on the ground and in *juridifying* the dispossession, displacement, and capital accumulation that had already taken place.[25]

[24] Although often conflated, the terms 'nation-building' and 'state-building' are conceptually distinct, with the former typically referring to efforts to craft new identities for a given 'people' and the latter ordinarily involving the foundation or re-foundation of state institutions, sometimes by way of external imposition. I prefer 'nation-building' in this book, but employ it expansively on account of the context at hand. This was a context in which Westernization-cum-modernization did not lend itself to cut-and-dry distinctions: the task of modifying the powerful state traditions bequeathed to Greece and Turkey was generally regarded as inseparable from the project of manufacturing new forms of national consciousness.

[25] There has been a resurgence of interest in recent years in the exchange among social and political historians. See especially Renée Hirschon, ed., *Crossing the Aegean: An Appraisal of the 1923 Compulsory Population Exchange between Greece and Turkey* (New York: Berghahn, 2003); Müfide Pekin, ed., *Yeniden Kurulan Yaşamlar: 1923 Türk–Yunan Zorunlu Nüfus Mübadelesi* (İstanbul: İstanbul Bilgi Üniversitesi Yayınları, 2005); Onur Yıldırım, *Diplomacy and Displacement: Reconsidering the Turco–Greek Exchange of Populations, 1922–1934* (New York: Routledge, 2006). A good bibliography of the literature until 2002 can be found in Müfide Pekin and Çimen Turan, eds., *Mübadele Bibliyografyası: Lozan Nüfus Mübadelesi İle İlgili Yayınlar ve Yayımlanmamış Çalışmalar* (İstanbul: Lozan Mübadilleri Vakfı, 2002). Notwithstanding the enormous value of this literature, discussion of the legal dimensions of the population exchange formalized at Lausanne is exceedingly

The exchange showcased the new pragmatism of the post-First World War international order, an increased willingness on the part of lawyers and politicians alike to adapt legal doctrine to local conditions, bringing greater, more sophisticated institutional resources to bear on crafting functionally suitable solutions to pressing problems.[26] The chief aim here was not to organize plebiscites or install protective mechanisms for under-resourced or under-represented minorities—both important aspects of the Allies' management of imperial disintegration in Europe after 1919. Nor was it to restructure all facets of a given economy and society in order to generate an entirely new legal system; this had often been the case with colonialism in Asia and Africa, and would characterize a good deal of the League's system of mandates. Instead, the aim of the Greek–Turkish exchange was to reshape the demographic composition of the two states in question, aligning *ethnos* with *demos* as tightly as possible with the help of a mechanism that was tailored to the region at hand. If Greece and Turkey were to be refashioned by way of a compulsory exchange, a mechanism whose status under international law was imprecise but with which many lawyers were nevertheless willing to work, this was due in no small part to the semi-peripheral character of Greece and Turkey, which both permitted and demanded reliance on a distinct procedure.

In developing this argument, I focus upon Ottoman and post-Ottoman Turkey to a greater degree than Greece, as it was through European engagement with the former that practices and doctrines of minority protection and population transfer (and also humanitarian intervention) were developed with greatest vigour. My argument proceeds in four stages. First, I provide a history of the international law of minority protection. The nation-building project the Greek–Turkish exchange facilitated was carried out against the background of a tradition of minority protection fostered by the nineteenth-century Concert of Europe system and furthered by twentieth-century experiences with League-sponsored minority governance. I trace this law's development from its classical origins in the 1814–15 Congress of Vienna, through the balance-of-power treaties concluded during the remainder of the nineteenth century, and finally to the minority-protection mechanisms introduced into a number of newly created or reconfigured states, Turkey included, after the First World War. Nineteenth-century intra-European treaties created minorities where they were not recognized legally, and crafted fresh entitlements for minorities where they already enjoyed formal recognition. Minority treaties backed by the Allied Powers after the Great War were driven by a broadly similar commitment to manage nationalism, but were designed under different conditions and with more in the way of institutional support to reinforce

rare. One overview can be found in Michael Barutciski, 'Les transferts de populations quatre-vingts ans après la Convention de Lausanne', *Canadian Yearbook of International Law* 41 (2003), 271. An analysis of Lausanne from the standpoint of self-determination is provided in Catriona J. Drew, 'Population Transfer: The Untold Story of the International Law of Self-Determination' (PhD dissertation, University of London, 2005), 93–110.

[26] On this see David Kennedy, 'The Move to Institutions', *Cardozo Law Review* 8 (1987), 841. See further Thomas Skouteris, *The Notion of Progress in International Law Discourse* (The Hague: T. M. C. Asser Press, 2010), chs. 2, 3.

their efforts. Post-Ottoman Greece and Turkey posed serious challenges here, in that neither a minority treaty nor a set of minority-protection provisions inserted into a peace treaty were believed to be enough to ensure stability. Ultimately, the minority-protection regime that was introduced into Turkey via the post-war settlement was not only weak (its application was limited to relatively small numbers of remaining non-Muslims and the rights it enshrined were less forceful than was the case elsewhere), but also conditioned upon a compulsory population exchange between Greece and Turkey. If much of what motivated minority protection, from the early nineteenth to the early twentieth century, was a desire to regulate nationalism on Europe's eastern margins, the exchange was the culmination of this commitment in a context that had come to be deemed too volatile for conventional minority-protection instruments alone.

Second, I offer a discussion of the Greek–Turkish exchange's immediate antecedents. The exchange is sometimes presented as a wholly *sui generis* development, an utterly anomalous phenomenon with no forerunners. But this is neither accurate from a descriptive standpoint nor adequate from an explanatory one. In truth, the exchange demands extensive contextualization, the specific socio-historical milieu in which it was conceived and executed having roots in a number of earlier experiments in the Balkans and Asia Minor. Forced migrations in the final decades of the nineteenth and first decades of the twentieth century had increased tensions between the Ottoman Empire's constituent ethno-confessional groups, fuelling bitterness and secessionism within non-Muslim communities and mobilizing ever larger numbers of Turkish-Muslim officers, bureaucrats, and intellectuals around the notion of a centralized, ethnically Turkish state. 'Voluntary' transfers were arranged between a variety of Muslim and Christian communities in the Balkans and Asia Minor during the 1910s in order to cope with war-related displacements or facilitate fresh movements with a view to ensuring national and regional 'security'. In the process, these transfers spurred the growth of a distinct body of international treaty law. By examining the legal and political background of the 1922–34 Greek–Turkish exchange, the first strictly compulsory endeavour of its kind, one gains an understanding of its foundations in late Ottoman governmental practice and also of its relation to a corpus of treaty law whose specific aim was to sanction and engineer large-scale population movements.

Third, I consider the text and *travaux préparatoires* of the convention by which the exchange was governed—a convention annexed to the Lausanne Peace Treaty as a key element of the package of international legal instruments that comprised the general peace settlement between Turkey and the Allied Powers in 1923.[27] Reading statements by delegates at the Conference of Lausanne,[28] I explain the

[27] For the text of the exchange convention, see Convention concerning the Exchange of Greek and Turkish Populations, and Protocol, signed at Lausanne, 30 January 1923, 32 LNTS 75. For that of the peace treaty, see Treaty of Peace, signed at Lausanne, 24 July 1923, 28 LNTS 11. For the entire package (itself often referred to simply as the 'Treaty of Lausanne'), see Treaty with Turkey and Other Instruments, signed at Lausanne, 24 July 1923, *AJIL Sup.* 18 (1924), 1.

[28] For the minutes in English see *Lausanne Conference on Near Eastern Affairs (1922–1923): Records of Proceedings and Draft Terms of Peace* (Cmd 1814) (London: His Majesty's Stationery Office,

convention's role in shaping the juridico-political architecture of post-Ottoman Turkey. As I demonstrate, nearly everyone at the negotiating table agreed that the exchange would need to be undertaken with the aid of 'technical' legal instruments. This, however, did not prevent such negotiators from drawing upon—and thereby legitimizing—the very ethno-nationalism they sought to elide through reliance upon legal 'technique'. Crucially, this strained engagement with ethno-nationalism found powerful expression in the question of how the exchange would bear upon the status of those non-Muslims who would remain in Turkey. The Mandate System, administratively indistinguishable in many cases from outright colonialism,[29] was often believed to be incompatible with conditions in Turkey. And the minority-protection instruments that had become popular in central and eastern Europe after the First World War were generally thought to be insufficient to ensure order. Recourse was thus had to the compulsory exchange, a mechanism which would keep the risk of majority–minority conflicts to an absolute minimum and whose roots in the Near East, with its own set of embedded legal and political practices, were known to most delegates at Lausanne.

Finally, I provide a contextual discussion of the Permanent Court of International Justice's 1925 advisory opinion in *Exchange of Greek and Turkish Populations*.[30] I first discuss the humanitarian background to the dispute that generated this opinion, examining the various relief organizations involved in resettlement and reconstruction initiatives immediately prior to and during the course of the formal exchange. Many such organizations boasted strong ties to missionary groups that had been active on Ottoman soil for some time; they employed analogous techniques, drew much of their membership from such groups, and, perhaps most revealingly, were frequently viewed by local actors as motivated by the same type of civilizing mission. From there I move on to the World Court's opinion, analysing the way in which it broached the question of Istanbul's *établis*, residents of the city exempted from the exchange on account of their status as Greeks. The Court's attempt to draw a sharp distinction between domestic and international law by maximizing the treaty-based rights of Istanbul's Greeks cannot, I argue, be understood without an appreciation of the broader context within which the dispute regarding their status came to the fore, particularly the widely felt desire to protect remaining minority communities by channelling assertions of sovereign right into a multilaterally coordinated programme of nation- and state-formation. As with the humanitarians of the League of Nations

1923). For the French, the language employed by most delegates, see *Conférence de Lausanne sur les affaires du Proche-Orient (1922–1923). Recueil des Actes de la Conférence*, 6 vols. (Paris: Imprimerie nationale, 1923).

[29] Susan Pedersen, 'The Meaning of the Mandates System: An Argument', *Geschichte und Gesellschaft* 32 (2006), 560, at 567 ff. See also Antony Anghie, *Imperialism, Sovereignty and the Making of International Law* (Cambridge: Cambridge University Press, 2005), ch. 3; Carsten Stahn, *The Law and Practice of International Territorial Administration: Versailles to Iraq and Beyond* (Cambridge: Cambridge University Press, 2008), ch. 2.

[30] *Exchange of Greek and Turkish Populations (Lausanne Convention VI, January 30th, 1923, Article 2)*, Advisory Opinion, PCIJ Rep. Series B No 10 (1925).

and organizations like Near East Relief, the World Court sought to ensure that the exchange procedure was managed internationally rather than nationally, supporting a new inter-state order formalized by treaty law rather than simply feeding an unruly and violent ethno-nationalism.

Considered as a totality, then, this book examines the Greek–Turkish population exchange as the context within which a unique mode of nation-building began to gain widespread legal currency. Notably, the legal status of population transfer, both of the explicitly compulsory and of the nominally voluntary kind,[31] was anything but settled at the time of the exchange. The Hague Conventions of 1899 and 1907 had made no mention of forcible displacement as such. In fact, with the exception of Article 23 of the 1863 Lieber Code, which contained a vague prohibition on the 'carr[ying] off to distant parts' of '[p]rivate citizens',[32] it would not be until after the Second World War that international legal instruments containing express or implied prohibitions of population transfer, such as the Genocide Convention and the Fourth Geneva Convention,[33] would begin to appear. Still, most interwar jurists were sceptical of its legality. Robert Redslob, for instance, branded transfer a political, not a legal, solution to the 'problem of nationalities', useful perhaps as a means of fostering 'national unity' but running counter to the kind of minority protection found 'in every peace treaty by virtue of customary law'.[34] Others noted that the population-transfer mechanism departed from established European techniques like the 'right of option'—the right, that is, of people inhabiting territories transferred from one sovereign to another to choose between retaining their existing nationalities (in which case they would be expected to move) and becoming nationals of the new sovereign (in which case they would remain where they were).[35] The 'brutal measure of expulsion and forced emigration' flouted such techniques, they argued, falling foul of the 'basic principles that are the foundation of the public law of civilized nations'.[36] A product mainly of Turkey's desire to liquidate its minorities 'completely and

[31] The distinction between 'compulsory' and 'voluntary' population transfers is important to understanding the revolutionary features of the Greek–Turkish exchange. However, in practice, nearly all 'voluntary' transfers have been accompanied by systematic intimidation and persecution. Pervasive reliance upon such coercive force renders the distinction between 'compulsory' and 'voluntary' transfers effectively problematic. As a result, while this book does not jettison the distinction, it also takes steps not to fetishize it.

[32] *Instructions for the Government of Armies of the United States, in the Field. Prepared by Francis Lieber, LL.D., and Revised by a Board of Officers* (New York: D. Van Nostrand, 1863), 8. Lincoln promulgated the code in the form of General Order No 100 on 24 April 1863.

[33] Convention on the Prevention and Punishment of the Crime of Genocide, 9 December 1948, 78 UNTS 277, Art 2, at 280; Geneva Convention relative to the Protection of Civilian Persons in Time of War, 12 August 1949, 75 UNTS 287, Arts 49, 147, at 318, 388.

[34] Robert Redslob, *Le principe des nationalités: les origines, les fondements psychologiques, les forces adverses, les solutions possibles* (Paris: Recueil Sirey, 1930), 166, 168.

[35] Josef L. Kunz, 'L'option de nationalité', *RCADI* 31 (1930-I), 107, at 134.

[36] Alexandre Devedji, *L'échange obligatoire des minorités grecques et turques en vertu de la convention de Lausanne du 30 janvier 1923* (Paris: Imprimerie du Montparnasse et de Persan-Beaumont, 1929), 84, 83–7 generally.

radically',[37] the exchange was 'an unfortunate regression in the evolution of the law of nations',[38] holding back its 'diplomatic, doctrinal and jurisprudential' development.[39] Some jurists differed in their assessment, though, and were willing to consider even overtly compulsory exchanges as minimally legal, though not necessarily deserving of moral or political praise. While Lausanne did not comply with prevailing principles of minority protection, one jurist admitted, it did offer an 'entirely different approach' to resolving conflict through law.[40] The 1922–34 Greek–Turkish exchange may have threatened to restore 'the wild and primitive conception of war', wrote another, but it had also been enshrined in 'a solemnly signed and legally ratified treaty'.[41] After all, the same author continued, while it might be the case that 'positive international law, in permitting compulsory exchange, was once again the slave of force', it could not be denied that positive international law did in fact grant such permission.[42] Indeed, no less an authority than the Permanent Court stated that the Greek–Turkish exchange was governed by a binding international treaty and that the interpretational dispute with which it was confronted 'involve[d] a question of international law'; the question of the treaty's legality, or even legitimacy, was simply not on the table.[43] Such views often exerted considerable influence over policymakers. British authorities in mandate-era Palestine were so impressed by the Greek–Turkish endeavour that they too would entertain an exchange. Whereas formerly 'the Greek and Turkish minorities had been a constant irritant', the Peel Commission's report declared, 'the ulcer ha[d] been clean cut out', placing relations between the two states on much firmer footing.[44]

Statements of the latter variety were hardly groundless. The instrument that regulated the Greek–Turkish exchange procedure was negotiated and drafted in the form of a treaty, deposited with the relevant authorities, registered with the League of Nations, published in its official compendium of treaties, entered into force with the requisite ratifications, and, most telling of all, accepted and understood by concerned parties, third states, and the World Court as a specifically legal document generating specifically legal obligations. To dismiss it as 'illegal' (or, perhaps, 'extra-legal') under such circumstances would be to fall prey to a naïve and ahistorical idealism, eliding the fact that international law and its various precursors (*jus gentium, droit des gens, droit public de l'Europe*, and so on) have

[37] M. F. de Jessen, 'Grèce et Turquie—protection des minorités—échange obligatoire des populations turques et grecques', *RGDIP* 30 (1923), 514, at 515.

[38] C. G. Ténékidès, 'Le statut des minorités et l'échange obligatoire des populations gréco–turques', *RGDIP* 31 (1924), 72, at 86.

[39] Stelio Séfériadès, 'L'échange des populations', *RCADI* 24 (1928-IV), 307, at 331.

[40] Leonidas Leontiades, 'Der griechisch–türkische Bevölkerungsaustausch', *ZaöRV* 5 (1935), 546, at 552.

[41] Th. P. Kiosséoglou, *L'échange forcé des minorités d'après le Traité de Lausanne* (Nancy: Imprimerie nancéienne, 1926), 100, 146.

[42] Kiosséoglou, *L'échange forcé* (n 41), 105.

[43] *Exchange* (n 30), 17.

[44] Palestine Royal Commission, *Report* (Cmd 5479) (London: His Majesty's Stationery Office, 1937), 390.

always been intrinsic to the exercise of state power, not least in the context of inter-state conflict.

During and after the Second World War, when, ironically, population transfer became a staple of statecraft, international lawyers like J. L. Brierly could be found arguing that '[l]aw never creates order', and that 'the most it can do is to help to sustain order when that has once been firmly established'.[45] Interwar jurists, however, were typically willing to attribute a significant degree of constitutive power to international law. Its rules and principles were not simply second-order reflections of existing states of affairs, but resilient, productive forces in their own right, equipped to recast whole regions if necessary. When backed up by treaty, shuffling whole communities from one place to another, by consent or by coercion, displayed and reinforced this constitutive power. Whether the formal exchange was understood to flout or conform to prevailing international legal norms, that it flowed in large part from a multilateral treaty intended to channel and constrain ethno-nationalism through regionally specific means was widely appreciated.

II. Distinguishing the Problem

That the Greek–Turkish exchange is the *locus classicus* of a distinct form of legal nation-building has a number of doctrinal and methodological implications. The first such implication stems from my concern with ethno-nationalism, the second pertains to the international law of self-determination, and the third relates to the multiple legal sources of Turkey's nation-building project and the regionally specific character of the population-exchange mechanism. In different but broadly analogous ways, all three involve issues arising from Turkey's experience as a former imperial power situated on the margins of Europe—a state with a strained, but uniquely non-colonial, relationship with the international law generated by Europe over the preceding centuries.

To begin with, many scholars of the Ottoman and post-Ottoman Balkans have taken issue with the tendency to associate the region with an exceptionally virulent strain of illiberal, chauvinistic nationalism. It has been argued that ethno-nationalism's popular affiliation with the Balkans is ideologically dubious, and that the conceptual distinction between 'civic' and 'ethnic' nationalism is far from clear, since even the most moderate forms of 'civic' nationalism tend ultimately to be premised upon a measure of racial or linguistic exclusion.[46] Reinforcing such concerns is the fact that nationalism, however understood, was a relative latecomer to the Ottoman Empire, and that, when it finally did arrive

[45] J. L. Brierly, *The Outlook for International Law* (Oxford: Clarendon Press, 1944), 74.

[46] See especially Maria Todorova, *Imagining the Balkans* (New York: Oxford University Press, 1997); and Isa Blumi, *Reinstating the Ottomans: Alternative Balkan Modernities, 1800–1912* (New York: Palgrave Macmillan, 2011).

on the scene, it generally found expression in a complex amalgam of ethnic, territorial, and confessional claims.

While understandable, such misgivings can be exaggerated to such a degree that they undermine the possibility of a form of nationalism that prioritizes ethnicity as the principal modality of socio-economic identification. This book is driven by a concern with the processes through which population transfer arose on Europe's south-eastern fringes as a legal instrument for managing preponderantly ethno-national forms of mobilization. But it makes no claim that 'ethnic' nationalism, whether explicitly racialized or grounded in Herderian notions of cultural and linguistic affinity, is uncontroversially distinguishable from 'civic' nationalism, generally identified with voluntary association with a particular polity. Nor, of course, does it assume that ethno-nationalism is, for some mysterious and indiscernible reason, a product solely of specifically Balkan experiences. Effecting large-scale population transfer through international treaty law may have had its origins in Anatolia and the Balkans, but ethno-nationalism itself was certainly not restricted to this region.

A second issue concerns self-determination. At first glance, self-determination may strike one as a promising lens for analysing legally coordinated population movements undertaken in the wake of the Great War. It cannot, after all, be denied that various conceptions of self-determination figured in negotiations surrounding the creation and dissolution of states after 1919, and even less that a diffuse fascination with the even hazier nineteenth-century 'principle of nationalities' continued to circulate at the time. This book is not, however, concerned with the international law of self-determination per se. To begin with, though it may have been ubiquitous as a political slogan, no single vision of self-determination had secured enough support to warrant characterization as an international legal norm by the time of the Greek–Turkish exchange. Ethnicity and other categories were used as criteria for redrawing borders and restructuring domestic arrangements, not to mention manufacturing new states, but self-determination itself—for many a 'catch-word' for 'muddled thinking'[47]—did not then belong to general international law.[48] Equally important is the fact that Turkish nationalists tended to be suspicious of the rhetoric of self-determination. With promises of an independent Armenia and Kurdistan still fresh in their minds, such nationalists had little intention of allowing self-determination to dominate the agenda in Lausanne.

[47] Noel Buxton and T. P. Conwil-Evans, *Oppressed Peoples and the League of Nations* (London: J. M. Dent & Sons, 1922), 27.

[48] The most famous illustration of this is offered by the 'Report of the International Committee of Jurists Entrusted by the Council of the League of Nations with the Task of Giving an Advisory Opinion upon the Legal Aspects of the Aaland Islands Question', *LNOJ* Spec. Sup. No 3 (1920), 3 (maintaining (at 5) that 'Positive International Law does not recognise the right of national groups, as such, to separate themselves from the State of which they form part by the simple expression of a wish, any more than it recognises the right of other States to claim such a separation'). See further Antonio Cassese, *Self-Determination of Peoples: A Legal Reappraisal* (Cambridge: Cambridge University Press, 1995), 27, 33; Karen Knop, *Diversity and Self-Determination in International Law* (Cambridge: Cambridge University Press, 2002), 63.

They preferred to speak of sovereignty and independence, and when they did draw upon self-determination, they typically relied upon a variant that veered somewhat closer to Lenin's Petrograd than Wilson's Washington.[49] And this, of course, was not without basis: 'As for the Turks', noted a historian and diplomat with experience in the Ottoman Empire, 'the world is little disposed to allow self-determination to peoples of the Moslem faith'.[50]

What is most distinctive about the population-exchange mechanism, as first developed in the Balkans and Asia Minor during the 1910s and 1920s, is not the fact that it showed up the less savoury features of self-determination.[51] Rather, it is the fact that it marked a departure both from the practice of introducing protective instruments for minorities—common in Europe throughout the long nineteenth century and augmented considerably after 1919—and from the practice of reconstructing entire economies and societies from scratch—the typical case of colonial and neo-colonial administration in Asia and Africa. Legally formalized population transfer was not called forth by the international law (or even political slogan) of self-determination so much as the commitment to craft functional solutions to challenging conflicts in a context framed neither as strictly European nor as strictly non-European.

A third and closely related point flows directly from this distinctiveness. Western legal traditions, both municipal and international, had exerted considerable influence over the Ottoman Empire for some time. In some respects, this had been driven by diplomacy, as with France both before and after 1789 (e.g. long-standing alliances reaching back as far as the sixteenth century, the enormous prestige bestowed upon the Code Napoléon in the nineteenth century). In others, it had run deeper, penetrating the Ottoman Empire's politico-economic core (e.g. a far-reaching regime of capitulatory privileges, and, in the late nineteenth century, control of the public debt by a consortium of European creditors). By the mid-nineteenth century, such engagement with the West had come to be intimately bound up with relations of dependence and debt-accumulation not unlike those in operation throughout the colonial world. Indeed, by the first decades of the twentieth century, even the most penetrating scholars of imperialism could be found suggesting as much: just as Hobson warned in 1902 that most of the remaining Turkish dominions would succumb to 'a slow, precarious process of absorption'[52] (the 'absorption', when it finally came, proved neither slow

[49] It was the Bolsheviks who insisted most forcefully on self-determination, investing it with the status of a revolutionary call to arms. Wilson appears to have adopted a highly attenuated form of this position only after it became clear that demands for representative government were being interpreted in stronger terms by subject nationalities. Thomas D. Musgrave, *Self-Determination and National Minorities* (Oxford: Oxford University Press, 1997), 23–4. For a classic reconstruction of the rivalry see Arno J. Mayer, *Wilson vs. Lenin: Political Origins of the New Diplomacy, 1917–1918* (Cleveland: World Publishing Co., 1964). For a reappraisal of Wilson's reception in the extra-European world, see Erez Manela, *The Wilsonian Moment: Self-Determination and the International Origins of Anticolonial Nationalism* (New York: Oxford University Press, 2007).

[50] Albert H. Lybyer, 'The Balkan Situation', *Journal of International Relations* 10 (1920), 404, at 405.

[51] As argued in the otherwise insightful analysis offered in Drew, 'Population Transfer' (n 25).

[52] J. A. Hobson, *Imperialism: A Study* (London: James Nisbet & Co., 1902), 236.

nor precarious), so too would Lenin, strategizing laterally in 1917, group Turkey with Persia and China in a class of 'semi-colonial countries'.[53] Nevertheless, this centuries-long encounter with the West—coming to the fore explicitly with the French-inspired Tanzimat reforms of the mid-nineteenth century and arguably reaching its zenith with the proclamation of a republic in 1923—involved the incremental marginalization of an otherwise powerful and predominantly patrimonial state, often through policies of its own devising, not colonialism in the sense of direct legal annexation or administration. If it is true that, in the nineteenth century, Ottoman Turkey was sometimes cast as the 'sick man of Europe', it is no less true that, even at this late stage, it made a point of styling itself the Islamic world's 'eternal state' (*devlet-i ebed-müddet*), or what one delegate at the Conference of Lausanne termed 'a great Islamic Power'.[54] It may never have been recognized as a fully fledged member of the 'family of civilized nations', at least not definitively, but late nineteenth-century jurists frequently felt a need to postulate an intermediate class for states of the type it was deemed to exemplify, thereby distinguishing them from 'savage' regions and *terrae nullius*.[55] Indeed, the influential classification of 'civilized', 'barbarous', and 'savage' humanity offered by James Lorimer—with Turkey as the archetypal illustration of the 'barbarous' (or 'semi-civilized') state—was intended to convey precisely this precariousness.[56] Just as the new social sciences tended to segregate the study of 'savage' populations (the principal sphere of the young discipline of anthropology) from that of non-European 'civilizations' (the core of most orientalist scholarship),[57] so too did the period's international legal scholarship taxonomize the rules and principles to be applied to different states and regions, marked as it was by a desire to fashion a

[53] V. I. Lenin, 'Imperialism, the Highest Stage of Capitalism' [1917], in V. I. Lenin, *Collected Works*, vol. 22, trans. Yuri Sdobnikov (Moscow: Progress Publishers, 1964), 185, at 257–60.

[54] Minutes of the Territorial and Military Commission's meeting on 10 January 1923, in *Lausanne Conference* (n 28), 321.

[55] Indeed, on the occasion of the Institut de droit international's consideration of the question of the '[a]pplication of the customary law of nations of Europe to Oriental nations', Travers Twiss, its vice-president, argued that '[t]he inhabitants of the Ottoman Empire, the Persians, the Chinese, [and] the Japanese must be distinguished from pagan and semi-savage peoples'. Travers Twiss, 'Rapport', *AIDI* 3–4 (1879–80), 301, at 301.

[56] James Lorimer, *The Institutes of the Law of Nations: A Treatise of the Jural Relations of Separate Political Communities*, vol. 1 (Edinburgh: William Blackwood & Sons, 1883), 101–3, also 239, 444. For the ideational context within which this (now infamous) vision of world order was elaborated, see Duncan Bell and Casper Sylvest, 'International Society in Victorian Political Thought: T. H. Green, Herbert Spencer, and Henry Sidgwick', *Modern Intellectual History* 3 (2006), 207, esp. at 231–7; Jennifer Pitts, 'Boundaries of Victorian International Law', in *Victorian Visions of Global Order: Empire and International Relations in Nineteenth-Century Political Thought*, ed. Duncan Bell (Cambridge: Cambridge University Press, 2007), 67. Lorimer may have been the most influential anglophone exponent of such views, but he was hardly the only jurist to hold them; for a pointed continental correlative see Franz von Liszt, *Das Völkerrecht, systematisch dargestellt* (Berlin: Verlag von O. Haering, 1898), 1–4 (distinguishing between *Kulturstaaten, halbcivilisierten Staaten*, and *nichtcivilisierten Staaten*).

[57] On this see Immanuel Wallerstein, *The Modern World-System IV: Centrist Liberalism Triumphant, 1789–1914* (Berkeley: University of California Press, 2011), 264–73.

workable 'standard' for grading and assessing competing claims to 'civilizational' status.[58]

Because of this distinctiveness, this book does not attempt to identify one or two Western 'parents' for Turkey's legal reconstitution through the population exchange, a key element of much post-colonial scholarship. Nor does it try to assimilate the Turkish case to a familiar narrative of nineteenth- and early twentieth-century attempts to craft responses to the European 'problem of nationalities'. Instead, it examines the processes through which shifting relations of power between a variety of actors and institutions facilitated Turkey's transition from empire to nation-state by way of the exchange. This calls for parsimonious engagement with existing scholarship. Inasmuch as my central task is that of capturing what was distinctive about the population exchange, scholarship geared toward state-building and international administration in what during the Cold War was termed the 'Third World' cannot serve as a basis for direct, one-to-one comparison. Similarly, since this book is not confined to examining the Greek–Turkish exchange in light of the international law that was developed in and for Europe in response to the 'problem of nationalities', it resists absorption into those bodies of international legal scholarship that foreground purely European modes of constituting order. Nathaniel Berman has examined the cultural roots and ramifications of early twentieth-century European and American jurists' ambivalence in regard to nationalism, suggesting that, when all is said and done, population transfer was a 'relatively marginal solution' to nationalist rivalry during the interwar period.[59] A central aim of this book is to explain why population transfer was indeed as marginal as it was—why, that is, it was legally sanctioned population transfer, and not some other mechanism, that had its provenance in Anatolia and the Balkans, why it came to be applied extensively in this region during the 1910s and 1920s, and what, if anything, this reveals about international law more generally.

III. Analysing an International Legal Field

This study marshalls a range of legal as well as historical and sociological material, notably from world-systems theory.[60] However, its methodological parameters

[58] The lengthiest discussion remains Gerrit W. Gong, *The Standard of 'Civilization' in International Society* (Oxford: Clarendon Press, 1984). See further Georg Schwarzenberger, 'The Standard of Civilisation in International Law', *Current Legal Problems* 8 (1955), 212; Martti Koskenniemi, *The Gentle Civilizer of Nations: The Rise and Fall of International Law 1870–1960* (Cambridge: Cambridge University Press, 2001), ch. 2; Anghie, *Imperialism* (n 29), 84–7.

[59] Nathaniel Berman, '"But the Alternative is Despair": European Nationalism and the Modernist Renewal of International Law', *Harvard Law Review* 106 (1993), 1792, at 1845.

[60] I am indebted to world-systems theory, for instance, in my usage of 'centre', 'periphery', and 'semi-periphery' in reference to different positions occupied by states in the international legal and economic order. For the reemergence of the concept of the semi-periphery in international legal scholarship, see Arnulf Becker Lorca, 'Universal International Law: Nineteenth-Century Histories of Imposition and Appropriation', *HILJ* 51 (2010), 475; and Umut Özsu, 'Agency, Universality, and

are defined to an important degree by those streams of post-realist socio-legal theory that are generally associated with the work of Pierre Bourdieu.[61] Following Bourdieu, I approach law neither as a policy tool nor as a formal system but as a 'social space',[62] a distinct arena of action that both defines and is defined by competition between agents wielding different quantities and qualities of social capital. Although law is, of course, capable of being utilized as an instrument, and though it may under certain conditions lend itself to exposition as a system distinguished by internal coherence and immanent rationality, it is best understood as a social field that translates competition between unequally endowed actors into a set of formalized practices, refracting political, economic, and other conflicts through a medium marked at least as much by normative constraint as by struggle for power.[63] As such, I examine international law from a historico-sociological rather than an instrumentalist or philosophical standpoint, analysing its operation in a particular context at a particular juncture with a view to illuminating the emergence and development of a particular mode of nation-building.

The exchange of minorities between Greece and Turkey recruited an astonishingly wide range of actors—lawyers, diplomats, bureaucrats, clergymen, philanthropists, military officers, and a variety of other 'brokers of the international'.[64] Some, like Nansen, saw themselves as responding to a pressing crisis, participating in a broader project of reorganization in order to bring stability to a region that had not known it for some time. The West had done precious little to rescue Armenians from genocide, and it could ill afford to stand by and watch as

the Politics of International Legal History', *HILJ Online* 51 (2010), 58, <http://www.harvardilj.org/2010/10/online_52_ozsu/>.

[61] The relevant literature is rich. Yves Dezalay and Bryant Garth have examined international commercial arbitration, legal and economic reforms in Latin America, and the legal dimensions of state-building projects in Asia. See, respectively, *Dealing in Virtue: International Commercial Arbitration and the Construction of a Transnational Legal Order* (Chicago: University of Chicago Press, 1996); *The Internationalization of Palace Wars: Lawyers, Economists, and the Contest to Transform Latin American States* (Chicago: University of Chicago Press, 2002); and *Asian Legal Revivals: Lawyers in the Shadow of Empire* (Chicago: University of Chicago Press, 2010). Nicolas Guilhot has considered the processes through which US foreign policy and the agendas of human rights organizations have come to be formulated through competition between different groups of lawyers and policymakers. See *The Democracy Makers: Human Rights and the Politics of Global Order* (New York: Columbia University Press, 2005). Still others influenced by Bourdieu have studied the transnational governance instruments produced by the post-1989 wave of legal transplants (David M. Trubek et al., 'Global Restructuring and the Law: Studies of the Internationalization of Legal Fields and the Creation of Transnational Arenas', *Case Western Reserve Law Review* 44 (1994), 407), focused on changes to criminal jurisdiction and the legal definition of terrorism ('Pacifier et punir' (symposium), *Actes de la recherche en sciences sociales* 173–4 (2008)), or examined the implications of his work for international law and international relations (' "A Different Reading of the International": Pierre Bourdieu and International Studies' (symposium), *International Political Sociology* 5 (2011)).

[62] Pierre Bourdieu, 'The Force of Law: Toward a Sociology of the Juridical Field', trans. Richard Terdiman, *Hastings Law Journal* 38 (1987), 805.

[63] Bourdieu, 'Force of Law' (n 62), 814–16.

[64] I borrow the expression from Yves Dezalay, 'Les courtiers de l'international: héritiers cosmopolites, mercenaires de l'impérialisme et missionnaires de l'universel', *Actes de la recherche en sciences sociales* 151–2 (2004), 5.

Greeks and Turks razed whole provinces in the name of this or that programme of ethno-national 'regeneration'. Others understood the exchange not simply as a means of achieving stability, but as an opportunity to realize particular aspirations they had nursed for years. Most members of the Turkish nationalist elite, for instance, were convinced that it was only through completing the project of ethno-national homogenization initiated by the Young Turks that the foundations of a viable order might be established in post-Ottoman Turkey. Still others threw their weight behind the claim that the exchange was driven by the demands of a world in which technocracy had begun to dominate both the form and content of international relations. The Great War had shown up the limits of cosmopolitanism. If a region as volatile as the Near East were to survive, let alone thrive, in this new order, it would need to be parcelled into discrete, easily manageable units, amenable to greater levels of political and economic control. Regardless of where they stood, though, all such actors operated within a common international legal field.

This approach has significant consequences for the account given in this book of the role of states and organizations external to the Near East. The great powers were instrumental in designing and executing the exchange, acting in and through the League of Nations' constituent organs and a variety of humanitarian organizations. The League had implanted minority-protection regimes throughout central and eastern Europe in an effort to forestall majority–minority conflicts, some of which were long-standing and others of which resulted from new distributions of sovereign authority. Since this was thought to be insufficient in Greece and Turkey, recourse was had to the compulsory exchange, a more radical and coercive measure that many believed 'would have been impossible in Central-Europe'.[65] Equally, this approach has important implications for my account of the crucial role that was played by Turkish nationalists in the exchange. The revolutionary vanguard led by Kemal was committed to the exchange, consenting to it, and the recalibration of Turkish law and society it entailed, in the name of a comprehensive programme of nation-building. Securing the new state's borders, homogenizing its population, and extending Ankara's authority over the length and breadth of the territory it had inherited from its imperial predecessor were, it was assumed, necessarily interrelated, part and parcel of the modernization project to which Kemal and his followers had dedicated themselves. If post-Ottoman Turkey was to bootstrap itself into modernity through defensive Westernization, displacing an old *noblesse d'épée* with a new *noblesse d'état* and thereby transitioning to a fully bureaucratic state,[66] it could do so only by deploying more modern techniques of legal organization.

65 Erwin Loewenfeld, 'The Protection of Private Property under the Minorities Protection Treaties', *TGS* 16 (1930), 41, at 41.

66 Pierre Bourdieu, 'From the King's House to the Reason of State: A Model of the Genesis of the Bureaucratic Field', in *Pierre Bourdieu and Democratic Politics: The Mystery of Ministry*, ed. Loïc Wacquant (Cambridge: Polity, 2005), 29. It should be noted, though, that the Ottoman state boasted well-resourced bureaucratic apparatuses, with impressive recruitment standards, administrative techniques, and traditions of relative autonomy, at least as early as the seventeenth century.

Because of its magnitude and its overtly coercive character, the Greek–Turkish population exchange has always strained the tolerance and imagination of international lawyers. Although often criticized, proposals for the exchange were not condemned with enough sincerity and consistency to impede its formalization and implementation. Neither, for that matter, did the Greek–Turkish experience, growing out of forces and relations specific to the region, render impossible the extension of the transfer procedure to other jurisdictions in the decades that followed. On the contrary, jurists and diplomats soon pressed ahead with legally formalized transfers in a variety of contexts. The mechanism was employed by Nazi and Soviet policymakers during the interwar years and the Allies immediately after the Second World War, and broadly analogous efforts found expression in the partition of British India in 1947, the exodus of Palestinian Arabs in 1948, the expulsion of ethnic Greeks from northern Cyprus in 1974–5, and the widespread use of forced migration in the former Yugoslavia during the early 1990s—all procedures that were subject to *ex ante* or *ex post* juridification. In the process, population transfer came to be regarded as one among a variety of conflict-resolution techniques that circulated as a 'global legal commodity' promising stability and development.[67] If we are to understand the popularity of population transfer throughout the twentieth century, and its tacit or express endorsement in some quarters even today, we must come to grips with its origins in a semi-peripheral region with a specific set of entrenched traditions and institutions.

See especially Rhoads Murphey, *Exploring Ottoman Sovereignty: Tradition, Image and Practice in the Ottoman Imperial Household, 1400–1800* (London: Continuum, 2008), ch. 9; and also Rifa'at 'Ali Abou-El-Haj, *Formation of the Modern State: The Ottoman Empire, Sixteenth to Eighteenth Centuries*, 2nd ed. (Syracuse: Syracuse University Press, 2005), 61–72. These apparatuses were subject to considerable expansion, consolidation, and differentiation in the nineteenth century, when new ministries (including, crucially, ministries of justice and foreign affairs) were established. For sustained treatment see Carter V. Findley, *Bureaucratic Reform in the Ottoman Empire: The Sublime Porte, 1789–1922* (Princeton: Princeton University Press, 1980), 167–90.

[67] I borrow the expression from Outi Korhonen, 'The "State-Building Enterprise": Legal Doctrine, Progress Narratives and Managerial Governance', in *The Role of International Law in Rebuilding Societies after Conflict: Great Expectations*, ed. Brett Bowden, Hilary Charlesworth, and Jeremy Farrall (Cambridge: Cambridge University Press, 2009), 15, at 15.

1

The Ottoman Empire and the International Law of Minority Protection, 1815–1923

This chapter demonstrates that the Greek–Turkish population exchange was rooted in a nation-building project developed in productive tension with an intra-European tradition of minority protection. I begin with the classic balance-of-power treaties of the nineteenth century, examining the degree to which they were associated not only with the extension of specific rights to recognized minorities, but also with the legal construction of minorities where none had previously been understood to exist. This phenomenon was especially pronounced in the case of the Ottoman Empire, with a significant portion of the minority-protection mechanisms that emerged during the nineteenth century being engineered in relation to the 'Eastern Question'. I then canvass the minority treaties concluded in the wake of the First World War. The technologies of protection called forth by these treaties overhauled state apparatuses and redistributed constitutional powers across an enormous swath of territory encircling Europe's politico-economic core. The League of Nations was enlisted not simply to the task of coordinating nation- and state-formation processes, but also to that of fashioning functional institutions of minority governance. Finally, I turn to the protective system introduced for non-Muslim minorities in post-Ottoman Turkey. Turkey bought its right to republicanism by agreeing to certain concessions on minority protection. Incorporated into the Lausanne Peace Treaty were a set of provisions according Turkey's non-Muslim communities rights akin to those afforded minorities in central and eastern Europe after 1919. Crucially, though, these provisions were not as onerous as was the case elsewhere: their application was strictly limited to non-Muslims, and, in practice, the entitlements they enshrined were effectively weak. Even more importantly, they were introduced only because the compulsory exchange with Greece, formalized at Lausanne a half year before the signature of the Peace Treaty, limited their reach significantly.

I. Managing Minorities in the Long Nineteenth Century

At some level the traditional assessment is undeniably accurate: international treaties have indeed been 'the paradigmatic instrument recognizing the right of minorities to fair treatment'.[1] This was certainly the case in Europe during much of the nineteenth century, when most of the entitlements associated with the international law of minority protection today—equal access to courts, the benefit of religious freedom, the right to gain employment in the civil service, and so on—were reinforced by way of treaty. The great powers of the period cultivated a host of new mechanisms to cope with the vagaries of colonialism and imperialism. The lease, the condominium, the protectorate—familiar instruments such as these were, as Hersch Lauterpacht later put it, 'devices of diplomacy', employed as 'preparations for annexation' or offering 'means of acquiring sufficient power where downright annexation was thought to be politically inexpedient'.[2] Minority protection offered another governmental technique, in this case typically for matters of broadly European concern. Territorial realignments, particularly in south-east Europe, would often leave one or another community, distinct from a cultural, linguistic, or religious standpoint from its neighbours, on the 'wrong side' of a new border. Preserving the continental balance was deemed paramount, and this was an end that could be achieved only if all parties could be made to keep the peace, be it through suasion or coercion. Specially drafted treaty provisions and similar instruments were believed to be adequate to this task, particularly when underwritten by great-power assurances of surgical intervention in the event that vulnerable communities were persecuted.

While the roots of the international law of minority protection are frequently traced to the 1648 Peace of Westphalia, and sometimes even earlier, it was in the early nineteenth century that most of the rules that came to be associated with minority protection were developed. Marking the conclusion of the Napoleonic Wars, which had raised the spectre of a generalized disintegration of Europe's *anciens régimes*, the 1814–15 Congress of Vienna generated a series of treaties that sought to contain France by establishing a new system of intra-European coordination that would restore the *status quo ante bellum*.[3] Importantly, in addition

[1] Patrick Thornberry, *International Law and the Rights of Minorities* (Oxford: Clarendon Press, 1991), 25.

[2] Hersch Lauterpacht, 'International Law and Colonial Questions, 1870–1914', in *International Law, Being the Collected Papers of Hersch Lauterpacht*, ed. Elihu Lauterpacht, vol. 2 (Cambridge: Cambridge University Press, 1975), 95, at 114.

[3] See, e.g., Joachim von Elbe, 'Peacemaking in 1815', *AJIL* 36 (1942), 470; Harold Nicolson, *The Congress of Vienna: A Study in Allied Unity: 1812–1822* (London: Constable & Co., 1946), esp. chs. 6, 14; H. G. Schenk, *The Aftermath of the Napoleonic Wars: The Concert of Europe—An Experiment* (London: Kegan Paul, 1947), ch. 6; F. R. Bridge and Roger Bullen, *The Great Powers and the European States System 1815–1914* (London: Longman, 1980), 13–15. The Ottoman Empire had not been immune from the wars that followed the French Revolution: Napoleon had invaded Egypt and Syria, while Russia had mounted campaigns in the Balkans and Caucasus. For the former see Juan Cole, *Napoleon's Egypt: Invading the Middle East* (New York: Palgrave Macmillan, 2007).

to reshuffling extra-European possessions, the congress introduced a variety of protective measures for certain subject nationalities in Europe. Thus, the first provision of the congress' final act famously stated that '[t]he Poles, subjects respectively of Russia, Austria, and Prussia, shall obtain a representation and National Institutions, regulated according to the mode of political existence that each of the Governments to which they belong deems useful and suitable to grant'.[4] This and related provisions have often been regarded as laying the foundations for what international lawyers would later term 'national minorities'.[5]

Although important elements of the Napoleonic model of statehood would find their way into the Restoration period,[6] it was widely assumed at Vienna that continental peace, strained by the French Revolution's diffusion of popular sovereignty,[7] was capable of being reinstated and safeguarded only through synchronized action on the part of great powers. When necessary, elites were now given to believe, these states would need to redistribute sovereign authority with a view to preserving the balance of power formalized in the increasingly critical 'public law of Europe'.[8] The creation of an independent Greece by Russia, Britain, and France—three of the five powers comprising the core of the Concert of Europe, the others being Austria and Prussia—offers a striking example of the transformative reach of this commitment, leveraging members of a non-Muslim Ottoman community into a position of statehood within little more than a decade. While initially reluctant to support the insurrection, overlapping diplomatic commitments, not to mention domestic pressure from liberals and socialists, drove the three powers to back Greek rebels agitating for independence from Istanbul.[9]

For the latter see Paul F. Shupp, *The European Powers and the Near Eastern Question 1806–1807* (New York: Columbia University Press, 1931).

[4] Act of the Congress of Vienna, signed between Austria, France, Great Britain, Portugal, Prussia, Russia, and Sweden, 9 June 1815, 64 CTS 453, Art 1, at 457.

[5] See, e.g., Charles de Visscher, 'Protection of Minorities', in Charles de Visscher, *The Stabilization of Europe: Lectures on the Harris Foundation, 1924* (Chicago: University of Chicago Press, 1924), 27, at 33; L. P. Mair, *The Protection of Minorities: The Working and Scope of the Minorities Treaties under the League of Nations* (London: Christophers, 1928), 26; C. A. Macartney, *National States and National Minorities* (London: Oxford University Press, 1934), 159–61. For a more recent example see André Liebich, 'Minority as Inferiority: Minority Rights in Historical Perspective', *Review of International Studies* 34 (2008), 243, at 253–6.

[6] See David Laven and Lucy Riall, 'Restoration Government and the Legacy of Napoleon', in *Napoleon's Legacy: Problems of Government in Restoration Europe*, ed. David Laven and Lucy Riall (Oxford: Berg, 2000), 1, at 10 ff.

[7] For the international legal dimensions see Boris Mirkine-Guetzévitch, 'L'influence de la Révolution française sur le développement du droit international dans l'Europe orientale', *RCADI* 22 (1928-II), 295; René-Jean Dupuy, 'La Révolution française et le droit international actuel', *RCADI* 214 (1989-II), 9. See also Chimène I. Keitner, *The Paradoxes of Nationalism: The French Revolution and Its Meaning for Contemporary Nation Building* (Albany: State University of New York Press, 2007), esp. ch. 4.

[8] Interestingly, some later jurists sought to maintain their distance from this phenomenon. Pasquale Fiore, for instance, spoke with venom of the '*meeting* of dictators' that sought to reinstate the pre-1789 order; see Pasquale Fiore, *Nouveau droit international public, suivant les besoins de la civilisation moderne*, 2nd ed., trans. Charles Antoine, vol. 1 (Paris: A. Durand & Pedone-Lauriel, 1885), 50 (emphasis in original).

[9] For the complex relations between revolutionary movements in western Europe and the Near East, compare Eric Hobsbawm, *The Age of Revolution: Europe, 1789–1848* (London: Weidenfeld

In 1827, when presenting the Ottomans with their conditions for 'reconciliation and peace', the great powers stated that they had resolved to join together to craft a formal treaty for the restoration of stability, 'as much by sentiments of humanity, as by the interests of the tranquility of Europe'.[10] The Sublime Porte, as the Ottoman government was then widely known in Europe, had already made noises of resistance, producing a state paper condemning intervention in its domestic affairs.[11] But it was ultimately forced to yield.[12] Through coordinated action of this sort, the Concert of Europe ensured that intra-European rivalries involving nationalism were managed. With dozens of conferences being convened in the decades prior to its final destruction in 1914, the Concert was the centrepiece of a world order premised on the bracketing of war within Europe and the concomitant intensification of competition for extra-European territories and resources.[13]

The 1856 Treaty of Paris, concluded in the aftermath of the Crimean War, modified and in some respects deepened the Concert system, altering relations between the great powers and the Ottoman Empire in the process.[14] As one of the war's 'victors', the Ottoman Empire gained 'admission' into the European state system with the treaty, its preamble addressing the need to preserve Turkey's integrity and independence through 'effective and reciprocal guarantees' and Article 7 famously according it the right 'to participate in the advantages of the public law and concert of Europe'.[15] The precise legal implications of these statements were always nebulous: it was doubtful that the Ottoman Empire had secured recognition as a state on the same footing as those comprising the Concert, and far likelier that it had simply been subordinated to European legal structures as a weaker sovereign.[16] Nevertheless, the key power-political assumptions were

and Nicolson, 1962), 116, 140; with Paul W. Schroeder, *The Transformation of European Politics 1763–1848* (Oxford: Clarendon Press, 1994), chs. 14–15.

[10] Treaty between France, Great Britain, and Russia for the Pacification of Greece, signed at London, 6 July 1827, 77 CTS 307, Preamble, Art 6, at 309, 312.

[11] For the English text see John L. Comstock, *History of the Greek Revolution, Compiled from Official Documents of the Greek Government...* (New York: William W. Reed & Co., 1828), 406–12.

[12] Efforts to terminate 'the Greek Affair in a way that shall be durable, and calculated to prevent all further discussion on this question', would ultimately come to a head in a final agreement; see Arrangement between France, Great Britain, and Russia, and Turkey, for the Definitive Settlement of the Continental Boundaries of Greece, signed at Constantinople, 21 July 1832, 82 CTS 477 (quotation from Preamble, at 479).

[13] Cf. Gerry Simpson, *Great Powers and Outlaw States: Unequal Sovereigns in the International Legal Order* (Cambridge: Cambridge University Press, 2004), 67–76, ch. 4; Matthias Schulz, '"Defenders of the Right"? Diplomatic Practice and International Law in the 19th Century: An Historian's Perspective', in *Constructing International Law: The Birth of a Discipline*, ed. Luigi Nuzzo and Miloš Vec (Frankfurt am Main: Klostermann, 2012), 251.

[14] General Treaty for the Re-Establishment of Peace between Austria, France, Great Britain, Prussia, Sardinia, and Turkey, and Russia, signed at Paris, 30 March 1856, 114 CTS 409 ('Treaty of Paris').

[15] Treaty of Paris (n 14), 410, 414. Interestingly, some saw the Porte as having been endowed with this right even before Paris; see, e.g., Robert Phillimore, *Commentaries upon International Law*, vol. 1 (Philadelphia: T. & J. W. Johnson, 1854), 101.

[16] The most sustained legal examination of the issue remains Hugh McKinnon Wood, 'The Treaty of Paris and Turkey's Status in International Law', *AJIL* 37 (1943), 262, esp. at 269, 273–4. For more recent consideration see Tetsuya Toyoda, 'L'aspect universaliste du droit international

never anything but obvious: it was widely believed that the treaty would neutralize the Black Sea, check Russian advances in the Balkans, and transfer Russia's long-standing claim to be the 'protector' of Ottoman Christians to west European states.[17] Importantly, this last objective received additional support from Article 9, which noted that the sultan had already issued a decree—'emanating spontaneously from his sovereign will' a month before the treaty's signature and reaffirming his 'generous intentions toward the Christian populations of his Empire'.[18] Coming at the height of the Tanzimat, a series of reforms designed to modernize the empire's legal and administrative institutions,[19] this decree promised to strengthen formal equality with regard to religious expression, educational opportunity, employment in the civil service, and legal adjudication (in the last case via mixed tribunals for the adjudication of disputes involving persons of different faith).[20] Christian communities in the Near East had figured prominently in relations between the Ottomans and Romanovs for some time already, making repeated appearances in the treaties that the Porte had concluded with Russia from the eighteenth century onwards.[21] Questions concerning their status had played a key role in the diplomatic crisis that precipitated the Crimean War,[22] and international lawyers were particularly sensitive to the implications, a tendency illustrated well by one jurist's observation that '[t]he cruelties in Servia, in 1815, the awful massacre at Scio, and the atrocities committed on the Christians in almost every city of the Turkish empire at the time of the Greek revolution, prove that the old Turkish mode of treating Christians is not forgotten'.[23]

européen du 19ème siècle et le statut juridique de la Turquie avant 1856', *Journal of the History of International Law* 8 (2006), 19.

[17] See, e.g., George Douglas Campbell Argyll, *The Eastern Question; From the Treaty of Paris 1856 to the Treaty of Berlin 1878, and to the Second Afghan War*, vol. 1 (London: Strahan & Co., 1879), ch. 1; Harold Temperley, 'The Treaty of Paris of 1856 and Its Execution', *Journal of Modern History* 4 (1932), 387 and 523 (in two parts); A. J. P. Taylor, *The Struggle for Mastery in Europe 1848–1918* (Oxford: Clarendon Press, 1954), 83–6. See also M. S. Anderson, *The Eastern Question 1774–1923: A Study in International Relations* (London: Macmillan, 1966), 139–48.

[18] Treaty of Paris (n 14), 414.

[19] Ed. Engelhardt, *La Turquie et le Tanzimat, ou Histoire des réformes dans l'Empire ottoman depuis 1826 jusqu'à nos jours*, 2 vols. (Paris: A. Cotillon & Cie, 1882–4); *Tanzimat I. Yüzüncü Yıldönümü Münasebetile* (İstanbul: Maarif Matbaası, 1940); Roderic H. Davison, *Reform in the Ottoman Empire, 1856–1876* (Princeton: Princeton University Press, 1963). For a tabulation of the legal reforms see Gülnihâl Bozkurt, 'Tanzimat and Law', in *Tanzimat'ın 150. Yıldönümü Uluslararası Sempozyumu: Ankara: 31 Ekim—3 Kasım 1989* (Ankara: Türk Tarih Kurumu Basımevi, 1994), 279.

[20] For the decree see 'Hatti Humayoun relatif aux réformes de l'Empire ottoman, 18 février 1856', reproduced in *Recueil d'actes internationaux de l'Empire ottoman*, ed. Gabriel Noradounghian, vol. 3 (Paris: Librairie Cotillon F. Pichon, 1902), 83.

[21] The most significant being a 1774 treaty concluded after the 1768–74 Russo–Turkish War and generally interpreted as having accorded Russia sweeping rights of guardianship over Christians on Ottoman territory; see Treaty of Perpetual Peace and Amity between Russia and Turkey, signed at Kuçuk Kainardji, 10/21 July 1774, 45 CTS 349, esp. Art 7, at 390. For Russian efforts to amplify these rights see Roderic H. Davison, '"Russian Skill and Turkish Imbecility": The Treaty of Kuchuk Kainardji Reconsidered', *Slavic Review* 35 (1976), 463.

[22] For detailed consideration see Candan Badem, *The Ottoman Crimean War (1853–1856)* (Leiden: Brill, 2010), ch. 2.

[23] C. M. Kennedy, *The Influence of Christianity upon International Law* (Cambridge: Macmillan, 1856), 115.

Paris was the culmination of these developments and tipped the balance in favour of Britain and France. The Ottoman Empire was to be 'admitted' to the system of European public law, or at least brought within its fold nominally. But this came at the price of its immersion in an increasingly far-reaching regime of surveillance that would enable the great powers to guard Christian interests throughout the empire. The Ottoman economic sphere, with its complex patterns of production, distribution, and consumption, had entered a period of sustained absorption into circuits of capital centred in north-western Europe in the late eighteenth century, a process facilitated by capitulatory concessions and also increasingly by bilateral treaties providing relatively unfettered access to Ottoman markets.[24] The Paris settlement consolidated this process of politico-economic assimilation, with the sultan permitting the creation of European-managed banks, encouraging the importation of European economic science, and agreeing to the establishment and augmentation of supervisory financial institutions staffed partly by foreigners.[25] The paradox, as a student of the 'Eastern Question' once noted, was striking: while the great powers had in some ways 'repudiated the right of interference' in the Ottoman Empire's domestic affairs, Paris was in other ways 'the point at which Turkey finally passed into a state of tutelage to the European Concert'.[26]

Ottoman statesmen were aware of the threat posed by Western encroachment, and took various steps to minimize it. The wording of Article 9 of the Treaty of Paris was, for instance, subject to contestation, with Ottoman negotiators resisting language that may have suggested quasi-contractual obligations growing out of the sultan's decree. The great powers would not be authorized 'to take note' (*prendre acte*) of the decree, since this turn of phrase, when rendered into Ottoman Turkish (as *kayıd ve derhatır etmek*), was understood by the Porte to entail a guarantee, something generating strict rights of supervision and enforcement. Instead, they would merely 'recognize the high value' (*constatent la haute valeur*) of its

[24] For classic analyses see Immanuel Wallerstein, Hale Decdeli, and Reşat Kasaba, 'The Incorporation of the Ottoman Empire into the World-Economy', in *The Ottoman Empire and the World-Economy*, ed. Huri İslamoğlu-İnan (Cambridge: Cambridge University Press, 1987), 88, at 92–4; Reşat Kasaba, *The Ottoman Empire and the World Economy: The Nineteenth Century* (Albany: State University of New York Press, 1988), 32–4, 54–6. The most well-known of these bilateral treaties, abolishing Ottoman monopolies and fixing import and export duties, was the Convention of Commerce and Navigation between Great Britain and Turkey, signed at Balta-Liman, 16 August 1838, 88 CTS 77. But see Orhan Kurmuş, 'The 1838 Treaty of Commerce Re-examined', in *Économie et sociétés dans l'Empire ottoman (fin du XVIIIe—début du XXe siècle). Actes du colloque de Strasbourg (1er–5 juillet 1980)*, ed. Jean-Louis Bacqué-Grammont and Paul Dumont (Paris: Éditions du Centre national de la recherche scientifique, 1983), 411; Donald Quataert, 'The Age of Reforms, 1812–1914', in *An Economic and Social History of the Ottoman Empire*, ed. Halil İnalcık and Donald Quataert, vol. 2 (Cambridge: Cambridge University Press, 1994), 759, at 764.

[25] For analysis see Kasaba, *Ottoman Empire* (n 24), 53; Edhem Eldem, 'Ottoman Financial Integration with Europe: Foreign Loans, the Ottoman Bank and the Ottoman Public Debt', *European Review* 13 (2005), 431, at 433 ff.

[26] J. A. R. Marriott, *The Eastern Question: An Historical Study in European Diplomacy* (Oxford: Clarendon Press, 1917), 274.

terms.[27] Nevertheless, the Ottomans were clearly on the back foot. Gone were the days when the empire could hazard the conceit of being a power confident in the eventual triumph of the *dār al-Islām* and oblivious to the demands of permanent diplomacy.[28] Having gained the right to partake in the European state system's 'advantages', it now had to comport itself accordingly: a foreign ministry had already been set up, and now it would be enlarged and strengthened, with French being adopted as a key working language, its staff and procedures undergoing professionalization, and a spate of new embassies being established in Europe and elsewhere.[29]

Finally, there is the 1878 Treaty of Berlin. Marking the end of the Russo–Turkish War of 1877–8 and tellingly styled an agreement 'for the Settlement of Affairs in the East', the Treaty of Berlin was the most ambitious attempt to institute a minority-protection regime prior to 1919. It laid out the most comprehensive set of minority guarantees to date, a development that owed much to successful lobbying on behalf of Romanian Jews by the Alliance israélite universelle.[30] In addition, it conditioned recognition of Serbia, Montenegro, and Romania as de jure sovereigns—and Bulgaria as a de facto independent state—on conformity to these guarantees. The relevant provisions were substantively identical in each case, forbidding, among other things, discrimination on the basis of faith 'in respect to the enjoyment of civil and political rights, admission to public employment, functions, and honours, or the exercise of different professions and industries'.[31] However, further requirements were introduced in the case of the Ottoman Empire. The Porte's heavy-handedness in suppressing rebellions in Bulgaria and elsewhere had raised the ire not only of Russia but also of the Western powers, 'bringing the fervor of humane impulse and of religious enthusiasm into one of the most confused problems of international law'.[32] As such, in

[27] Roderic H. Davison, 'Ottoman Diplomacy at the Congress of Paris (1856) and the Question of Reforms', in *VII. Türk Tarih Kongresi (Ankara: 25–29 Eylül 1970)—Kongreye Sunulan Bildiriler*, vol. 2 (Ankara: Türk Tarih Kurumu Basımevi, 1973), 580, at 584–5; Temperley, 'Treaty of Paris' (n 17), 410–11. See also Treaty of Paris (n 14), 414.

[28] Not until the final decade of the eighteenth century did the Ottomans open their first permanent embassy in Europe. (They did so in London.) See J. C. Hurewitz, 'Ottoman Diplomacy and the European State System', *Middle East Journal* 15 (1961), 141, at 145; A. Nuri Yurdusev, 'The Ottoman Attitude toward Diplomacy', in *Ottoman Diplomacy: Conventional or Unconventional?*, ed. A. Nuri Yurdusev (Houndmills: Palgrave Macmillan, 2004), 5, at 27.

[29] J. C. Hurewitz, 'The Europeanization of Ottoman Diplomacy: The Conversion from Unilateralism to Reciprocity in the Nineteenth Century', *Belleten* 25 (1961), 455, esp. at 462–4. See also Carter V. Findley, 'The Legacy of Tradition to Reform: Origins of the Ottoman Foreign Ministry', *International Journal of Middle East Studies* 1 (1970), 334; Carter V. Findley, 'The Foundation of the Ottoman Foreign Ministry', *International Journal of Middle East Studies* 3 (1972), 388.

[30] Carole Fink, *Defending the Rights of Others: The Great Powers, the Jews, and International Minority Protection, 1878–1938* (Cambridge: Cambridge University Press, 2004), 15–38.

[31] Treaty between Austria–Hungary, France, Germany, Great Britain, Italy, Russia, and Turkey for the Settlement of Affairs in the East, signed at Berlin, 13 July 1878, 153 CTS 171 ('Treaty of Berlin'), Arts 5, 27, 35, 44, at 176 (Bulgaria), 182 (Montenegro), 184 (Serbia), 187 (Romania).

[32] Joseph P. Thompson, 'The Intercourse of Christian with Non-Christian Peoples' [1876], in Joseph P. Thompson, *American Comments on European Questions, International and Religious* (Boston: Houghton, Mifflin & Co., 1884), 104, at 105. The classic illustration is W. E. Gladstone's

addition to having to strengthen the right to offer evidence in Ottoman courts for all its nationals, refrain from restricting the movement of clerics and pilgrims, and adopt a number of other measures to protect minorities and foreigners, the Ottoman Empire was compelled to undertake 'improvements' and 'reforms' in provinces with large Armenian populations.[33] Although Ottoman authorities never complied with this stipulation, they were acutely aware of the fact that it internationalized the 'Armenian question'. Just as the conflict that had given rise to the Treaty of Berlin was often couched as 'a veritable war of humanity', so too would its terms be taken as illustrations of a growing tendency toward the 'collective intervention of humanity'.[34] As late as 1914, a reform plan for six Ottoman provinces with significant Armenian populations was designed with an eye to the Treaty of Berlin's attempt to protect Armenians from Kurds and Circassians, with whom they frequently competed for land, as well as from persecution or simply indifference on the part of Ottoman state authorities.[35]

That no such mechanisms of minority protection were mandated for the great powers of the time (Britain, France, Germany, Austria–Hungary, Italy, and Russia) was lost neither on Western observers nor on Ottoman elites. In Europe the inconsistency of European interventionism had already established itself as a recurring theme in both scholarly and journalistic writing, with Mazzini famously denouncing non-intervention as 'Intervention on the wrong side; Intervention by all who choose, and are strong enough, to put down free movements of peoples against corrupt governments'.[36] Critical sentiments only received further support in Berlin's wake. Shortly after the treaty was ratified, Gladstone wrote that it was not 'a little amusing to observe with what edifying zeal all the great States of

widely circulated *Bulgarian Horrors and the Question of the East* (London: John Murray, 1876). For the context see especially Davide Rodogno, *Against Massacre: Humanitarian Interventions in the Ottoman Empire 1815–1914* (Princeton: Princeton University Press, 2012), 147–57; Matthias Schulz, 'The Guarantees of Humanity: The Concert of Europe and the Origins of the Russo–Ottoman War of 1877', in *Humanitarian Intervention: A History*, ed. Brendan Simms and D. J. B. Trim (Cambridge: Cambridge University Press, 2011), 184, esp. at 193–4.

33 Treaty of Berlin (n 31), Arts 61–2, at 189–90.

34 André Mandelstam, *La Société des Nations et les puissances devant le problème arménien* (Paris: A. Pedone, 1926), 17–18 (de-emphasized from original). Russian jurists of the late nineteenth and early twentieth centuries were no less given to adopting the vocabulary of 'civilization' than their Western counterparts. See Eric Myles, '"Humanity", "Civilization" and the "International Community" in the Late Imperial Russian Mirror: Three Ideas "Topical for our Days"', *Journal of the History of International Law* 4 (2002), 310; Peter Holquist, 'The Russian Empire as a "Civilized State": International Law as Principle and Practice in Imperial Russia, 1874–1878', National Council for Eurasian and East European Research grant document (2004), <http://www.ucis.pitt.edu/nceeer/2004_818-06g_Holquist.pdf>.

35 Roderic H. Davison, 'The Armenian Crisis, 1912–1914', *American Historical Review* 53 (1948), 481, at 496–7 ff; Michael A. Reynolds, *Shattering Empires: The Clash and Collapse of the Ottoman and Russian Empires, 1908–1918* (Cambridge: Cambridge University Press, 2011), 74–7. As it turned out, the plan (which was designed by André Mandelstam, an international lawyer then serving as Russian dragoman in Istanbul) was never implemented. For details see André Mandelstam, *Le sort de l'Empire ottoman* (Paris: Librairie Payot & Cie, 1917), 217–27.

36 Giuseppe Mazzini, 'On Nonintervention' [1851], in *A Cosmopolitanism of Nations: Giuseppe Mazzini's Writings on Democracy, Nation Building, and International Relations*, ed. Stefano Recchia and Nadia Urbinati (Princeton: Princeton University Press, 2009), 213, at 217.

Europe united to force religious liberty upon those new-fledged bantlings of politics, on their first view of the light of day; and yet these great States have hardly in any case learned . . . to adopt it at home'.[37] Ottoman statesmen were alive to the phenomenon, and had already taken numerous steps to counteract it. The 1876 Ottoman constitution, prepared partly as a response to European pressure but still the first such document in the Islamic world,[38] had, for instance, included as its first provision a statement to the effect that the imperial polity comprised 'an indivisible whole, no part of which can ever be detached for any reason whatsoever'.[39] Ottoman sensitivity was heightened further by what transpired in Berlin. Echoing François Guizot, who had branded the Ottoman Empire 'a Muslim Poland',[40] Grand Vezier Saffet Paşa likened the great powers' stance during the negotiations to that which they had adopted in respect to Poland's partitions.[41]

The Treaty of Berlin and similar instruments testify to the growing strength of a distinctly European understanding of international order, one in which strategic intervention—intervention in the name of the European state system and the 'humanity' whose rights and interests it purportedly safeguarded—came increasingly to be invested with greater value.[42] As it turned out, the Berlin settlement was not enforced as stringently as many had hoped. It could not, for instance, prevent continued persecution of Romania's Jews. Nor could it save Anatolia's Armenians and Assyrians from massacre in the mid-1890s. But it did go some way to reinforce the minority-protection regime inaugurated tentatively at Vienna and bolstered significantly at Paris. This regime licensed ever deeper intrusions into the domestic legal systems of 'oriental' states—states whose status as nominal vassals of the Porte (e.g. Bulgaria) restricted them to one or another form of 'semi-sovereignty',[43] or whose

[37] W. E. Gladstone, *The Berlin Treaty and the Anglo–Turkish Convention* (London: Liberal Central Association, 1878), 14.

[38] A fact which led Lorimer to denounce it as a political ploy to remove 'from the other parties to the Treaty of Paris the last formal pretext for interference in the internal affairs of the Ottoman Empire'. James Lorimer, 'Does the Corân Supply an Ethical Basis on Which a Political Superstructure Can Be Raised?' [1877–8], in James Lorimer, *Studies National and International, Being Occasional Lectures Delivered in the University of Edinburgh 1864–1889* (Edinburgh: William Green & Sons, 1890), 132, at 142.

[39] See 'Constitution, promulguée le 7 zilhidje 1293 (11/23 décembre 1876)', reproduced in *Législation ottomane, ou Recueil des lois, réglements, ordonnances, traités, capitulations et autres documents officiels de l'Empire ottoman*, ed. Aristarchi Bey, vol. 5 (Constantinople: Imprimerie frères Nicolaïdes, 1878), 7, at 7.

[40] François Guizot, *Mémoires pour servir à l'histoire de mon temps*, vol. 7 (Paris: Michel Lévy frères, 1865), 263.

[41] Roderic H. Davison, 'The Ottoman Empire and the Congress of Berlin', in *Der Berliner Kongress von 1878: Die Politik der Grossmächte und die Probleme der Modernisierung in Südosteuropa in der zweiten Hälfte des 19. Jahrhunderts*, ed. Ralph Melville and Hans-Jürgen Schröder (Wiesbaden: Franz Steiner Verlag, 1982), 205, at 213.

[42] Even before Berlin, Gustave Rolin-Jaequemyns had felt comfortable writing that the great powers were entrusted with the mission of representing 'the whole of Europe' and acting 'in the interest of humanity' in their relations with 'oriental peoples'. Gustave Rolin-Jaequemyns, 'Le droit international et la phase actuelle de la question d'Orient', *RDILC* 8 (1876), 293, at 368 (partly de-emphasized from original).

[43] See, e.g., K. Omer Lutfi, *Die völkerrechtliche Stellung Bulgariens und Ostrumeliens* (Erlangen: E. Th. Jacob, 1903); M. Boghitchévitch, *Halbsouveränität: Administrative und politische Autonomie seit dem Pariser Vertrage (1856)* (Berlin: Verlag von Julius Springer, 1903).

formal independence (Serbia, Montenegro, Romania, and the Ottoman Empire itself) was conditioned on recognition as subordinates in the European system. Small wonder it became fashionable at this juncture—when fascination with the European state form ran high—to refer to sovereign equality as a principle 'rapidly becoming obsolete'.[44]

A key feature in most such treaties—snapshots of a diffuse and deeply contradictory process rather than foundational reference-points for a coherent body of law of the sort that Thomas Erskine Holland seems to have had in mind when imagining a '*corpus iuris publici orientalis*'[45]—is a commitment to regulate nationalism by arming recognized minorities with greater rights. European powers frequently claimed rights of guardianship over Ottoman Christians and were reluctant to tolerate the disorder that accompanied persecution and inter-communal strife, particularly as this could pose a threat to the state system they sought to govern. As a result, they pressured the Ottomans into augmenting existing protections and policed situations of actual or perceived crisis, or at least made a show of their ability to do so.[46] In addition, one also finds a commitment to manufacture legal minorities where none had formally been deemed to exist, frequently as part of territorial realignments, inducements for domestic reform, or shifts in broader alliance networks. Certain communities were not recognized as such under domestic and international law. The introduction of minority protection would go some way to 'rectify' this 'anomaly', and also make it possible for great powers to intervene on their behalf. Nationalism was not simply something to be honed and hedged in. It was also, at least under certain circumstances, something to be cultivated and channelled.

Both tendencies—*shielding* minorities where they already existed at law, *constituting* them legally where this was thought needed—were facilitated, or at least mediated, by the Ottoman Empire's indigenous legal traditions. The *millet* system, considered by most scholars to have been operational in various complex forms for centuries, had long ensured that non-Muslim communities within the Ottoman Empire were afforded a measure of internal sovereignty.[47] The arrangements it made possible pluralized the Ottoman legal order to a significant degree, but they also contained important elements of hierarchy: during most of the *millet* system's existence, many Orthodox Christians (Albanians, Bulgarians, Georgians, Greeks,

44 T. J. Lawrence, 'The Primacy of the Great Powers', in T. J. Lawrence, *Essays on Some Disputed Questions in Modern International Law*, 2nd ed. (Cambridge: Deighton, Bell, & Co., 1885), 208, at 209.

45 Thomas Erskine Holland, ed., *The European Concert in the Eastern Question: A Collection of Treaties and Other Public Acts* (Oxford: Clarendon Press, 1885), 2.

46 On this 'policing' function see Georges-Henri Soutou, 'Le Concert européen, de Vienne à Locarno', in *L'ordre européen du XVIe au XXe siècle. Actes du colloque de l'Institut des recherches sur les civilisations de l'Occident moderne, 15–16 mars 1996*, ed. Jean Bérenger and Georges-Henri Soutou (Paris: Presses de l'Université de Paris-Sorbonne, 1998), 117, at 122 ff.

47 The standard reference for the system's development remains Benjamin Braude and Bernard Lewis, eds., *Christians and Jews in the Ottoman Empire: The Functioning of a Plural Society*, 2 vols. (New York: Holmes & Meier, 1982). See also M. O. H. Ursinus, 'Millet', in *The Encyclopaedia of Islam: New Edition*, vol. 7, ed. C. E. Bosworth et al. (Leiden: Brill, 1990), 61.

Romanians, Serbs, and others) were deemed members of the *millet-i Rum* ('Greek nation'), and therefore placed under the authority of the Greek Orthodox patriarch, while other Christians (Armenians, Chaldeans, Copts, Ethiopians, and others) fell within the jurisdiction of the Armenian Gregorian patriarch.[48] The system was subject to considerable expansion, refinement, and institutionalization in the nineteenth century. Reforms established mixed courts and supplemented existing mechanisms of intra-confessional administration with a general right of equality applicable to all Ottoman subjects.[49] And entirely new minorities were created through the extension of formal recognition to certain communities, as when autonomous Catholic and Protestant *millets* were constituted legally through sultanic decree.[50] No such *millets* had previously existed in law: Protestants had enjoyed no recognition as such, and Catholics, though present in large numbers throughout the empire for centuries, had simply been subsumed beneath the jurisdiction of the Greek and Armenian patriarchs.

The consolidation of the *millet* system ran alongside enhanced reliance upon the Ottoman capitulations. Originally little more than unilateral pledges by the sultan, the capitulations had been introduced centuries earlier with a view to managing relations with the empire's political allies and trading partners. Most capitulations provided a variety of tax and customs exemptions, privileges of temporary residence on or safe passage through Ottoman territory, and partial if not complete immunity from the jurisdiction of Islamic courts,[51] spurring the growth of chartered companies like the Levant Company.[52] By the mid-nineteenth century, though, many European and American jurists had become accustomed to presenting the capitulations not as unilateral concessions but as bilateral treaties—treaties that imposed binding legal obligations upon the Ottoman sultan and thereby invited intervention in the event that he failed to satisfy these obligations.[53] This

[48] On the ramifications for the eventual growth of nationalism see Fatma Müge Göçek, 'The Decline of the Ottoman Empire and the Emergence of Greek, Armenian, Turkish, and Arab Nationalisms', in *Social Constructions of Nationalism in the Middle East*, ed. Fatma Müge Göçek (Albany: State University of New York Press, 2002), 15, at 18–19 ff.

[49] See generally Davison, *Reform* (n 19). For the mixed courts see in particular Jasper Yeates Brinton, *The Mixed Courts of Egypt* (New Haven: Yale University Press, 1930).

[50] For key decrees see 'Patriarcat arménien catholique, bérat, 5 janvier 1831' and 'Firman en faveur des sujets ottomans protestants, 14 novembre 1850', reproduced in *Corps de droit ottoman: Recueil des codes, lois, règlements, ordonnances et actes les plus importants du droit intérieur, et d'études sur le droit coutumier de l'Empire ottoman*, ed. George Young, vol. 2 (Oxford: Clarendon Press, 1905), 103 and 108 respectively. This had particularly far-reaching implications for the integrity of the Ottoman Armenian community; see Vartan H. Artinian, 'The Formation of Catholic and Protestant Millets in the Ottoman Empire', *Armenian Review* 28 (1975), 3, esp. at 8, 11.

[51] For the terms of most capitulations see Nasim Sousa, *The Capitulatory Régime of Turkey: Its History, Origin, and Nature* (Baltimore: The Johns Hopkins Press, 1933), esp. 70–86; Maurits H. van den Boogert, *The Capitulations and the Ottoman Legal System: Qadis, Consuls, and* Beratlıs *in the 18th Century* (Leiden: Brill, 2005), ch. 1.

[52] M. Epstein, *The Early History of the Levant Company* (London: George Routledge & Sons, 1908); Alfred C. Wood, *A History of the Levant Company* (London: Oxford University Press, 1935).

[53] That the capitulations were treaties *sensu stricto* was often asserted rather than argued. Thus, the most comprehensive pre-Lausanne study of the capitulations began with the claim that '[t]he condition of foreigners in the Ottoman Empire is regulated by a series of treaties concluded between the Porte and most Christian states of Europe and America, which are commonly given the name

delegitimized the Porte's claim to what had come to be viewed as a key attribute of full statehood—the capacity to exercise exclusive, or near-exclusive, sovereign power over a delimited territory.[54] It also encouraged abuse of the capitulations by Western merchants and the growing number of local Ottoman 'protégés' with whom they collaborated.[55] So deeply entrenched had the capitulations become by the mid-nineteenth century that only with the introduction of European legal institutions was it believed possible to entertain their abrogation. Thus, while they admitted that the capitulations 'circumscribe the authority of the Porte within unfortunate limits',[56] European negotiators at the 1856 Congress of Paris insisted that the privileges and immunities the capitulations extended to resident aliens and loyal 'protégés' would need to remain in place for the foreseeable future.[57] Friedrich Martens was only expressing a widely held sentiment when he claimed that extraterritoriality would remain indispensable until 'oriental' states demonstrated their capacity to guarantee the personal and proprietary rights of non-Muslim foreigners and 'protégés'.[58]

In sum, it was in the nineteenth century that much of what is now recognized as the international law of minority protection was developed. The Concert of Europe fashioned, apportioned, and reconstituted states, devoting a good part of

of Capitulations': G. Pélissié du Rausas, *Le régime des capitulations dans l'Empire ottoman*, vol. 1 (Paris: Arthur Rousseau, 1902), 1. For recent consideration see Viorel Panaite, *The Ottoman Law of War and Peace: The Ottoman Empire and Tribute Payers* (Boulder: East European Monographs, 2000), 239–48; Edhem Eldem, 'Capitulations and Western Trade', in *The Cambridge History of Turkey*, vol. 3, ed. Suraiya N. Faroqhi (Cambridge: Cambridge University Press, 2006), 283.

[54] '[T]he sovereign which represents the state in its international relations must be able . . . to extend his or its power equally throughout the whole of his or its domains. When this cannot be done, the state and its sovereign either fall out of the pale of the international law, or are admitted by other states and sovereigns upon sufferance. . . . The present condition and treatment of the Ottoman Empire afford a striking illustration of this practice.' John Norton Pomeroy, *Lectures on International Law in Time of Peace*, ed. Theodore Salisbury Woolsey (Boston: Houghton, Mifflin, & Co., 1886), 51.

[55] For attempts by Ottoman authorities as early as the late eighteenth century to limit the proliferation of *berats*, in some cases by issuing new *berats* to 'loyal' (Muslim and non-Muslim) merchants, see van den Boogert, *Capitulations* (n 51), 105–12; Ali İhsan Bağış, *Osmanlı Ticaretinde Gayrî Müslimler: Kapitülasyonlar—Avrupa Tüccarları—Beratlı Tüccarlar—Hayriye Tüccarları (1750–1839)* (Ankara: Turhan Kitabevi, 1983), esp. ch. 2; Bruce Masters, 'The Sultan's Entrepreneurs: The *Avrupa Tüccarıs* and the *Hayriye Tüccarıs* in Syria', *International Journal of Middle East Studies* 24 (1992), 579.

[56] 'Protocole no. 14—séance du 25 mars 1856', in *Protocols of Conferences Held at Paris Relative to the General Treaty of Peace* (London: Harrison & Sons, 1856), 52, at 54.

[57] Treaty of Paris (n 14), Art 32, at 419 (precluding the renewal or replacement of 'Treaties or Conventions' with the Porte in the absence of Western consent).

[58] F. Martens, *Das Consularwesen und die Consularjurisdiction im Orient*, trans. H. Skerst (Berlin: Weidmannsche Buchhandlung, 1874), 320. Such views would remain common for decades to come. See, e.g., Travers Twiss, *On Consular Jurisdiction in the Levant, and the Status of Foreigners in the Ottoman Law Courts* (London: William Clowes & Sons, 1880), 20–1, 23–4; Nicolas Politis, 'Les capitulations et la justice répressive ottomane à propos de l'affaire Joris', *Revue de droit international privé et de droit pénal international* 2 (1906), 659, at 682; Frank E. Hinckley, *American Consular Jurisdiction in the Orient* (Washington: W. H. Lowdermilk & Co., 1906), 14–15, ch. 7; André Mandelstam, *La justice ottomane dans ses rapports avec les puissances étrangères* (Paris: A. Pedone, 1908), 273–4; Léon Ostroróg, *Pour la réforme de la justice ottomane* (Paris: Pedone, 1912); Henry G. Hodges, *The Doctrine of Intervention* (Princeton: Banner Press, 1915), 116–17.

its energy to the regulation of majority–minority dynamics in the Ottoman Empire and the various states formed from its gradual 'retreat from Europe'. In the words of Holland, it 'remade the map of Europe in 1815, liberated Greece in 1827, . . . regulated the Ottoman Empire in 1856, freed the Balkan States in 1878, and later meddled with the navigation of the Danube and the Suez Canal, the boundaries of Greece, and the fate of Crete'.[59] Minority protection—a means both of arming and of generating minorities—was essential to the Concert's capacity to deploy force in the name of inter-state equilibrium. It was also crucial to its self-constitution as an integrated 'Europe', confident in the normative supremacy of its models of statehood and disposed to see minority protection as an instrument applicable principally on its eastern margins.

II. Minority Protection, the League of Nations, and a New World Order

Historians of international law have long characterized 1919 as a watershed, transforming the discipline—its theory, doctrine, and practice—from top to bottom. International law had proven no more able to control industrial and military rivalry between Manchester and the Rhineland than to manage majority–minority relations in the few multinational states that remained. Inter-state competition, reaching toxic levels as 1914 neared, fuelled struggles throughout Asia, Africa, and the Americas. All of this, it is regularly said, rendered classic international law a thing of the past, a resource to be mined here and there, perhaps, but hardly the lynchpin of international relations it had previously been. 'Sovereignty', however understood, was now to be disaggregated and disciplined in the name of a new world order.

Such assessments are often exaggerated, resting on an overly static understanding of nineteenth- and early twentieth-century international law and overstating post-Versailles international law's claim to novelty. The latter half of the nineteenth century had brought with it rapid professional organization and increased codification of positive law. The Institut de droit international and International Law Association were up and running by the time its final decades rolled around, treatise writers worked hard to cobble together a 'scientific' canon capable of withstanding charges of imprecision and ineffectiveness, the first professional journals of international law entered into circulation, international arbitration became increasingly commonplace, the 1899 and 1907 Hague Conferences developed a legal framework that sought to cast a regulatory net over the conduct of warfare, and new treaties were fused with bits and pieces of state practice and *opinio juris* to generate a barrage of international crimes, such as the prohibitions against the slave trade that surfaced toward the *fin de siècle*.[60] Lawyers were effusive in their praise for such developments.

[59] Thomas Erskine Holland, *Lectures on International Law*, ed. Thomas Alfred Walker and Wyndham Legh Walker (London: Sweet & Maxwell, 1933), 105.

[60] The strongest general account of the period remains that provided in Martti Koskenniemi, *The Gentle Civilizer of Nations: The Rise and Fall of International Law 1870–1960* (Cambridge: Cambridge

In 1912, for instance, one commentator observed that '[t]he half century beginning with the Declaration of Paris in 1856 and ending with the London Conference in 1909 has seen greater progress in the direction of internationalism and more successful attempts to improve and codify international law than any other in history, or perhaps more than all previous half-centuries combined'.[61] Considered from this standpoint, the League of Nations itself could be characterized as a fundamentally reformatory rather than revolutionary project. Indeed, it is arguable that, far from supplanting the Concert of Europe, or, as Carl Schmitt would have put it, facilitating a 'leap into the nothingness of a universality lacking any grounding in space or on land',[62] the League sublimated characteristically nineteenth-century obsessions with alliance networks and multilateral diplomacy into an aspirationally, if not actually, global system of interdependence, one in which the rule of great powers was not replaced so much as updated and institutionalized.[63] Jan Smuts' proposals for a 'future world-government' modelled on the idea of a British Commonwealth exerted considerable influence,[64] and many advocates of the League pressed vehemently for greater regionalism, often for the sake of strengthening established spheres of influence.[65] But the League of Nations remained faithful to the core tenets of the Concert of Europe system.

Yet the customary periodization—premised upon the idea that the system inaugurated in 1919 departed from the international law produced by the European Concert—is not entirely without merit. Something new had indeed emerged. For most observers the cast of great powers had been altered, with Austria, Russia, and Prussia/Germany falling from grace, and Japan and the United States rising

University Press, 2001). See also Martti Koskenniemi, 'The Legacy of the Nineteenth Century', in *Routledge Handbook of International Law*, ed. David Armstrong (London: Routledge, 2009), 141.

[61] Amos S. Hershey, 'History of International Law since the Peace of Westphalia', *AJIL* 6 (1912), 30, at 50.

[62] Carl Schmitt, *The* Nomos *of the Earth in the International Law of the* Jus Publicum Europaeum, trans. G. L. Ulmen (New York: Telos, 2003 [1950]), 237.

[63] Interwar jurists frequently admitted as much. See, e.g., Philip Marshall Brown, *International Society: Its Nature and Interests* (New York: Macmillan, 1923), 126–7 ('The "Primacy of the Great Powers" thus finds its full recognition and the equality of nations its full repudiation in the organization and control of the [League] Council'); Manley O. Hudson, *Progress in International Organization* (Stanford: Stanford University Press, 1932), 34 (underscoring the fact that 'the hegemony of the Great Powers was recognized' in the League Council). The assessment has proven popular; see, e.g., Inis L. Claude Jr, *Swords into Plowshares: The Problems and Progress of International Organization*, 3rd ed. (New York: Random House, 1964), 50 (arguing that the League 'was intended to introduce radical changes in the operation of the multistate system, rather than to accomplish or even to presage the replacement of that system').

[64] J. C. Smuts, *The League of Nations: A Practical Suggestion* (London: Hodder and Stoughton, 1918), 30 ff. For analysis see Mark Mazower, *Governing the World: The History of an Idea* (New York: Penguin, 2012), 131–5, ch. 5 generally.

[65] For a useful overview of the European scene see Jean-Michel Guieu, 'The Debate About a European Institutional Order among International Legal Scholars in the 1920s and Its Legacy', *Contemporary European History* 21 (2012), 319. Of course, as Guieu himself notes (at 322 ff), this was by no means a purely European phenomenon, with Latin American jurists often finding regionalism an attractive counterweight to the League's growing power. For analysis of Alejandro Álvarez, the leading exponent of 'American international law' at the time, see 'The Periphery Series: Alejandro Álvarez' (symposium), *Leiden Journal of International Law* 19 (2006).

to take their place. With varying degrees of persuasiveness, many international lawyers of the period made a point of casting their predecessors as voluntarists whose overarching commitment to state sovereignty rendered international order untenable. This spoke less to the decline of legal form in the face of political power than to the gradual development of a pragmatic international law that embraced the flexibility and functionalism thought to be required of international organization.[66] Whereas the old law of nations had not contained many 'rules for its own modification', the Kelsenian Josef Kunz later reflected, the new international law, aiming 'to eliminate war as an institution', was 'under a necessity to develop dynamic rules' that would limit the threat of conflict.[67] Nowhere was this felt with greater force than with respect to minority protection. Since tensions between majority and minority communities had been integral to the Great War's eruption, minority protection was placed at the forefront of reconstruction efforts after the war.

Minority protection was not designed to apply to the war's principal victors, or indeed to any Western powers at all—a structural bias made manifest in the fact that its normative architecture was clearly developed in reference to eastern Europe. International lawyers were anything but reluctant to admit as much. In its *Greco–Bulgarian 'Communities'* opinion, for instance, the Permanent Court of International Law associated the term 'community' with the Balkans: 'the material benefits which from time immemorial in the East individuals of the same race, religion, language and traditions, have derived from uniting into communities, are well known', it stated, adding that the instrument in question in that case—a 1919 convention regulating the 'voluntary' population exchange between Greece and Bulgaria—approached 'the conception of a "community" from the point of view of [the] exclusively minority character which it has had for centuries past in the East'.[68] If minority protection came after 1919 to be seen as a necessary precondition for statehood, this was so only inasmuch as the state to which recognition was to be extended was always already assumed to deviate from dominant Western paradigms of national statehood. Centuries of state-formation in western Europe, frequently involving massive forced migration, had generated societies with more or less cohesive national identities. Where nationhood had not been 'achieved', though, minority protection was to provide a palliative. An influential 1943 volume on minority protection put the matter bluntly when it observed

[66] *Contra* Stephen Wertheim, 'The League of Nations: A Retreat from International Law?', *Journal of Global History* 7 (2012), 210 (relying upon an unsustainably rigid conception of legality to argue that the League Covenant, with its 'gaps and discretion', destroyed 'the dream of replacing politics with law' (at 228–9)).

[67] Josef L. Kunz, 'The Law of Nations, Static and Dynamic', *AJIL* 27 (1933), 630, at 630.

[68] *The Greco–Bulgarian 'Communities'*, Advisory Opinion, PCIJ Rep. Series B No 17 (1930), 20, 21–2. The Court defined 'community' as 'a group of persons living in a given country or locality, having a race, religion, language and traditions of their own and united by this identity of race, religion, language and traditions in a sentiment of solidarity, with a view to preserving their traditions, maintaining their form of worship, ensuring the instruction and upbringing of their children in accordance with the spirit and traditions of their race and rendering mutual assistance to each other' (21).

that, in the aftermath of the First World War, 'the initiative for protecting minorities came, not from the minorities themselves, but from outside'—from, that is, a West inclined to view minority protection as a technology of governance applicable mainly in eastern Europe.[69]

Broached taxonomically, techniques of minority protection available after the First World War tended to fall into four classes: custom-tailored minority treaties, the most typical solution (Czechoslovakia, Greece, Poland, Romania, and the Serb-Croat-Slovene state); specific bilateral and multilateral agreements enshrining minority protection for particular regions (Danzig, Memel, and Upper Silesia); chapters concerning minority protection inserted into general peace treaties (Austria, Bulgaria, Hungary, and Turkey); and declarations required of certain states upon admission to the League (Albania, Estonia, Finland, Latvia, and Lithuania).[70] One or another form of minority protection was thus implanted in a string of states running from the Baltic to the Mediterranean, the so-called 'minorities belt', with the instrument in question being selected and attuned *in situ*. (The 'belt' would later be extended to Iraq, which was compelled to issue a declaration of commitment to minority protection as a condition of its emancipation from the Mandate System and consequent admission to the League.)[71] As outlined by the Permanent Court in an oft-quoted passage from its 1935 advisory opinion in *Minority Schools in Albania*, the system had two basic objectives. On the one hand, it aimed to 'secure for certain elements incorporated in a State, the population of which differs from them in race, language or religion, the possibility of living peaceably alongside that population and co-operating amicably with it'. On the other hand, it sought to preserve 'the characteristics which distinguish them from the majority' with a view to 'satisfying the ensuing special needs'.[72]

[69] Jacob Robinson et al., *Were the Minorities Treaties a Failure?* (New York: Institute of Jewish Affairs, 1943), 6.

[70] For a cross-section see *Protection of Linguistic, Racial and Religious Minorities by the League of Nations: Provisions Contained in the Various International Instruments at Present in Force*, LN Doc. C.L.110.1927.I (Geneva: League of Nations, 1927). For useful discussions see Francesco Capotorti, *Study on the Rights of Persons Belonging to Ethnic, Religious and Linguistic Minorities*, UN Doc. E/CN.4/Sub.2/384/Rev.1 (1979), 18, 16–26 generally; Athanasia Spiliopoulou Åkermark, *Justifications of Minority Protection in International Law* (The Hague: Kluwer, 1997), 104–8; Natan Lerner, 'The Evolution of Minority Rights in International Law', in *Peoples and Minorities in International Law*, ed. Catherine Brölmann, René Lefeber, and Marjoleine Zieck (Dordrecht: Nijhoff, 1993), 77, at 83; Anna Meijknecht, *Towards International Personality: The Position of Minorities and Indigenous Peoples in International Law* (Antwerp: Intersentia, 2001), 123; Janne E. Nijman, 'Minorities and Majorities', in *The Oxford Handbook of the History of International Law*, ed. Anne Peters and Bardo Fassbender (Oxford: Oxford University Press, 2012), 95, at 111–13.

[71] The issue of minority protection entered Iraq in full force only in 1930, and the Permanent Mandates Commission, the League organ authorized to supervise the Mandate System, was not convinced that Britain's formal withdrawal would bode well for the country's Kurds, Assyrians, and other minorities. See Susan Pedersen, 'Getting Out of Iraq—in 1932: The League of Nations and the Road to Normative Statehood', *American Historical Review* 115 (2010), 975, at 992–8; and also Nelida Fuccaro, 'Minorities and Ethnic Mobilisation: The Kurds in Northern Iraq and Syria', in *The British and French Mandates in Comparative Perspectives*, ed. Nadine Méouchy and Peter Sluglett (Leiden: Brill, 2004), 579, at 586 ff.

[72] *Minority Schools in Albania*, Advisory Opinion, PCIJ Rep. Series A/B No 64 (1935), 17. As the Court explained (at 17), this approach had two implications: 'The first is to ensure that nationals

The most ambitious of the available mechanisms was the minority treaty. The first and most critical such treaty—the 'Little Treaty of Versailles'—was concluded with Poland in 1919.[73] Partitioned and resoldered time and again over the course of the preceding centuries, beleaguered, territorially fractured Poland had long served as a fulcrum for intra-European rivalry. For Mazzini, it had been 'a nation thrown into the grave alive'.[74] For Marx, it had been nothing less than 'the cement which holds together the three great military despots: Russia, Prussia and Austria'.[75] With Europe's imperial houses now in disarray, it was to be reconstituted, armed with a new batch of legal and political institutions, and reinserted into an international legal order that was itself in the process of being overhauled. Article 1 set the tone, ensuring that the next seven provisions would be 'recognised as fundamental laws, and that no law, regulation or official action shall conflict or interfere with these stipulations'. Article 2 explained that Poland undertook to 'assure full and complete protection of life and liberty to all inhabitants of Poland without distinction of birth, nationality, language, race or religion'. And Article 7 provided similarly across-the-board guarantees of equality, stating that '[a]ll Polish nationals shall be equal before the law and shall enjoy the same civil and political rights without distinction as to race, language or religion'. The term 'nationals' was defined broadly in Articles 3 to 6, including, among others, Austrian, German, Hungarian, and Russian subjects resident habitually in Poland at the time of the treaty's entry into force or born on Polish soil to parents resident habitually in the country at this time. Rights pertaining to religious practice, the use of language, and the establishment and maintenance of educational and other institutions were enshrined in Articles 2, 7, 8, and 9. Provisions were inserted to provide the Jewish minority with rights in connection with the allocation of public funds for education, as well as a guarantee that its members would not be required to work on the Sabbath (Articles 10 and 11 respectively). Article 12 made it clear that these stipulations constituted 'obligations of international concern' and would be 'placed under the guarantee of the League of Nations', with disputes arising from a 'difference of opinion as to questions of law or fact' being referable to the World Court.[76]

belonging to racial, religious or linguistic minorities shall be placed in every respect on a footing of perfect equality with the other nationals of the State. The second is to ensure for the minority elements suitable means for the preservation of their racial peculiarities, their traditions and their national characteristics.'

[73] Minorities Treaty between the Principal Allied and Associated Powers (the British Empire, France, Italy, Japan, and the United States) and Poland, signed at Versailles, 28 June 1919, 225 CTS 412 ('Polish Minority Treaty').

[74] Giuseppe Mazzini, 'The European Question: Foreign Intervention and National Self-Determination' [1847], in *A Cosmopolitanism of Nations: Giuseppe Mazzini's Writings on Democracy, Nation Building, and International Relations*, ed. Stefano Recchia and Nadia Urbinati (Princeton: Princeton University Press, 2009), 193, at 194.

[75] Karl Marx and Friedrich Engels, 'For Poland' [1875], trans. Paul Jackson, in Karl Marx, *The First International and After*, ed. David Fernbach (Harmondsworth: Penguin/New Left Review, 1974), 388, at 391.

[76] For these provisions see Polish Minority Treaty (n 73), 416–19. See also Treaty of Peace with Germany, signed at Versailles, 28 June 1919, *AJIL Sup.* 13 (1919), 151, Arts 87–93, at 194–202.

No less telling is the letter that Georges Clemenceau, French prime minister and president of the Paris Peace Conference, sent to Polish officials along with the treaty.[77] Clemenceau explained that international law had long shielded minorities from persecution, albeit with somewhat different mechanisms: instead of being enmeshed in a system of institutions centralized in Geneva, as it would now be, minority protection had been nested in balance-of-power networks coordinated by the Concert of Europe. That it was the League, and not some set of great powers, that would be responsible for monitoring compliance with the Polish treaty should, he argued, assuage Warsaw's concerns of illegitimate intervention. Whereas '[u]nder the older system the guarantee for the execution of similar provisions was vested in the Great Powers', this had proven to be 'ineffective' and had now been replaced with a new system in which 'the guarantee [was] entrusted to the League of Nations'.[78] This was a position that would find a home in many studies of international law before long. It became routine to claim that the minority treaties were designed partly to counter long-standing accusations that the great powers had abused their 'rights' of intervention in the domestic affairs of weaker states.[79]

A passage from Clemenceau's letter illustrates well the power dynamics at work beneath the Polish treaty. Underscoring the point that Poland's reconstitution had been achieved by the great powers, he left no room for doubt as to who held the reins:

> I must also recall to your consideration the fact that it is to the endeavours and sacrifices of the Powers in whose name I am addressing you that the Polish nation owes the recovery of its independence. It is by their decision that Polish sovereignty is being re-established over the territories in question and that the inhabitants of these territories are being incorporated in the Polish nation. It is on the support which the resources of the Powers will afford to the League of Nations that for the future Poland will to a large extent depend for the secure possession of these territories. There rests, therefore, upon these Powers an obligation, which they cannot evade, to secure in the most permanent and solemn form guarantees for certain essential rights which will afford to the inhabitants the necessary protection whatever changes may take place in the internal constitution of the Polish State.[80]

The great powers were determined to maintain control over a minority-protection regime of which they were the principal authors. They were also committed to

[77] 'Letter Addressed to M. Paderewski by the President of the Conference Transmitting to Him the Treaty to be Signed by Poland under Article 93 of the Treaty of Peace with Germany', reproduced in *A History of the Peace Conference of Paris*, ed. H. W. V. Temperley, vol. 5 (London: Henry Frowde and Hodder & Stoughton, 1921), 432.

[78] 'Letter Addressed to M. Paderewski' (n 77), 434.

[79] See, e.g., Helmer Rosting, 'Protection of Minorities by the League of Nations', *AJIL* 17 (1923), 641, at 647; P. E. Corbett, 'What is the League of Nations?', *BYIL* 5 (1924), 119, at 145; Raymond Leslie Buell, 'The Protection of Minorities', *International Conciliation* 11 (1926), 348, at 356. Cf. Alphonse Heyking, 'The International Protection of Minorities—The Achilles' Heel of the League of Nations', *TGS* 13 (1927), 31, at 47.

[80] 'Letter Addressed to M. Paderewski' (n 77), 434.

making this determination known, in Warsaw and elsewhere. Poland's reintegration as an independent sovereign state equipped to resist a resurgent Germany or revolutionary Russia had occurred at an exceptionally volatile juncture, and it involved a state of affairs that could only be sustained through ongoing involvement on the part of great powers. The force of Clemenceau's words here can hardly be overemphasized: it was through the 'decision' of these powers that Poland's independence had been restored, and it was upon their 'support' that its economy and society would depend for the foreseeable future.[81]

A new set of institutional apparatuses was to ensure that the League's minority-protection system functioned adequately. Predicated on the idea that minorities should be able to access the League Council when their rights had been violated and domestic avenues of redress exhausted, a 'Minorities Section' was established within the League Secretariat to review complaints sent to Geneva. For a petition to be deemed examinable and transmitted to a 'Minorities Committee', convened by and comprised of Council member states, it had to be vetted for formal 'receivability' by the Minorities Section. The League laid out five conditions that petitions would have to satisfy in order to complete this vetting procedure. The petition had to 'have in view the protection of minorities in accordance with the Treaties', could not have been 'submitted in the form of a request for the severance of political relations between the minority in question and [the] State of which it forms a part', must not have derived 'from an anonymous or unauthenticated source', could not include 'violent language', and needed to 'contain information or refer to facts which have not recently been the subject of a petition submitted to the ordinary procedure'.[82] The fourth and least precise criterion—regarding 'violent language'—often proved to be the most determinative, its vagueness bolstering the vetting officials' already considerable discretionary authority.[83] Unsurprisingly, navigating the petitions system—a system involving a large number of procedural rules[84]—proved

[81] Cf. Carole Fink, 'The Minorities Question at the Paris Peace Conference: The Polish Minority Treaty, June 28, 1919', in *The Treaty of Versailles: A Reassessment After 75 Years*, ed. Manfred F. Boemeke, Gerald D. Feldman, and Elisabeth Glaser (Washington: German Historical Institute/ Cambridge: Cambridge University Press, 1998), 249, at 273 (analysing Poland as 'a fragile republic encumbered by extraordinary internationally imposed controls on its domestic legislation and administration').

[82] 'Resolution Adopted by the Council on September 5th, 1923', reproduced in *Protection of Linguistic, Racial or Religious Minorities by the League of Nations: Resolutions and Extracts from the Minutes of the Council, Resolutions and Reports Adopted by the Assembly, Relating to the Procedure to be Followed in Questions Concerning the Protection of Minorities*, LN Doc. C.24.M.18.1929.I (Geneva: League of Nations, 1929), 7, at 7.

[83] On this see Jane K. Cowan, 'Who's Afraid of Violent Language? Honour, Sovereignty and Claims-Making in the League of Nations', *Anthropological Theory* 3 (2003), 271; Jane K. Cowan, 'The Success of Failure? Minority Supervision at the League of Nations', in *Paths to International Justice: Social and Legal Perspectives*, ed. Marie-Bénédicte Dembour and Tobias Kelly (Cambridge: Cambridge University Press, 2007), 29.

[84] For general discussion of the system see H. B. Calderwood, *The Protection of Minorities by the League of Nations* (Geneva: Geneva Research Information Committee, 1931), 7–9; Julius Stone, 'The Legal Nature of the Minorities Petition', *BYIL* 12 (1931), 76; Julius Stone, *International Guarantees of Minority Rights: Procedure of the Council of the League of Nations in Theory and Practice* (London: Oxford University Press, 1932), pt. 2; Pablo de Azcárate, *League of Nations and National*

challenging.[85] Turkey was subject to many petitions, frequently from Armenian citizens of the new republic troubled by their precarious status.[86] But the main sources were central and east European in origin—chiefly from ethnic Germans in Poland and Hungarians in Czechoslovakia and Romania, until recently at the helm of powerful empires and dissatisfied with the post-war settlement, but also from Jews in Romania, Albanians in Greece, and others.

Crucial to the implementation of the minority-protection system was the delimitation of the space in which it was to apply. The League Covenant contained no provision necessitating universal observance of minority rights. Wilson's second draft of the Covenant had included an article requiring 'all new States to bind themselves as a condition precedent to their recognition as independent or autonomous States, to accord to all racial or national minorities within their several jurisdictions exactly the same treatment and security, both in law and in fact, that is accorded the racial or national majority of their people'.[87] This would not have amounted to strict universalization, as it would have been restricted to 'new States'. Even so, both it and a number of related proposals, such as the Japanese delegation's insistence that a racial equality clause be inserted into the Covenant,[88] had been rejected.[89]

The entire system would eventually break down, in no small part due to charges of double standards stemming from such partial application. In September 1934, roughly five years after the Institut de droit international had adopted a declaration on the 'international rights of man',[90] Józef Beck of Poland proposed that

Minorities: An Experiment (Washington: Carnegie Endowment for International Peace, 1945), 102–9. See further Jennifer Jackson Preece, *National Minorities and the European Nation-States System* (Oxford: Clarendon Press, 1998), 80–3.

[85] For an especially challenging context see Julius Stone, *Regional Guarantees of Minority Rights: A Study of Minorities Procedure in Upper Silesia* (New York: Macmillan, 1933); and Christian Raitz von Frentz, *A Lesson Forgotten: Minority Protection under the League of Nations—The Case of the Germany Minority in Poland, 1920–1934* (Münster: Lit Verlag, 1999), ch. 4.

[86] See Gustave Kövér, *L'erreur initiale de la Société des Nations: Documents pour servir à l'histoire de la question minoritaire* (Genève: Éditions du Bureau central des minorités, 1940), 45–66; and also Gustave Kövér, *Histoire d'une trahison: le calvaire des minorités nationales et la Société des Nations* (Genève: Éditions du Bureau central des minorités, 1939), 35–40.

[87] David Hunter Miller, *The Drafting of the Covenant*, vol. 2 (New York: G. P. Putnam's Sons, 1928), 91.

[88] Naoko Shimazu, *Japan, Race and Equality: The Racial Equality Proposal of 1919* (London: Routledge, 1998); Paul Gordon Lauren, 'Human Rights in History: Diplomacy and Racial Equality at the Paris Peace Conference', *Diplomatic History* 2 (1978), 257.

[89] David Hunter Miller, adviser to the American delegation in Paris, had found Wilson's proposal both too weak, in that it was to apply only to 'new States', and too strong, given the practical difficulty of generalizing many rights. See the commentary in Miller, *Drafting of the Covenant*, vol. 2 (n 87), 91; and also David Hunter Miller, *The Drafting of the Covenant*, vol. 1 (New York: G. P. Putnam's Sons, 1928), 47. For discussion see Malcolm D. Evans, *Religious Liberty and International Law in Europe* (Cambridge: Cambridge University Press, 1997), 88.

[90] For the text see 'Déclaration des droits internationaux de l'homme', *AIDI* 35 (1929-II), 298. For commentary see André Mandelstam, 'La Déclaration des droits internationaux de l'homme adoptée par l'Institut de droit international', *Revue de droit international* 5 (1930), 59; and James Brown Scott, 'La Déclaration internationale des droits de l'homme', *Revue de droit international* 5 (1930), 79.

the League's minority-protection obligations be extended to all League members, going so far as to index continued Polish cooperation to such generalization. This proposal received support from other delegates, eventually snowballing into a broader movement. Like Japan, Germany—a long-standing critic of Anglo-French interpretations of minority rights,[91] and now a staunch supporter of its ethnic kin in Poland and elsewhere[92]—had already pulled out of the League. Poland's decision to condition further cooperation on the universalization of minority protection, combined with the support it received from other League members, brought this process to a head. Some of the last nails in the coffin may well have come from the establishment of bilateral regimes escaping League control, and, even more importantly, Geneva's abysmal track record in constraining conflict and the use of force, exemplified by Italy's invasion of Abyssinia and the Spanish Civil War. Ultimately, though, it was disputes about the scope of minority protection that deracinated the League: if minority protection was not applicable to all, then it could not be applicable to any, in which case the League dream of managing nationalism turned out to be little more than a chimera.[93]

I have already noted that the League's minority treaties and related techniques have often been understood as a radical augmentation of the minority-protection provisions inserted into the balance-of-power treaties of the nineteenth century. I have also noted that this claim is frequently supported with a sharp distinction between pre- and post-1919 international law. Hard-and-fast epochal divisions of this sort are always misleading, and it would be incorrect to posit an unbridgeable gap between the international law of the nineteenth century and that of the interwar period. Yet, once again, it cannot be denied that international law experienced far-ranging changes after Versailles. The rigid model of absolute sovereignty found in so many classic nineteenth-century discussions of 'civilized' states underwent relaxation after the war. Aiming for an efficient distribution of territory while arbitrating the 1928 *Island of Palmas* dispute, the sociologically minded Max Huber could, for instance, write that 'the establishment of sovereignty may be the outcome of a slow evolution, of a progressive

[91] As early as 1917 German and Austrian authorities had denounced as hypocritical claims that the Allied war effort was driven by a dedication to self-determination (pointing as evidence to Ireland, Finland, the Boer Republics, and North African territories under British, French, and Italian colonial rule). Antonio Cassese, *Self-Determination of Peoples: A Legal Reappraisal* (Cambridge: Cambridge University Press, 1995), 24.

[92] A number of German grievances found themselves before the Permanent Court in the interwar period. See *German Settlers in Poland*, Advisory Opinion, PCIJ Rep. Series B No 6 (1923); *Case concerning Certain German Interests in Polish Upper Silesia (The Merits)* (*Germany v Poland*) PCIJ Rep. Series A No 7 (1926); *Case concerning the Factory at Chorzów (Claim for Indemnity) (Merits)* (*Germany v Poland*) PCIJ Rep. Series A No 17 (1928); *Rights of Minorities in Upper Silesia (Minority Schools)* (*Germany v Poland*) PCIJ Rep. Series A No 15 (1928); *Case concerning the Polish Agrarian Reform and the German Minority (Interim Measures of Protection)* (*Germany v Poland*) PCIJ Rep. Series A/B No 58 (1933).

[93] As one commentator would later put it, minority protection was delegitimized by the fact that it was 'treated as a mere expedient, to be adopted with discriminatory effect, not as an expression of a universally valid, normative approach to problems of human relations'. Inis L. Claude Jr, *National Minorities: An International Problem* (Cambridge: Harvard University Press, 1955), 36.

intensification of State control'[94]—a depiction with which many pre-1919 treatise writers, accustomed to presenting European sovereignty as a crypto-metaphysical 'supreme power' or 'supreme authority',[95] would have been somewhat uncomfortable, at least when discussing specifically European affairs.[96] The drive to institute minority-protection regimes under the supervision of the League testified to the breadth of this change. Regardless of whether nineteenth-century scholarship was studied carefully,[97] earlier attempts to extend protection to minorities or to regulate majority–minority relations appeared makeshift in comparison, outgrowths of temporary, unsustainable truces in a game of inter-imperial rivalry rather than harbingers of a properly cosmopolitan future in which sovereignty might be modulated and calibrated in the name of international peace.

Part of this shift can be explained by a move toward a mode of pragmatic institutionalism that was viewed as critical to managing conflict, manufacturing viable states, and preventing the outbreak of yet another *bellum omnium contra omnes*—with the important qualification that the post-First World War turn to pragmatism was more an internal refinement of positivism, itself deeply intertwined with natural law,[98] than a clean break from it. Writing in the *American Political Science Review*, for instance, one student of international relations argued that the League was 'neither an anomaly nor a so-called superstate, but simply a corporation—that very convenient invention for getting joint business accomplished with which we are all familiar'.[99] This was a characterization that would have been all but unthinkable in respect to an international organization even a few years earlier and that clearly suggested sympathy with a managerialism

[94] *Island of Palmas* (*Netherlands v United States*) 2 RIAA 829 (1928), 867.

[95] Although such notions are typically associated with nineteenth-century German legal theory, they were common in a number of traditions. For Britain and the United States see, e.g., Henry Wheaton, *Elements of International Law, With a Sketch of the History of the Science* (Philadelphia: Carey, Lea & Blanchard, 1836), 210, 263, 271; Herbert Wolcott Bowen, *International Law: A Simple Statement of Its Principles* (New York: G. P. Putnam's Sons, 1896), 3; L. Oppenheim, *International Law: A Treatise*, 2nd ed., vol. 1 (London: Longmans, Green, & Co., 1912), 177.

[96] Nineteenth-century European authorities often regarded the sovereign claims of extra-European states and peoples as subject to considerable gradation. In respect to Indian states, for instance, British colonial officials deftly manipulated constitutional and international law to afford local rulers only limited sovereignty. Lauren Benton, *A Search for Sovereignty: Law and Geography in European Empires, 1400–1900* (Cambridge: Cambridge University Press, 2010), ch. 5. For a juxtaposition of the development of divisible sovereignty for the extra-European world and the consolidation of sovereign equality for 'civilized' European states in the nineteenth century, see Edward Keene, *Beyond the Anarchical Society: Grotius, Colonialism and Order in World Politics* (Cambridge: Cambridge University Press, 2002), ch. 4.

[97] On this see Anthony Carty, '19th Century Textbooks and International Law' (PhD dissertation, University of Cambridge, 1972), i–xxiii.

[98] Koskenniemi, *Gentle Civilizer* (n 60), 130–2; and also Martti Koskenniemi, 'Into Positivism: Georg Friedrich von Martens (1756–1821) and Modern International Law', *Constellations* 15 (2008), 189, at 190, 201–3. For a suggestive argument to the effect that this tension between positivism and naturalism contributed to the popularization of evolutionary modes of thinking among late nineteenth-century British international lawyers, see Casper Sylvest, 'International Law in Nineteenth-Century Britain', *BYIL* 75 (2004), 9, at 12, 40–1, 48.

[99] Dayton Voorhees, 'The League of Nations: A Corporation, not a Superstate', *American Political Science Review* 20 (1926), 847, at 847.

derived from the United States' recently acquired great-power status, not to mention the formative influence of Wilson over the League project. 'Suppress the League', argued William Rappard, a senior League diplomat heavily involved in the Mandate System, 'and you liberate instincts of domination, which are at present at least restrained. Fortify the League, on the other hand, and you bridle and repress these dangerous instincts which threaten not only the welfare of millions of Europeans, but thereby also the peace of the world.'[100] Another writer was even more mellifluous, suggesting that the 'new world order' would be realized only if 'international coöperation', understood both as 'a matter of law' and as 'a matter of policy, self-interest, and spiritual attitude', succeeded in taming nationalistic sovereignty, 'so firmly fixed in the minds of men and the consciousness of states that we may not expect it to disappear'.[101]

Such pragmatism had profound repercussions on the state. Already under attack, not least from solidaristic and pluralistic legal theories propounded by the likes of Léon Duguit and Harold Laski,[102] state sovereignty entered the post-1919 world battered from war and bruised by calls for supranational institution-building. Jurists spoke of 'the growing interdependence of nations and the appearance of rudimentary organs of international government',[103] or at least of an interlocking system of 'International Legislation, International Administration of Justice, and International Mediation'[104]—claims which, ironically enough, proved fatal to attempts to ratify the League Covenant in Washington. Although sovereignty would not, of course, disappear in this new world order, the path had been cleared for 'a new conception of the State, wider and more just than that of absolute territorial sovereignty'.[105] The League sought, with varying degrees of success, to reconcile state sovereignty and world order under conditions that frequently blurred classical boundaries. One result was that the line between municipal and international law became ever more difficult to draw. Some toyed with the idea that the League was following in the footsteps of early British constitutional history by instituting dispute-resolution mechanisms without extinguishing traditional claims to sovereignty.[106] Others were puzzled about how much could be shielded from international scrutiny through characterization as a 'matter of domestic

[100] William E. Rappard, *International Relations as Viewed from Geneva* (New Haven: Yale University Press, 1925), 56.

[101] Frederick Charles Hicks, *The New World Order: International Organization, International Law, International Coöperation* (Garden City: Doubleday, Page, & Co., 1920), 15–16.

[102] See, e.g., Léon Duguit, *Le droit social, le droit individuel et la transformation de l'Etat*, 2nd ed. (Paris: Félix Alcan, 1911); Harold J. Laski, *Studies in the Problem of Sovereignty* (New Haven: Yale University Press, 1917).

[103] S. W. Armstrong, 'The Doctrine of the Equality of Nations in International Law and the Relation of the Doctrine to the Treaty of Versailles', *AJIL* 14 (1920), 540, at 563.

[104] L. Oppenheim, *The League of Nations and Its Problems: Three Lectures* (London: Longmans, Green, & Co., 1919), 41.

[105] Paul Vinogradoff, 'Historical Types of International Law' [1923], in *The Collected Papers of Paul Vinogradoff, With a Memoir by The Right Hon. H. A. L. Fisher*, vol. 2 (Oxford: Clarendon Press, 1928), 248, at 318.

[106] A. F. Pollard, *The League of Nations: An Historical Argument* (Oxford: Clarendon Press, 1918), 52–7; Geoffrey Butler, 'Sovereignty and the League of Nations', *BYIL* 1 (1920–1), 35, at 40–1.

jurisdiction' pursuant to paragraph eight of Article 15 of the League Covenant,[107] a provision of unstable scope and content even at the drafting stage.[108] The new system of minority protection was of central importance here. By restructuring mechanisms of international supervision in respect to minorities in central and eastern Europe, it was hoped that the League would be able to manage nationalism with greater dexterity than had previously been the case.

III. Before and After the Compulsory Greek–Turkish Exchange

Considered superficially, Turkey's encounter with the interwar international law of minority protection may seem conventional, more or less in keeping with experiences in central and eastern Europe after the fall of the Habsburgs, Hohenzollerns, and Romanovs. The Allies succeeded in inserting into the Lausanne Peace Treaty a set of provisions guaranteeing basic civil and political rights to Turkey's non-Muslim communities. These provisions were retailored variants of the protective clauses the Allies had built into the treaties with Poland and other states. On closer inspection, though, what occurred in Turkey was instructively distinctive. To begin with, the Turkish political class flatly refused to extend legal minority status to Muslim communities. In this it followed the *millet* system, which had afforded certain non-Muslim communities a measure of autonomy but had not contemplated similar treatment for non-Turkish Muslim communities. In addition, the rights extended to non-Muslims in Turkey tended to be less effective than those made available to minorities in central and eastern Europe. When operationalized, the minority-related provisions of the Lausanne Peace Treaty were frequently weaker in practice than the corresponding provisions of the European minority treaties, themselves anything but resounding successes. Finally, and most crucially, the system as a whole was made contingent on the Greek–Turkish population exchange. The Turkish delegation consented to the comparatively meagre minority-protection clauses that were built into the Lausanne Peace Treaty only on the condition that the number of individuals to

[107] 'If the dispute between the parties is claimed by one of them, and is found by the Council to arise out of a matter which by international law is solely within the domestic jurisdiction of that party, the Council shall so report, and shall make no recommendation as to its settlement.' Covenant of the League of Nations Adopted by the Peace Conference at Plenary Session, 28 April 1919, *AJIL Sup.* 13 (1919), 128, at 134.

[108] Kelsen called this 'one of the worst drafted provisions of the Covenant', rejecting outright the notion that 'there are objects which by their nature escape from the control of international law'. Hans Kelsen, *Legal Technique in International Law: A Textual Critique of the League Covenant* (Geneva: Geneva Research Centre, 1939), 125, 127. Trenchant criticisms came from a variety of other directions. See, e.g., J. L. Brierly, 'Matters of Domestic Jurisdiction', *BYIL* 6 (1925), 8, at 13–14; and, for a broader and more charged discussion, Georg Schwarzenberger, *The League of Nations and World Order: A Treatise on the Principle of Universality in the Theory and Practice of the League of Nations* (London: Constable & Co., 1936), ch. 3.

whom they would apply was curtailed through a compulsory exchange of minorities with Greece. Turkey's conformity to even the most rudimentary elements of the Versailles system of minority protection was thus tethered to the exchange's implementation. If the Lausanne settlement was 'the international birth certificate of the new Turkey',[109] the population exchange exercised guardianship rights over minority protection in the new state.

These points require independent analysis. Members of the Turkish delegation at Lausanne tended to see themselves neither as heirs of a vanquished Central Power nor as forerunners of a new state with limited bargaining power, but as victors in a national liberation struggle seeking both to resist partition and to depose a despotic *ancien régime*. Turkey was finally to take its place in the 'family of civilized nations'—not as a marginal participant, as in previous arrangements like the Treaty of Paris, but on its own terms, as an entity formidable enough to turn 'civilizational' rhetoric to its advantage,[110] even at the risk of inviting further dependence upon the West. Accordingly, as with other matters with serious politico-economic implications, like the question of how to handle the concessions the Ottomans had granted to European companies for large-scale projects like railroad construction, an especially thorny issue given the Turkish Republic's status as the Ottoman Empire's legal successor,[111] they pressed hard on the question of minority protection.

This position of perceived—if not actual—strength, departing markedly from the situation Poland found itself in 1919, enabled the Turkish delegation to push the Allies on a problem of first-order importance—that of determining the meaning and scope of the term 'minority' in the context at hand. Allied delegates suggested, if only half-heartedly, that 'minority' should be understood in a broad sense, including, in addition to non-Muslims, those communities that shared the Islamic faith but were distinct from an ethnic, cultural, or linguistic standpoint from the Turkish majority. In response, Turkey argued that minority status should be attached to non-Muslims alone. This, Turkish delegates contended, would accord with realities on the ground, particularly as centuries of living with the *millet* system had brought about a situation in which social relations were mediated by differences of faith and 'no distinction was made either in theory or in practice between the various elements of the Moslem population'.[112]

[109] René Albrecht-Carrié, *A Diplomatic History of Europe since the Congress of Vienna* (New York: Harper & Brothers, 1958), 403.

[110] The term 'civilization'—key to the rhetoric of Turkish nationalism in the early twentieth century—first entered Ottoman Turkish in the 1830s; see Tuncer Baykara, *Osmanlılar'da Medeniyet Kavramı ve Ondokuzuncu Yüzyıla Dair Araştırmalar* (İzmir: Akademi Kitabevi, 2000), 1, 12, 29.

[111] An instrument concluded at Lausanne established the republic's successorship respecting concessionary contracts and related agreements in territories not detached from Turkey; see Protocol relating to Certain Concessions Granted in the Ottoman Empire and Declaration, signed at Lausanne, 24 July 1923, 28 LNTS 203. For analysis see Jean Teyssaire, 'Les concessions et le Traité de Lausanne', *RGDIP* 35 (1928), 447.

[112] Minutes of the Territorial and Military Commission's meeting on 9 January 1923, in *Lausanne Conference on Near Eastern Affairs (1922–1923): Records of Proceedings and Draft Terms of Peace* (Cmd 1814) (London: His Majesty's Stationery Office, 1923), 301. For analysis of the debate at Lausanne see Derya Bayır, *Minorities and Nationalism in Turkish Law* (Farnham: Ashgate, 2013), 83–4.

Turkey's stance on this issue, which proved insurmountable, is reflected in the terms of the final agreement. Nowhere in the section of the Lausanne Peace Treaty that concerned minority protection—Articles 37 to 44, with Article 45 as something of a reciprocity clause vis-à-vis Greece to ensure similar treatment for Muslims in western Thrace[113]—did the term 'minority' appear unaccompanied by 'non-Moslem'. Article 39, the most generally framed of the lot, declared that 'Turkish nationals belonging to non-Moslem minorities will enjoy the same civil and political rights as Moslems'.[114] With respect to specific rights, Article 40 granted members of these same communities the right to 'establish, manage and control at their own expense any charitable, religious and social institutions', Article 41 obliged the state to make instruction in native languages available in 'those towns and districts, where a considerable proportion of non-Moslem nationals are resident', and so on.[115] At no point in these or any other provisions—all of which were 'placed under the guarantee of the League of Nations' by Article 44[116]—were similar entitlements extended to non-Turkish Muslims. In each case, the noun 'minority' was qualified by the immediately preceding adjective, 'non-Moslem'. That minority status was conceptualized in this manner followed directly from the Ottoman *millet* system. Religion had been the primary formal marker of identity under the *millet* system, and Muslims had only rarely, and exceptionally, been distinguished along ethnic or linguistic lines for purposes of legal administration. Indeed, not only did the Peace Treaty contain no requirement that Turkey recognize its non-Turkish Muslim communities as national minorities, but it effectively restricted the application of minority status to those non-Muslim communities which had traditionally commanded dominant positions within the *millet* system: the Greeks, Armenians, and Jews. In this respect, Lausanne did not deviate from Ottoman tradition.[117]

As has so often been the case, it was the Kurds—the most sizable non-Turkish group inhabiting the territory that would comprise the Turkish Republic[118]—who

[113] Treaty of Peace, signed at Lausanne, 24 July 1923, 28 LNTS 11 ('Lausanne Peace Treaty'), at 31–7.

[114] Lausanne Peace Treaty (n 113), 33.

[115] Lausanne Peace Treaty (n 113), 33–5.

[116] Lausanne Peace Treaty (n 113), 35–7. See further 'League of Nations Guarantee in respect of the Provisions contained in Articles 1 to 15 of the Treaty of Sèvres between the Principal Allied Powers and Greece', *LNOJ* 5 (1924), 1343; 'League of Nations Guarantee in respect of the Provisions contained in Articles 37 to 43 of the Treaty of Peace between the Principal Allied Powers, Greece, Roumania and the Kingdom of the Serbs, Croats and Slovenes, of the One Part, and Turkey, of the Other Part', *LNOJ* 5 (1924), 1344.

[117] See Baskın Oran, *Türkiye'de Azınlıklar: Kavramlar, Teori, Lozan, İç Mevzuat, İçtihat, Uygulama* (İstanbul: İletişim Yayınları, 2004), 47–60; B. Ali Soner, 'Citizenship and the Minority Question in Turkey', in *Citizenship in a Global World: European Questions and Turkish Experiences*, ed. E. Fuat Keyman and Ahmet İçduygu (London: Routledge, 2005), 289, at 294 ff. Religion continued to be viewed as the primary marker of minority status in many other post-Ottoman territories; for a particularly complex case see Benjamin Thomas White, *The Emergence of Minorities in the Middle East: The Politics of Community in French Mandate Syria* (Edinburgh: Edinburgh University Press, 2011), 49–60.

[118] The republic's first census—conducted in 1927 and including details on religious affiliations and native languages, some for the first time—put the number of Kurds at nearly 1,200,000, approximately 10 per cent of the total population.

bore the brunt of this restriction. Not only were the Kurds overwhelmingly Muslim, but most were affiliated with the same tradition of Sunni *Sharī'a* as the majority of Turks, albeit typically of the *Shāfi'ī* rather than *Hanafī* variety. Mustafa Kemal's nationalists had made a point of peddling the idea of a federal, consociational 'land of Turks and Kurds' during the Greek–Turkish War, with Kemal himself resorting to the rhetoric of pan-Islamic solidarity in an effort to galvanize the anti-imperialist cause.[119] But at Lausanne, promises of regional autonomy to Kurds were laid aside.[120] The Kurds, who would soon rebel and face successive waves of internal displacement,[121] were not alone in this regard. Arabs, present in large numbers in south-eastern Anatolia, and a number of other Muslim groups, such as Albanians, Bosnians, and Circassians, were denied minority status. Despite the fact that some members of these groups resisted Turkish nationalist authorities,[122] the latter typically deemed them amenable to assimilation to a greater degree than non-Muslims. Further, if references to minorities in the Lausanne Peace Treaty had not been accompanied by the modifier 'non-Moslem', groups like the Alevi—a quasi-Shi'i sect commanding the allegiance of nearly a fifth of all Muslims in Turkey today[123]—may well have qualified as minorities under domestic and international law.[124]

Even if one brackets the question of religious faith, one cannot help but be struck by the fact that those provisions that did make their way from the post-war minority treaties to the Lausanne Peace Treaty were often effectively diluted. To be sure, both in style and in substance, most of these provisions echoed those in

[119] On the legal implications see Bayır, *Minorities and Nationalism* (n 112), 70–9; Bülent Gökay, 'The Kurdish Question in Turkey: Historical Roots, Domestic Concerns and International Law', in *Minorities, Peoples, and Self-Determination: Essays in Honour of Patrick Thornberry*, ed. Nazila Ghanea and Alexandra Xanthaki (Leiden: Nijhoff, 2005), 315, at 321.

[120] For revealing glosses from a doyen of international law in Turkey (and the editor of the Conference of Lausanne's Turkish-language minutes), see Seha L. Meray, *Devletler Hukukuna Giriş*, vol. 1 (Ankara: Ajans-Türk Matbaası, 1959), 51, 191 ff. On the background dynamics see David McDowall, *A Modern History of the Kurds*, 3rd ed. (London: Tauris, 2004), 137–43; Wadie Jwaideh, *The Kurdish National Movement: Its Origins and Development* (Syracuse: Syracuse University Press, 2006), 133–8.

[121] For various episodes see Robert W. Olson, *The Emergence of Kurdish Nationalism and the Sheikh Said Rebellion, 1880–1925* (Austin: University of Texas Press, 1989); İsmail Beşikçi, *Tunceli Kanunu (1935) ve Dersim Jenosidi* (İstanbul: Belge Yayınları, 1990); Hamit Bozarslan, 'Kurdish Nationalism in Turkey: From Tacit Contract to Rebellion (1919–1925)', in *Essays on the Origins of Kurdish Nationalism*, ed. Abbas Vali (Costa Mesa: Mazda, 2003), 163; Jwaideh, *Kurdish National Movement* (n 120), ch. 12; Uğur Ümit Üngör, *The Making of Modern Turkey: Nation and State in Eastern Anatolia, 1913–1950* (Oxford: Oxford University Press, 2011), ch. 3.

[122] For the Circassians, the strongest example, see Ryan Gingeras, *Sorrowful Shores: Violence, Ethnicity, and the End of the Ottoman Empire, 1912–1923* (Oxford: Oxford University Press, 2009), esp. chs. 4, 5.

[123] Although the Alevi were not subject to systemic group persecution at the time, many Turkish nationalists feared that they would exert a destabilizing influence. For a useful general discussion see Hamit Bozarslan, 'L'alévisme et l'impossible équation du nationalisme en Turquie', in *Nationalismes en mutation en Méditerranée orientale*, ed. Alain Dieckhoff and Riva Kastoryano (Paris: CNRS Éditions, 2002), 133.

[124] Baskın Oran, 'The Minority Concept and Rights in Turkey: The Lausanne Peace Treaty and Current Issues', in *Human Rights in Turkey*, ed. Zehra F. Kabasakal Arat (Philadelphia: University of Pennsylvania Press, 2007), 35, at 37.

the central and east European minority treaties: Articles 37, 38, 39, 40, and 44 of the Lausanne Peace Treaty were, for instance, closely related to Articles 1, 2, 7, 8, and 12 of the Polish Minority Treaty, respectively.[125] Be that as it may, important divergences persisted, particularly in respect to their enforcement and implementation. Article 42 provides a strong illustration. With this provision, Turkey agreed 'to take, as regards non-Moslem minorities, in so far as concerns their family law or personal status, measures permitting the settlement of these questions in accordance with the customs of those minorities'.[126] At face value, this entailed a clear limitation of the authority of the new Turkish state: just as the *millet* system had preserved a certain sphere of internal autonomy for non-Muslim communities in regard to family law, so the 'new Turkey' was to ensure that these communities would participate in the construction of a great many legal structures to which they would be subjected as members of the republic. A systematically revamped legal system, grounded in codes imported from continental Europe, was to be fashioned. This process would not unfold behind the backs of Turkey's Greeks, Armenians, and Jews. On the contrary, it would involve them at every stage.

Yet this was not the entire story. Article 42 proved to be the most problematic of the various provisions bundled together under the rubric of minority protection in the Lausanne Peace Treaty. This was due to the fact that it involved an intriguing procedure for legal reform, calling for the establishment of 'special Commissions composed of representatives of the Turkish Government and of representatives of each of the minorities concerned in equal number' to review relevant proposals. 'In case of divergence' with respect to the pace or trajectory of reform, it went on to explain, 'the Turkish Government and the Council of the League of Nations will appoint in agreement an umpire chosen from amongst European lawyers' to negotiate a compromise.[127] Unsurprisingly, the work of these commissions proved deeply divisive, with government officials being at pains to find pretexts for their liquidation and many members of the *millets*-turned-minorities themselves expressing doubts as to their usefulness. In 1925, roughly two years after Lausanne and one year after the entry into force of the first complete republican constitution, the commissions informed the Turkish ministry of justice that sufficient progress had been achieved and that there was no longer any reason why their activities should continue. A significant amount of pressure had been applied to assure such conformity: state authorities had curtailed the activities of educational institutions and co-opted or hand-picked minority representatives, going as far as to arrest recalcitrant commission members in some cases.[128] What at first

[125] Lausanne Peace Treaty (n 113), 31–7; Polish Minority Treaty (n 73), 416–19.

[126] Lausanne Peace Treaty (n 113), 35.

[127] Lausanne Peace Treaty (n 113), 35.

[128] Aron Rodrigue, *French Jews, Turkish Jews: The Alliance Israélite Universelle and the Politics of Jewish Schooling in Turkey, 1860–1925* (Bloomington: Indiana University Press, 1990), 164–5; Rıfat N. Bali, *Cumhuriyet Yıllarında Türkiye Yahudileri: Bir Türkleştirme Serüveni (1923–1945)* (İstanbul: İletişim Yayınları, 1999), 54–101; Ayhan Aktar, 'Cumhuriyetin İlk Yıllarında Uygulanan "Türkleştirme" Politikaları', in Ayhan Aktar, *Varlık Vergisi ve 'Türkleştirme' Politikaları* (İstanbul: İletişim Yayınları, 2000), 101, at 112–13; Samim Akgönül, *Türkiye Rumları: Ulus-Devlet Çağından Küreselleşme Çağına Bir Azınlığın Yok Oluş Süreci*, trans. Ceylan Gürman (İstanbul: İletişim Yayınları, 2007), 67–74.

may have appeared as an attempt to salvage bits and pieces of Ottoman pluralism was thereby channelled into a full-blown programme of neo-Jacobin centralization, a key element in the drive to subordinate minorities to the sovereignty of the new nationalist state.

Seeing as how the Polish Minority Treaty had served as a standard-bearer for later minority treaties, and by extension the League's minority-protection system as a whole, the fact that similarities should have existed between it and the Lausanne Peace Treaty is not especially noteworthy. What *is* noteworthy is that Lausanne's relevant provisions were generally weaker and less effective. As one contemporaneous scholar observed, '[o]f the nationality provisions of the Peace Treaties, those of the Lausanne Treaty' were 'the most defective'; flimsy assurances of supervision from the League Council aside, 'the authority permitted to Turkey for promulgating such Nationality Laws as she pleases' was essentially 'supreme'.[129] Indeed, so removed was Turkey from central and eastern Europe's minority-protection paradigm that Erik Colban, director of the League's Minorities Section, was led to assert that 'the minorities procedure adapted for the European States does not give the desired result when applied to Turkey'.[130]

As though these deficiencies were not enough, the value of Turkey's minority-protection system was diminished by the fact that the Lausanne Peace Treaty was concluded a half year after the Convention concerning the Exchange of Greek and Turkish Populations. The Exchange Convention set out the basic parameters of the population transfers, establishing an internationally staffed organization (the 'mixed commission') to supervise the movement of displaced persons, liquidate both movable and immovable property, and dispense compensation for losses incurred during the procedure. All parties to the Lausanne negotiations, particularly Greece and Turkey, regarded the population exchange as a prerequisite not simply to a lasting peace, but to a decisive resolution of the eastern Mediterranean's 'minority problems'.[131] And since the exchange, in combination with the Armenian genocide and other First World War-related displacements, 'cleansed' Turkey of the vast majority of its remaining non-Muslim population, it also reduced the relevance of Lausanne's minority-protection provisions to an exceedingly small segment of the new Turkish Republic's citizenry. Rendered marginal from a demographic standpoint, non-Muslim minorities could thenceforth be coerced or cajoled all the more easily into toeing the line favoured by the Turkish-Muslim majority. Reports prepared for the Paris Peace Conference had frequently recommended the creation of a truncated Turkish state in central Anatolia, suggesting that with its 'solid block of Turkish Moslems', this region would serve as a natural home for post-Ottoman Turkey, '[n]ot the least of its

[129] William O'Sullivan Molony, *Nationality and the Peace Treaties* (London: George Allen & Unwin, 1934), 101.

[130] Quoted in Martin Scheuermann, *Minderheitenschutz contra Konfliktverhütung? Die Minderheitenpolitik des Völkerbundes in den zwanziger Jahren* (Marburg: Verlag Herder-Institut, 2000), 369, fn.

[131] See the discussion in ch. 3.

assets' being 'freedom from the burden of governing alien peoples of different faith, whose oppression by the Turk has reacted upon him morally and politically, with well-known evil effects'.[132] The Treaty of Sèvres had been drafted in the general spirit of such recommendations, providing a 'national home' for Armenians and autonomy (with the prospect of potential independence) for Kurds in addition to an extensive set of guarantees for minority protection.[133] Seeing as how this project had come to naught, it was now believed that stable and peace-abiding nation-states could be constructed only by way of full-scale population transfer, a more muscular and decisive mechanism of achieving security and furthering development.

[132] 'Outline of Tentative Report and Recommendations Prepared by the Intelligence Section, in Accordance with Instructions, for the President and the Plenipotentiaries, January 21, 1919', reproduced in David Hunter Miller, *My Diary at the Conference of Paris, with Documents*, vol. 4 (New York: Appeal Printing Co., 1924), 209, at 257.

[133] Treaty of Peace between the Allied Powers and Turkey, signed at Sèvres, 10 August 1920, *AJIL Sup.* 15 (1921), 179, Arts 62–4, 88–93, 140–51, at 192–3, 198–9, 208–13.

2

Early Experiments in Population Transfer, 1913–19

In 1954 Thomas Baty, a British jurist who had served as adviser to the Japanese government, observed that the word 'state' lent itself to two interpretations. The first envisioned the state as an independent sovereign entity, the other as the economic and social organization requisite for the existence of this entity—the state's 'national' bedrock, as it were. Each interpretation was hardwired into the term's genealogy, and each illuminated something essential about the concept of the state. '[N]ot only', wrote Baty, 'has the word "state," now used as a technical term of international law, connotations of ideas of pompous magnificence on the one hand, and mere "condition" on the other, but . . . it has actually been derived etymologically from . . . both of the two'.[1]

Others had shared Baty's sensitivity to this ambiguity for some time. Only a few years earlier, Carl Schmitt had concluded an analysis of a sentence from book one of Rousseau's *Du contrat social* with the observation that Rousseau made full use of the ambivalence inherent in the French *état*. Since this word's initial character may appear in upper as well as in lower case (the former being the traditional form for the sovereign state, the latter typically being used as a placeholder for a particular condition), Rousseau's decision to retain the lower case for the one sense just as much as the other was, he suggested, both politically and theoretically significant, implying that the state ought not to be deemed absolute.[2] In Schmitt's eyes, though, this move—a most 'perplexing and almost primitive artifice'—obfuscated statehood's solemnity, obliterating at one stroke 'the whole rationalizing power of the concept "state"'.[3] *Un État* should never be conflated with *un état*, he emphasized, least of all for the sake of 'word-play'.[4]

[1] Thomas Baty, *International Law in Twilight* (Tokyo: Maruzen Co., 1954), 311. On Baty's international legal theory see especially Anthony Carty, 'Thomas Baty: An International Lawyer as Public Intellectual between Imperial Japan and the Republic of China', *Japanese Yearbook of International Law* 56 (2013), 70.

[2] See the translator's note in Jean-Jacques Rousseau, *The Social Contract and Other Later Political Writings*, ed. Victor Gourevitch (Cambridge: Cambridge University Press, 1997), xliv, at lii–liii.

[3] Carl Schmitt, *The* Nomos *of the Earth in the International Law of the* Jus Publicum Europaeum, trans. G. L. Ulmen (New York: Telos, 2003 [1950]), 149–50.

[4] Schmitt, Nomos *of the Earth* (n 3), 150.

Initial reaction to the Greek–Turkish population exchange often underscored its novelty, with Stelios Seferiades articulating a widely shared sentiment when he wrote that the expression 'exchange of populations' was 'completely new in the history of treaties'.[5] Such claims were not without basis, as the notion of a large-scale compulsory exchange of minorities, undertaken with the assistance of international and humanitarian organizations, was indeed novel. Yet the Greek–Turkish exchange must also be understood as the culmination of a series of transfers designed in the Balkans and Asia Minor in the 1910s. The internal connection between the two meanings of 'state' outlined by the likes of Baty and Schmitt—the one underscoring the sovereignty essential to the state's political power and legal authority, the other speaking to the 'national' preconditions for the exercise of such sovereignty—is no less discernible in these earlier projects of demographic engineering than in the compulsory Greek–Turkish exchange of the 1920s and 1930s.[6] Each of these movements was driven by the need to align ethnicity with territory, nation with state. Absent such an alignment—such a subsumption of *état* under *État*—prospects for security and development in Greece and Turkey would remain remote.

This chapter begins by situating the compulsory Greek–Turkish exchange in a body of international treaty law concerning population transfer that was developed in the 1910s. It then proceeds to explain the socio-economic preconditions of demographic engineering in the Balkans and Asia Minor at the time. The two facets of my analysis are intertwined. Understanding the legally formalized population movements of the 1910s demands consideration of the forces at work in the crystallization of a specifically Turkish-Muslim mode of nationalism in the late Ottoman Empire. Similarly, the processes whereby such nationalism made itself manifest can be appreciated only by examining the body of treaty law through which population displacements were legitimized.

I. The First Legally Mediated Transfers

In a sense, the history of the Ottoman Empire, and of the post-Ottoman Balkans and Middle East, is a history of population movements.[7] Ottoman elites shifted

[5] Stelio Séfériadès, 'L'échange des populations', *RCADI* 24 (1928-IV), 307, at 335.

[6] I borrow the expression 'demographic engineering' from a rapidly growing literature on late Ottoman population politics. See especially Nesim Şeker, 'Demographic Engineering in the Late Ottoman Empire and the Armenians', *Middle Eastern Studies* 43 (2007), 461; Fuat Dündar, *Modern Türkiye'nin Şifresi: İttihat ve Terakki'nin Etnisite Mühendisliği (1913–1918)* (İstanbul: İletişim Yayınları, 2008); Erik Jan Zürcher, 'The Late Ottoman Empire as Laboratory of Demographic Engineering', *Il mestiere di storico* 1 (2009), 7; Uğur Ümit Üngör, '"Turkey for the Turks": Demographic Engineering in Eastern Anatolia, 1914–1945', in *A Question of Genocide: Armenians and Turks at the End of the Ottoman Empire*, ed. Ronald Grigor Suny, Fatma Müge Göçek, and Norman M. Naimark (Oxford: Oxford University Press, 2011), 287. For an earlier and broader discussion see John McGarry, '"Demographic Engineering": The State-Directed Movement of Ethnic Groups as a Technique of Conflict Regulation', *Ethnic and Racial Studies* 21 (1998), 613.

[7] For incisive variations on this theme see Reşat Kasaba, *A Moveable Empire: Ottoman Nomads, Migrants, and Refugees* (Seattle: University of Washington Press, 2009).

communities from one province to another for centuries. While the practice of relocating Christian children to Istanbul and elsewhere for training as members of the sultan's elite order of Janissary guards—termed *devşirme*, literally 'collection'—was effectively discontinued by the late sixteenth or early seventeenth century, the custom of resettling Muslims and non-Muslims throughout the empire continued long afterwards.[8] Elites in newly independent or semi-autonomous states in the Balkans, where such resettlement initiatives have often been associated with regional 'backwardness',[9] expelled large numbers of Muslims in the late nineteenth century. Nevertheless, despite the residual influence of these and related practices, it was not until the first decades of the twentieth century that legally formalized transfers and exchanges appeared on the scene in full force. Indeed, moving over the terrain that commences with the outbreak of the First Balkan War in 1912 and concludes with the cessation of the Greek–Turkish War in 1922, one cannot help but notice the incremental normalization of a new form of statecraft: transfers of minority populations governed at least partly by international treaty law. If, as one commentator wrote of the Balkan Wars' conclusion, 'the end of the Ottoman Empire, long foreseen and long dreaded as the certain prelude to Armageddon, had come, and come in the best possible way', with 'young nations of high promise' having 'been brought to the birth',[10] then forced migrations regulated by international law played a key role in facilitating this transformation.

The first attempt to coordinate an exchange of populations in the Balkans took place in 1913. The Ottoman Empire had been defeated in the First Balkan War of 1912–13 by Bulgaria, Greece, Serbia, and Montenegro, members of an unstable anti-Ottoman 'Balkan League', but had managed to regain some of its European possessions during the Second Balkan War of 1913. Determined to control the resulting displacements—the latest in a series of migrations both before and after Bulgaria's formal independence in 1908[11]—Bulgarian and Ottoman authorities agreed to oversee a formal population exchange along their new border in Thrace, this and adjacent areas having long been contested and heterogeneous.[12] While

[8] See Halil İnalcık, 'Ottoman Methods of Conquest', *Studia Islamica* 2 (1954), 103, at 122–9; Ömer L. Barkan, 'Osmanlı İmparatorluğunda Bir İskan ve Kolonizasyon Metodu Olarak Sürgünler', *İstanbul Üniversitesi İktisat Fakültesi Mecmuası* 11, 13, and 15 (1949–50, 1951–2, and 1953–4), 524, 56, and 209 (in three parts). See also Cengiz Orhonlu, *Osmanlı İmparatorluğunda Aşiretlerin İskânı* (İstanbul: Eren Yayıncılık ve Kitapçılık, 1987).

[9] See, e.g., Wayne S. Vucinich, 'The Nature of Balkan Society under Ottoman Rule', *Slavic Review* 21 (1962), 597; Nikolai Todorov, 'Sur quelques aspects du passage du féodalisme au capitalisme dans les territoires balkaniques de l'Empire ottoman', *Revue des études sud-est européennes* 1 (1963), 103. See also Perry Anderson, *Lineages of the Absolutist State* (London: Verso, 1979), 361–94.

[10] J. A. R. Marriott, *The Eastern Question: An Historical Study in European Diplomacy* (Oxford: Clarendon Press, 1917), 407.

[11] For the circumstances of independence see especially R. J. Crampton, *Bulgaria* (Oxford: Oxford University Press, 2007), 174–9.

[12] A particularly important site of contestation had been 'Eastern Rumelia', constituted as an autonomous province of the Ottoman Empire in 1878 but effectively annexed by Bulgaria in 1885. For Ottoman–Bulgarian rivalry over this quasi-sovereign territory, and the ensuing migrations of Muslims and others, see Anna M. Mirkova, '"Population Politics" at the End of Empire: Migration and Sovereignty in Ottoman Eastern Rumelia, 1877–1886', *Comparative Studies in Society and*

this was couched as a 'voluntary' affair, and while Muslims in territories ceded to Bulgaria were provided with a nominal right of option in respect to nationality,[13] the formal procedure was designed to confer legitimacy upon movements that had already taken place and to encourage many of those who remained to move without delay. To this end the instrument governing the exchange—a protocol annexed to the peace treaty concluded between the two countries after the war—stated that Bulgaria and the Ottoman Empire had reached agreement 'to facilitate the optional, reciprocal exchange of Bulgarian and Muslim populations, as well as their properties, within an area extending to 15 kilometres along the entirety of the common border'.[14] A mixed Bulgarian–Ottoman commission, to be established pursuant to the protocol, was to do much of the heavy lifting, being entrusted with the task of managing the movement of peoples and overseeing compensatory efforts.[15] Although spatially circumscribed, the exchange spoke to the desire of the two countries' elites to win recognition as vanguards of genuinely modern nation-states—states boasting distinct national identities and capable of exercising effective control over their respective territories and populations. The outbreak of the First World War blocked full implementation of the agreement, particularly of the mixed commission's work. But the enterprise nevertheless served as a rough-and-ready point of reference for the exchanges that would soon be carried out in Asia Minor and the Balkans.[16]

History 55 (2013), 955. The region had also been home to a small and short-lived republic of Pomaks, or Bulgarian-speaking Muslims, in the years following the 1877–8 Russo–Turkish War. For some details see A. G. Drandar, *Les événements politiques en Bulgarie depuis 1876 jusqu'à nos jours* (Bruxelles: T. Falk & Cie, 1896), 373–81. Within the Ottoman Empire, the Balkan Wars solidified Thrace's image as a tenuous frontier, one in which non-Muslims could often 'turn against' Muslims; see Eyal Ginio, 'Paving the Way for Ethnic Cleansing: Eastern Thrace During the Balkan Wars (1912–1913) and Their Aftermath', in *Shatterzone of Empires: Coexistence and Violence in the German, Habsburg, Russian, and Ottoman Borderlands*, ed. Omer Bartov and Eric D. Weitz (Bloomington: Indiana University Press, 2013), 283, esp. at 288–93.

[13] Traité de paix, signed at Constantinople, 16/29 September 1913, reproduced in G. Fr. de Martens, *Nouveau recueil général de traités et autres actes relatifs aux rapports de droit international*, 3rd series, ed. Heinrich Triepel, vol. 8 (Leipzig: Librairie Dieterich, 1914), 78 ('Turkish–Bulgarian Peace Treaty'), Art 7, at 82. Note that Bulgarian officials had sought to exercise greater control over Muslims after Bulgaria's de facto independence in 1878. The means were varied, ranging from cultural assimilation programmes and the supervision of Turkish clerics and schools to sweeping land reforms and outright encouragement of emigration. See André Girard, *Les minorités nationales ethniques et religieuses en Bulgarie* (Paris: Marcel Giard, 1933); R. J. Crampton, 'The Turks in Bulgaria, 1878–1944', in *The Turks of Bulgaria: The History, Culture and Political Fate of a Minority*, ed. K. H. Karpat (Istanbul: Isis Press, 1990), 43, esp. at 47–58; Ali Eminov, *Turkish and Other Muslim Minorities in Bulgaria* (London: C. Hurst & Co., 1997), 48–50; Mary Neuburger, *The Orient Within: Muslim Minorities and the Negotiation of Nationhood in Modern Bulgaria* (Ithaca: Cornell University Press, 2004), 41–4, 174–8. Such pressure would continue long after the conclusion of the Second Balkan War.

[14] Turkish–Bulgarian Peace Treaty (n 13), 86. On the implications of this protocol for the tenability of a right of option, see Dimitrije Djordjević, 'Migrations During the 1912–1913 Balkan Wars and World War One', in *Migrations in Balkan History*, ed. Ivan Ninić (Belgrade: Serbian Academy of Sciences and Arts, 1989), 115, at 117; and also Peter Loizos, 'Ottoman Half-Lives: Long-Term Perspectives on Particular Forced Migrations', *Journal of Refugee Studies* 12 (1999), 237, at 239.

[15] Turkish–Bulgarian Peace Treaty (n 13), 86.

[16] It also received tacit or express support from Western authorities, with the International Commission to Inquire into the Causes and Conduct of the Balkan Wars, established by the

This first effort was followed by a second in 1914. In 1913, partly in retaliation against the flight and expulsion of large numbers of Muslims from the Balkans,[17] Ottoman forces were instructed to have Greek farmers and townspeople removed from eastern Thrace and the Aegean coast. In mid-1914, by which time Ottoman authorities had launched a brutal campaign of persecution and intimidation that foreshadowed the Armenian genocide,[18] Venizelos, then prime minister of Greece, and Galip Kemali Bey, Ottoman ambassador in Athens, took steps to stabilize the situation by rendering these and related movements permanent. A 'voluntary' exchange between the Muslims of Macedonia and Epirus and the ethnic Greeks of Ionia and eastern Thrace would, it was thought, go some way to structuring movements between the two states. As with the 1913 initiative, this exchange was to be administered by a mixed commission.[19]

Although the institutional mechanisms of this procedure were never truly set in motion, it constituted a slightly more ambitious undertaking than the sort of frontier tinkering that characterized the proposed exchange between Turkey and Bulgaria in 1913.[20] Nevertheless, there was considerable continuity between the two enterprises. Like the Turkish–Bulgarian arrangement, the 1914 exchange was guided to a significant degree by the assumption that ethno-national tension could be minimized if minority protection and the right of option—provision for which had been made as recently as the 1913 Treaty of Athens between Greece and the Ottoman Empire[21]—were supplemented with organized movements of

Carnegie Endowment for International Peace, suggesting that a 'happy beginning' had been made to normalizing Turkish–Bulgarian relations with the 1913 treaty: *Report of the International Commission to Inquire into the Causes and Conduct of the Balkan Wars* (Washington: Carnegie Endowment for International Peace, 1914), 157. On this see further Howard Adelman and Elazar Barkan, *No Return, No Refuge: Rites and Rights in Minority Repatriation* (New York: Columbia University Press, 2011), 31–2.

[17] This was often stressed by publicists sympathetic to the Ottoman position; see, e.g., 'Les musulmans en Grèce', *Revue du monde musulman* 28 (1914), 323.

[18] See Taner Akçam, *The Young Turks' Crime Against Humanity: The Armenian Genocide and Ethnic Cleansing in the Ottoman Empire* (Princeton: Princeton University Press, 2012), xvii–xviii, ch. 3; and also Matthias Bjørnlund, 'The 1914 Cleansing of Aegean Greeks as a Case of Violent Turkification', *Journal of Genocide Research* 10 (2008), 41. For contemporaneous reports see Alexander Papadopoulos, *Persecution of the Greeks in Turkey Before the European War* (New York: Oxford University Press, 1919).

[19] For details on the initiative see Dündar, *Modern Türkiye'nin Şifresi* (n 6), 191–225; Ayhan Aktar, 'Nüfusun Homojenleştirilmesi ve Ekonominin Türkleştirilmesi Sürecinde Bir Aşama: Türk–Yunan Nüfus Mübadelesi 1923–1924', in Ayhan Aktar, *Varlık Vergisi ve 'Türkleştirme' Politikaları* (İstanbul: İletişim Yayınları, 2000), 17, at 26–32; Yannis G. Mourelos, 'The 1914 Persecutions and the First Attempt at an Exchange of Minorities between Greece and Turkey', *Balkan Studies* 26 (1985), 389.

[20] Indeed, it has been argued that it is here that 'the beginnings of a conscious policy of demographic restructuring and ethnic homogenization' should be located. See Mark Levene, 'Creating a Modern "Zone of Genocide": The Impact of Nation- and State-Formation on Eastern Anatolia, 1878–1923', *Holocaust and Genocide Studies* 12 (1998), 393, at 407.

[21] Traité de paix, signed at Athens, 1/14 November 1913, reproduced in G. Fr. de Martens, *Nouveau recueil général de traités et autres actes relatifs aux rapports de droit international*, 3rd series, ed. Heinrich Triepel, vol. 8 (Leipzig: Librairie Dieterich, 1914), 93, esp. Arts 4, 6, 11–12, at 94–5, 96–8. For discussion see Charalambos N. Fragistas, 'Le droit musulman en Grèce', *Annales de la Faculté de droit d'Istanbul* 4 (1954), 129; Samim Akgönül, 'Les vestiges du système ottoman dans le traitement des minorités en Grèce et en Turquie', in *La perception de*

minority peoples in strategically sensitive areas. Similarly, the 1914 enterprise foresaw a professional mixed commission charged with coordinating movements and overseeing the appraisal and liquidation of property.[22] The Great War suspended its work, but the idea of a semi-autonomous body in which competing rights and interests might be mediated continued to prove enticing for many of the region's statesmen. Whatever its family resemblance to programmes of mass resettlement underway in other contexts,[23] population transfer had clearly begun to come into its own as a distinct technique of facilitating and formalizing nation-building through international law, one with deep roots in Asia Minor and the Balkans.

This brings one to what is the most ambitious precedent of all, and the first to be fully implemented—the 1919 agreement between Greece and Bulgaria for a 'voluntary' exchange of minorities. This endeavour did not simply make a 'non-coercive' exchange of populations possible between two rivals, embroiled in a decades-long struggle over Macedonia and Thrace that had spilled over into regular conflict (the Balkan Wars and the First World War) as well as irregular conflict (bands of guerrillas launching raids in rural areas).[24] It also succeeded in establishing a set of complex institutions for the management of the upheaval, chief among them a League-supported mixed commission. In large part a product of Venizelos' nationalist foreign policy, the implementation of the agreement—a convention signed at Neuilly-sur-Seine in tandem with Bulgaria's general post-war peace treaty[25]—proved somewhat sluggish, with the bulk of the actual movements occurring after 1923, not least due to the confusion caused by Greece's near-constant efforts to absorb Asia Minor refugees.[26] Nevertheless, its chief purpose—facilitating a smooth 'reciprocal emigration' between the two

l'héritage ottoman dans les Balkans, ed. Sylvie Gangloff (Paris: L'Harmattan, 2005), 43, at 46; Konstantinos Tsitselikis, *Old and New Islam in Greece: From Historical Minorities to Immigrant Newcomers* (Leiden: Nijhoff, 2012), 60–2.

22 For details see Stephen P. Ladas, *The Exchange of Minorities: Bulgaria, Greece and Turkey* (New York: Macmillan, 1932), 22.

23 Comparisons with contemporaneous German policy, in France, Belgium, and elsewhere, were not uncommon; see, e.g., Félix Sartiaux, 'Le sac de Phocée et l'expulsion des Grecs ottomans d'Asie-Mineure en juin 1914', *Revue des deux mondes* 24 (1914), 654, at 655.

24 All of this had taken a toll: between 1912 and 1917 alone, the number of Bulgarians and Turks in Macedonia is recorded in one source as having fallen by approximately 50,000 and 40,000 respectively, with the total number of Greeks increasing by roughly 130,000. J. Ivanoff, *Les Bulgares devant le Congrès de la Paix: Documents historiques, ethnographiques et diplomatiques* (Berne: Paul Haupt. Librairie académique, 1919), 299.

25 Art 56 of the peace treaty Bulgaria had signed in 1919 stated that Sofia undertook 'to recognise such provisions as the Principal Allied and Associated Powers may consider opportune with respect to the reciprocal and voluntary emigration of persons belonging to racial minorities'. Treaty of Peace between Belgium, the British Empire, China, Cuba, Czechoslovakia, France, Greece, the Hedjaz, Italy, Japan, Poland, Portugal, the Serb-Croat-Slovene State, Siam, and the United States, and Bulgaria, signed at Neuilly-sur-Seine, 27 November 1919, 226 CTS 332, at 344. It was from this provision that the population exchange grew; see Convention between Greece and Bulgaria respecting Reciprocal Emigration, signed at Neuilly-sur-Seine, 27 November 1919, 1 LNTS 67 ('Convention of Neuilly-sur-Seine').

26 For a thorough account see Theodora Dragostinova, *Between Two Motherlands: Nationality and Emigration among the Greeks of Bulgaria, 1900–1949* (Ithaca: Cornell University Press, 2011), ch. 4.

countries—was reinforced by a host of mechanisms that would go on to resurface in the 1922–34 Greek–Turkish exchange. 'The High Contracting Parties recognise', the first article of the convention stated, 'the right of those of their subjects who belong to racial, religious or linguistic minorities to emigrate freely to their respective territories'.[27] In terms that would be reproduced nearly verbatim in the convention regulating the Greek–Turkish exchange, Article 5 explained that '[e]migrants shall lose the nationality of the country which they leave the moment they quit it and shall acquire that of the country of destination from the moment of their arrival there'.[28] And as with its predecessors, the bulk of the convention's remaining provisions—Articles 6 to 13[29]—established a regime for transferring and liquidating movable and immovable property that was to be directed by a mixed commission financed by 'the Governments concerned'.[30] Mixed commissions had been called into existence by the 1913 and 1914 arrangements, but neither endeavour had yielded anything on the scale of the commission established for the Greek–Bulgarian exchange in 1919. The Greek–Bulgarian commission had a small army of 'agents and instrumentalities', including 'neutral technical advisers', at its disposal.[31] These and other officials were stationed in a number of different locations and affiliated with a number of different centres and sub-committees, with the principal nodes of the logistical network that grew out of their interactions being located in Sofia, Salonica, and Komotini.[32]

Each of these early experiments—the projected exchange between Turkey and Bulgaria in 1913, the design for an exchange between Greece and Turkey in 1914, and, finally, the 1919 exchange agreement between Greece and Bulgaria—played an important role in the development of a corpus of legal precedents in respect to the management of large-scale displacement. But the 1922–34 Greek–Turkish exchange's regional antecedents do not end here. In 1919, when presenting the Greek case as the culmination of a long-standing drive to 'civilize' the eastern Mediterranean,[33] Venizelos pressed the Paris Peace Conference for a reciprocal exchange between Greece and what would remain of Turkey once it had been stripped of Istanbul, the western coast of Asia Minor, and those eastern provinces once home to large numbers of Armenians.[34] Exchanges were also contemplated for Kosovo, claimed by rival factions of (Christian) Serbs and (predominantly

[27] Convention of Neuilly-sur-Seine (n 25), 68–9.
[28] Convention of Neuilly-sur-Seine (n 25), 69.
[29] Convention of Neuilly-sur-Seine (n 25), 69–71.
[30] Convention of Neuilly-sur-Seine (n 25), Art 13, at 71.
[31] The language belongs to Ladas, *Exchange of Minorities* (n 22), 64.
[32] Ladas, *Exchange of Minorities* (n 22), 65 ff. See further André Wurfbain, *L'échange gréco-bulgare des minorités ethniques* (Lausanne: Librairie Payot & Cie, 1930).
[33] For this tendency in Venizelos' diplomatic strategy, see Michael Llewellyn Smith, 'Venizelos' Diplomacy, 1910–23: From Balkan Alliance to Greek–Turkish Settlement', in *Eleftherios Venizelos: The Trials of Statesmanship*, ed. Paschalis M. Kitromilides (Edinburgh: Edinburgh University Press, 2008), 134, at 138, 166.
[34] Eleutherios Venizelos, *La Grèce devant le Congrès de la Paix* (Paris: Imprimerie Chaix, 1919), 17–18. See further N. Petsalis-Diomidis, *Greece at the Paris Peace Conference (1919)* (Thessaloniki: Institute for Balkan Studies, 1978), 125.

Muslim) Albanians,[35] and Karabakh, a deeply contested territory over which Armenian and Azeri forces were embroiled in conflict.[36] Even more importantly, the Treaty of Sèvres called for a 'reciprocal and voluntary' population exchange between Greece and Turkey in a brief and generally ignored provision.[37] Sèvres never entered into force, and the exchange for which it called was never realized, but the fact that this scheme was considered seriously points to a growing recognition that it constituted an acceptable means of nation-building in the Near East. Indeed, if Sèvres was supposed to have been about 'the liberation of a large part of the people under Turkish domination, as a supreme humanitarian intervention on the part of Europe',[38] it was also about the crisp partition of a region whose 'mixed' character was so widely regarded as unsustainable that even the idea of mandates over a partitioned Ottoman Empire was occasionally floated in 1919.[39]

The 1922–34 Greek–Turkish endeavour relied on these early experiences, but it also went beyond them on account of its magnitude and explicitly compulsory character. The similarities between the justifications advanced for these earlier enterprises and the logic at work behind the compulsory Greek–Turkish exchange, particularly the desire to 'unmix' peoples in response to uncoordinated displacements, are not difficult to discern. And here too it was thought necessary to place a significant measure of authority in the hands of an institution armed with enough *savoir faire* to stand above the fray, in form if not necessarily in substance. Since it was thought that Greece and Turkey could be transformed into stable nation-states neither through enhanced reliance upon international minority protection nor through a Mandate System-style programme of full-scale reconstruction, it was believed that their constituent peoples needed to be segregated physically, a precondition for economic growth and political stability. Crucially, it was only after ostensibly 'voluntary' exchanges came to be viewed as insufficient that recourse was had to a compulsory procedure. What had formerly been attempted only on a comparatively small scale and through ostensibly 'non-coercive' means was now to be undertaken as part of a broader and even more forceful exercise in conflict resolution.

[35] The proposal would be laid aside as impractical, given the acrimony between the different groups. See Margaret MacMillan, *Paris 1919: Six Months That Changed the World* (New York: Random House, 2001), 361–2.

[36] See Donald Bloxham, *The Great Game of Genocide: Imperialism, Nationalism, and the Destruction of the Ottoman Armenians* (Oxford: Oxford University Press, 2005), 160.

[37] Treaty of Peace between the Allied Powers and Turkey, signed at Sèvres, 10 August 1920, *AJIL Sup.* 15 (1921), 179, Art 143, at 209–10.

[38] Alexandre Devedji, *L'échange obligatoire des minorités grecques et turques en vertu de la convention de Lausanne du 30 janvier 1923* (Paris: Imprimerie du Montparnasse et de Persan-Beaumont, 1929), 41.

[39] 'Report of the American Section of the International Commission on Mandates in Turkey', reproduced in *Papers Relating to the Foreign Relations of the United States: The Paris Peace Conference 1919*, vol. 12 (Washington: United States Government Printing Office, 1947), 751. See Harry N. Howard, *The King-Crane Commission: An American Inquiry in the Middle East* (Beirut: Khayats, 1963); and also Leonard V. Smith, 'Wilsonian Sovereignty in the Middle East: The King-Crane Commission Report of 1919', in *The State of Sovereignty: Territories, Laws, Populations*, ed. Douglas Howland and Luise White (Bloomington: Indiana University Press, 2009), 56.

For many international lawyers, the Ottoman Empire had long served as something of an exception. In 1894 Westlake had written that '[t]he case of Turkey' needed to 'be left out of sight, because of the anomalous position of that empire, included on account of its geographical situation in the political system of Europe, but belonging in other respects rather to the second group of contrasted populations'. 'She may', he had continued, 'benefit by European international law so far as it can be extended to her without ignoring plain facts, but her admission to that benefit cannot react on the statement of the law, which is what it is because it is the law of the European peoples'.[40] Likewise, the third edition of Lassa Oppenheim's seminal treatise, published only three years before the Lausanne settlement, had noted that the Ottoman Empire's 'position as a member of the Family of Nations was anomalous, because her civilisation fell short of that of the Western States', explaining further that '[i]t was for that reason that the so-called Capitulations were still in force, and that other anomalies still prevailed'.[41] Such 'exceptionalism' underwrote the popularity of population transfer in Anatolia and the Balkans during the final years of the Ottoman Empire. Indeed, as one interwar student of the last phase of the 'Eastern Question' would write, the late Ottoman Empire comprised 'an interesting laboratory for the study of the dynamic changes in international law', as it was in this, 'perhaps better than in any other single area', that one could observe at close hand 'the terrific forces which make for international change'.[42] In order to appreciate how such 'international change' took root, I turn now from the population transfer treaties of the 1910s to the broader socio-historical processes through which demographic engineering came into its own as a distinct mode of nation-building.

II. Dynamics of Displacement

Neither the rationales offered for the various experiments in demographic engineering that preceded the compulsory Greek–Turkish exchange nor the methods through which they were implemented can be appreciated fully without understanding the specific context within which they were planned. To be sure, willingness to design or redesign nations and states through forced migration was not unknown elsewhere at the time. Tsarist and Bolshevik authorities, for instance, were both given to employing public administrators with technocratic experience

[40] John Westlake, *Chapters on the Principles of International Law* (Cambridge: Cambridge University Press, 1894), 103. This assessment is still mild in comparison to Westlake's account of 'uncivilized peoples', whom he regarded as typically requiring 'the training and discipline which results from European government or control'. John Westlake, 'Territorial Sovereignty, Especially with Relation to Uncivilised Regions', in *The Collected Papers of John Westlake on Public International Law*, ed. Lassa Oppenheim (Cambridge: Cambridge University Press, 1914), 131, at 180.

[41] L. Oppenheim, *International Law: A Treatise*, 3rd ed., ed. Ronald F. Roxburgh, vol. 1 (London: Longmans, 1920), 34.

[42] Wilbur Wallace White, 'The Status in International Law of the Fragments of the Ottoman Empire' (PhD dissertation, University of Chicago, 1935), 331.

to oversee far-reaching land reforms and resettlement programmes in Siberia and central Asia.[43] Yet such efforts were typically undertaken with a view to optimizing management of productive resources within territorially integrated states. It was in Anatolia and the Balkans that the idea of orchestrating large-scale migrations between states first gained wide currency as a legally legitimized technique of nation-building.

It was against the background of the ethno-nationalist ideology the Young Turks began to cultivate after they wrested control of the Ottoman government in 1908–9, particularly the administrative centralization to which they had recourse in an effort to keep the empire from disintegrating in the face of secessionist nationalism and great-power intrigue, that notions of legally regulated population transfer began to gain popularity. The Young Turks' principal organ, the Committee of Union and Progress (İttihat ve Terakki Cemiyeti), initially included many non-Turks and non-Muslims within its ranks, officially committed as it was to a vision of shared Ottoman citizenship whose roots reached back to the mid-nineteenth century.[44] Over time, though, it grew increasingly reliant upon policies structured to strengthen the Turkish-Muslim 'core' of Ottoman society (the empire's Muslims had long been characterized as the *millet-i hâkime*, or 'ruling nation'). Over the course of 1908 and 1909, it deposed the reigning sultan, curtailed his successor's powers, and inaugurated a period of quasi-parliamentary rule by restoring the 1876 Ottoman constitution after nearly three decades of suspension.[45] In the years that followed, numerous attempts were made to tighten Istanbul's grip over the provinces, not least through the institution of sweeping powers of martial law, the curtailment of freedom of association and freedom of the press, the establishment of well-organized police, gendarmerie, and security services, and the calculated use of militias and paramilitary organizations to snuff out resistance. Materially, this push for centralization was intended to safeguard the state by stifling opposition and cultivating an indigenous Turkish-Muslim commercial class that could reverse comprador-facilitated economic intervention. Ideologically, it reflected Istanbul's desire to deflect European charges of 'backwardness': since the Ottoman state form, with its overlapping authorities and complex networks of intermediaries,[46] was widely viewed as archaic and inefficient, falling well short of Western standards of public administration, it was only by attenuating Ottoman traditions of legal and political pluralism that the

[43] Peter Holquist, '"In Accord with State Interests and the People's Wishes": The Technocratic Ideology of Imperial Russia's Resettlement Administration', *Slavic Review* 69 (2010), 151.

[44] References to 'Young Turkey' surfaced as early as the mid-1850s, roughly a decade before a heterogenous group of liberal publicists and civil servants popularly known as the 'Young Ottomans' began rallying around modernization programmes with Islamic and proto-nationalistic overtones. Şerif Mardin, *The Genesis of Young Ottoman Thought: A Study in the Modernization of Turkish Political Ideas* (Princeton: Princeton University Press, 1962), 40.

[45] For a detailed account of the *ancien régime*'s supplanting, see Aykut Kansu, *The Revolution of 1908 in Turkey* (Leiden: Brill, 1997), ch. 4.

[46] See especially Karen Barkey, *Empire of Difference: The Ottomans in Comparative Perspective* (Cambridge: Cambridge University Press, 2008).

committee believed it stood a chance of 'catching up' to the 'contemporary civilization' typified by national statehood.

These efforts often backfired. Centralization in the name of 'national sovereignty' (the expression seems to have entered Ottoman Turkish, as *hakimiyet-i milliye*, through the committee's publications)[47] was frequently resisted. In fact, the committee's policies often retrenched precisely those insurgent nationalisms they were meant to suppress. Far from being passive recipients of a modernization initiative imposed from above, provincial notables, castigated as 'oriental' by many members of the Istanbul elite,[48] frequently turned governmental innovations to their own advantage, augmenting political and economic structures derived from administrative reforms or the *millet* system in order to consolidate incipient national identities.[49] The committee's official prioritization of Ottoman citizenship as an overarching point of reference for all of the empire's constituent groups went some way to temper such peripheral movements, particularly in Arab provinces where secessionism does not appear to have emerged as a serious source of political mobilization until the mid-1910s.[50] Yet undergirding this public commitment was a dedication to the 'Turkification' of the empire's economy and society—an ethno-nationalism that, among other things, inspired the committee's policies in respect to engineered population movements. Accompanied by

[47] M. Şükrü Hanioğlu, *A Brief History of the Late Ottoman Empire* (Princeton: Princeton University Press, 2008), 165.

[48] On the general phenomenon see Ussama Makdisi, 'Ottoman Orientalism', *American Historical Review* 107 (2002), 768.

[49] This was not a new development. For the view that Bulgarian notables' engagement with Tanzimat-era administrative councils and financial institutions was key to the production of new modes of governance, see M. Safa Saraçoğlu, 'Some Aspects of Ottoman Governmentality at the Local Level: The Judicio-Administrative Sphere of the Vidin County in the 1860s and 1870s', *Ab Imperio* 2008 (2008-II), 223. For an argument that such processes struck even deeper into everyday life, see Milen V. Petrov, 'Everyday Forms of Compliance: Subaltern Commentaries on Ottoman Reform, 1864–1868', *Comparative Studies in Society and History* 46 (2004), 730. See also Yonca Köksal, 'Rethinking Nationalism: State Projects and Community Networks in 19th-Century Ottoman Empire', *American Behavioral Scientist* 51 (2008), 1498, at 1509–10.

[50] C. Ernest Dawn, 'The Rise of Arabism in Syria', in C. Ernest Dawn, *From Ottomanism to Arabism: Essays on the Origins of Arab Nationalism* (Urbana: University of Illinois Press, 1973), 148, at 152–4; C. Ernest Dawn, 'The Quality of Arab Nationalism', in *Arab Nation, Arab Nationalism*, ed. Derek Hopwood (Houndmills: Macmillan, 2000), 41, at 44; Hasan Kayalı, *Arabs and Young Turks: Ottomanism, Arabism, and Islamism in the Ottoman Empire, 1908–1918* (Berkeley: University of California Press, 1997), 12–13; Adeed Dawisha, *Arab Nationalism in the Twentieth Century: From Triumph to Despair* (Princeton: Princeton University Press, 2003), 33, ch. 2 generally. Even those accounts of Arabism that seek to demonstrate its influence before 1914 tend to concede that it did not generate public calls for independence until the Great War was under way; see, e.g., Rashid Khalidi, 'Ottomanism and Arabism in Syria Before 1914: A Reassessment', in *The Origins of Arab Nationalism*, ed. Rashid Khalidi et al. (New York: Columbia University Press, 1991), 50. The most notable exception is Egypt, formally bound to Istanbul until 1914 but effectively autonomous or under European administration after Muhammad Ali. For Muhammad Ali see especially Khaled Fahmy, *All the Pasha's Men: Mehmed Ali, His Army and the Making of Modern Egypt* (Cambridge: Cambridge University Press, 1997). The implications for Egyptian identity formation are analysed in Will Hanley, 'When Did Egyptians Stop Being Ottomans? An Imperial Citizenship Case Study', in *Multilevel Citizenship*, ed. Willem Maas (Philadelphia: University of Pennsylvania Press, 2013), 89.

unilateral expulsions and organized exchanges, not to mention outright massacre, the Committee of Union and Progress' heavy-handed drive toward centralization often engendered more *ressentiment* than it did *solidarité*.

The stance adopted by the Committee of Union and Progress with regard to the galvanization of the empire's Turkish-Muslim 'core' was closely associated with an awareness of the consequences of the Ottoman Empire's numerous territorial losses before and after the 1908–9 revolution. While some of these losses had followed domestic rebellions, others, such as the loss of Tripolitania to Italy in 1912 or the near-total disintegration of Ottoman power in south-east Europe during the 1912–13 Balkan Wars, resulted from international armed conflict. A point of particular sensitivity was the mass displacement of Muslims from Crimea, the Caucasus, and the Balkans—a process that had commenced in the late 1850s and continued essentially without pause since the early 1860s.[51] Stemming largely from Russia's southward expansion and the Ottoman Empire's military and diplomatic weakness, these migrations had focused sizable chunks of the Ottoman state's Turkish-Muslim population around new or hitherto marginal causes, contributing to the gradual popularization of Islamism and proto-nationalism.[52] The devastating Balkan Wars further reconfigured the Turkish-Muslim socio-economic imaginary, with the ensuing *en masse* expulsion of Muslims playing a key role in the growth of Young Turk revanchism and chauvinism, something of a default Ottoman 'policy' throughout the course of the Great War.[53]

[51] From a large and growing literature see especially Stanford J. Shaw, 'Ottoman Population Movements during the Last Years of the Empire, 1885–1914: Some Preliminary Remarks', *Osmanlı Araştırmaları* 1 (1980), 191; Kemal H. Karpat, *Ottoman Population, 1830–1914: Demographic and Social Characteristics* (Madison: University of Wisconsin Press, 1985), esp. ch. 4; Bilâl N. Şimşir, ed., *Rumeli'den Türk Göçleri*, 3 vols. (Ankara: Türk Tarih Kurumu Basımevi, 1989); Nedim İpek, *Rumeli'den Anadolu'ya Türk Göçleri (1877–1890)* (Ankara: Türk Tarih Kurumu Basımevi, 1994); Alexandre Toumarkine, *Les migrations des populations musulmanes balkaniques en Anatolie (1876–1913)* (Istanbul: Les éditions Isis, 1995); Justin McCarthy, *Death and Exile: The Ethnic Cleansing of Ottoman Muslims, 1821–1922* (Princeton: Darwin Press, 1995); Stephen D. Shenfield, 'The Circassians: A Forgotten Genocide?', in *The Massacre in History*, ed. Mark Levene and Penny Roberts (Oxford: Berghahn, 1999), 149; Brian Glyn Williams, '*Hijra* and Forced Migration from Nineteenth-Century Russia to the Ottoman Empire: A Critical Analysis of the Great Crimean Tatar Emigration of 1860–1861', *Cahiers du monde russe* 41 (2000), 79; David Cuthell, 'The Circassian Sürgün', *Ab Imperio* 2003 (2003-II), 139; James H. Meyer, 'Immigration, Return, and the Politics of Citizenship: Russian Muslims in the Ottoman Empire, 1860–1914', *International Journal of Middle East Studies* 39 (2007), 15; Irma Kreiten, 'A Colonial Experiment in Cleansing: The Russian Conquest of Western Caucasus, 1856–65', *Journal of Genocide Research* 11 (2009), 213; Oktay Özel, 'Migration and Power Politics: The Settlement of Georgian Immigrants in Turkey (1878–1908)', *Middle Eastern Studies* 46 (2010), 477; Dawn Chatty, *Displacement and Dispossession in the Modern Middle East* (Cambridge: Cambridge University Press, 2010), ch. 3; Walter Richmond, *The Circassian Genocide* (New Brunswick: Rutgers University Press, 2013).

[52] For an influential typology of late Ottoman political theory, see Yusuf Akçura, *Üç Tarz-ı Siyaset* (Ankara: Türk Tarih Kurumu Basımevi, 1976 [1904]). On these and related typologies see Niyazi Berkes, *The Development of Secularism in Turkey* (Montreal: McGill University Press, 1964), 337–46, 359–66; and Feroz Ahmad, *The Young Turks: The Committee of Union and Progress in Turkish Politics, 1908–1914* (Oxford: Clarendon Press, 1969), 154–5.

[53] Fikret Adanır and Hilmar Kaiser, 'Migration, Deportation, and Nation-Building: The Case of the Ottoman Empire', in *Migrations et migrants dans une perspective historique: Permanences et innovations*, ed. René Leboutte (Bruxelles: P. I. E.–Peter Lang, 2000), 273, at 279–80; Çağlar Keyder, 'Bir Türk Milliyetçilik Tarihi ve Coğrafyası', in Çağlar Keyder, *Memâlik-i Osmaniye'den*

The conviction that Anatolia served as a kind of sanctuary for displaced Turks and Muslims, who frequently found themselves forced to compete for land and resources with Greeks, Armenians, and others, quickly gained traction in this volatile and rapidly changing environment. Assuming that this was the last territory upon which Turkish nationalism might concentrate its energies, the Committee of Union and Progress sought consciously to redesign Anatolia, its chief point of ideological reference, in accordance with an idealized 'homeland'. So crucial an element of the committee's domestic and foreign policies was demographic engineering that local and provincial officials were regularly instructed to collect detailed information on the wealth, social status, and educational credentials of those within their jurisdiction, all with a view to ensuring that resettlement programmes furthered the demographic predominance of Muslims, above all Turkish Muslims.[54] Resettlement of displaced persons was only one aspect of a multi-faceted programme of demographic engineering in which non-Muslims and Muslims alike—Armenians, Assyrians, Greeks, and Jews, as well as Albanians, Arabs, Bosnians, Circassians, Kurds, and others—were shuffled from one region to another in the name of 'national security'.

These tendencies only grew stronger in response to the Allied Powers' drive to dismember the Ottoman Empire along the lines of the 1916 Sykes–Picot Agreement after the First World War,[55] as well as the closely related British-backed Greek invasion of western Anatolia in 1919, which Turkish nationalists would eventually succeed in countering with substantial Soviet support in arms and capital.[56] Many of the committee's highest-ranking officials quickly came to form

Avrupa Birliği'ne (İstanbul: İletişim Yayınları, 2003), 73, at 77–9; Kemal H. Karpat, 'The Muslim Minority in the Balkans', in Kemal H. Karpat, *Studies on Turkish Politics and Society: Selected Articles and Essays* (Leiden: Brill, 2004), 523, at 529 ff; Nicholas Doumanis, *Before the Nation: Muslim-Christian Coexistence and Its Destruction in Late Ottoman Anatolia* (Oxford: Oxford University Press, 2013), 148–61.

[54] Dündar, *Modern Türkiye'nin Şifresi* (n 6), 142–70; Akçam, *Young Turks' Crime* (n 18), 31–40; Taner Akçam, 'The Young Turks and the Plans for the Ethnic Homogenization of Anatolia', in *Shatterzone of Empires: Coexistence and Violence in the German, Habsburg, Russian, and Ottoman Borderlands*, ed. Omer Bartov and Eric D. Weitz (Bloomington: Indiana University Press, 2013), 258, esp. at 261–4. The importation of European statistical methods had been integral to the Ottoman bureaucracy's modernization in the nineteenth century. See Fatma Müge Göçek and M. Şükrü Hanioğlu, 'Western Knowledge, Imperial Control, and the Use of Statistics in the Ottoman Empire', in *Cultural Horizons: A Festschrift in Honor of Talat S. Halman*, ed. Jayne L. Warner (Syracuse: Syracuse University Press/İstanbul: Yapı Kredi Yayınları, 2001), 105, at 111; Kemal H. Karpat, 'The Ottoman Adoption of Statistics from the West in the 19th Century', in Kemal H. Karpat, *Studies on Ottoman Social and Political History: Selected Articles and Essays* (Leiden: Brill, 2002), 132.

[55] For the Sykes–Picot Agreement, see Correspondance relative à la reconnaissance et à la protection d'un État arabe en Syrie, 9–16 May 1916, reproduced in G. Fr. de Martens, *Nouveau recueil général de traités et autres actes relatifs aux rapports de droit international*, 3rd series, ed. Heinrich Triepel, vol. 10 (Leipzig: Librairie Dieterich, 1920), 350.

[56] See Stefanos Yerasimos, *Türk–Sovyet İlişkileri: Ekim Devriminden 'Millî Mücadele'ye* (İstanbul: Gözlem Yayınları, 1979); and Bülent Gökay, *A Clash of Empires: Turkey between Russian Bolshevism and British Imperialism, 1918–1923* (London: Tauris, 1997). The relationship was not merely one of 'assistance'; between 1921 and 1923, trade with Turkey appears to have comprised roughly a quarter of Russia's total trade in Asia. See Violet Conolly, *Soviet Economic Policy in the East: Turkey, Persia, Afghanistan, Mongolia and Tana Tuva, Sin Kiang* (London: Oxford University Press, 1933), 36.

the backbone of the Ankara-based nationalist movement, comprising much of the leadership of Mustafa Kemal's 'National Forces' (Kuva-i Milliye). And the very terms of the movement's 'National Pact' (Misak-ı Millî) made it clear that Anatolia would constitute the geographical centrepiece of the new, post-Ottoman Turkish state, with Kemal and his followers pledging to continue the war until such time as their position on the matter had secured international recognition.[57] Although the compulsory Greek–Turkish exchange had yet to be realized, the resettlement policies of the committee had already redistributed communities so 'efficiently' that Kemal's nationalist movement inherited an Anatolia more thoroughly Turkish-Muslim—and therefore more likely to submit to mobilization as part of an anti-imperialist resistance movement—than at any earlier time.

The precise extent to which the policies put in place by the Committee of Union and Progress' intelligentsia can be linked to the administrative mechanisms favoured by the Kemalist movement is open to some debate. What cannot be denied, though, is that their membership overlapped significantly, and that both groups were home to many who were prepared to exploit pervasive frustrations for the sake of a supposedly all-encompassing national struggle. Those who comprised the core of the Committee of Union and Progress and the Kemalist movement shared a common class background, virtually identical educational credentials, a strikingly analogous set of political commitments, and a similar willingness to track, and in many cases simply import, the legal and political innovations of the West. Crucially, as with so many other nationalizing elites on Europe's south-eastern margins,[58] their members frequently traced their origins to borderlands from which their families had fled or been evicted.[59] Indeed, it is no accident that most of those responsible for the deportation and massacre of Christians during the First World War—including, most notoriously, Mehmed Reşid, the Young Turk governor of Diyarbekir province, a major focal point for government action against Armenians and other Christians—were descendants of Muslims who had been expelled from the Balkans and Caucasus, often under conditions of brutal violence and with considerable loss of property.[60] Save for the

[57] See the text of the 'National Pact', reproduced in Arnold J. Toynbee, *The Western Question in Greece and Turkey: A Study in the Contact of Civilisations* (London: Constable & Co., 1922), 207. For the Turkish original see Reşat Ekrem, *Osmanlı Muahedeleri ve Kapitülâsiyonlar, 1300–1920, ve Lozan Muahedesi, 24 Temmuz 1923* (İstanbul: Muallim Ahmet Halit Kitaphanesi, 1934), 267–8.

[58] The Montenegrin case is especially telling; see Isa Blumi, 'Agents of Post-Ottoman States: The Precariousness of the Berlin Congress Boundaries of Montenegro and How to Define/Confine People', in *War and Diplomacy: The Russo–Turkish War of 1877–1878 and the Treaty of Berlin*, ed. M. Hakan Yavuz with Peter Sluglett (Salt Lake City: University of Utah Press, 2011), 226, at 243–4.

[59] On this see especially the work of Erik Jan Zürcher: 'The Young Turks: Children of the Borderlands?', *International Journal of Turkish Studies* 9 (2003), 275, esp. at 279–82; 'How Europeans Adopted Anatolia and Created Turkey', *European Review* 13 (2005), 379; and also *The Young Turk Legacy and Nation Building: From the Ottoman Empire to Atatürk's Turkey* (London: I.B. Tauris 2010), chs. 8–9. For an earlier rendition of the argument see also Erik Jan Zürcher, *The Unionist Factor: The Rôle of the Committee of Union and Progress in the Turkish National Movement, 1905–1926* (Leiden: Brill, 1984).

[60] Uğur Ümit Üngör, *The Making of Modern Turkey: Nation and State in Eastern Anatolia, 1913–1950* (Oxford: Oxford University Press, 2011), 43–7, 61–3 ff.

Ottoman nobility, this ambitious and rather unruly generation—an upwardly mobile cadre of 'reformers' fixated on nationalist renewal—had little standing in the way of its seizing power, which it did first with the Young Turks' palace revolution in 1908–9 and then through the consolidation of Kemal's nationalist movement in Anatolia.

It is a matter of no small importance that this prioritization of ethnic homogenization owed much to the writings of European intellectuals sympathetic to economic nationalization.[61] Friedrich List, theorist of the aptly termed 'national system' of economics, nineteenth-century British free-trade doctrine's protectionist rival, was a mainstay, supplementing the reception of French positivist literature on social engineering.[62] But far and away the most influential figure was Alexander Helphand, the Second International theoretician and arms dealer widely credited with having proposed an embryonic form of the theory of uneven and combined development that would later be picked up and developed by Trotsky. According to Helphand, a resident of Istanbul and financial adviser to the committee in the 1910s,[63] the Ottoman state had no choice but to abrogate the capitulations, do away with the Public Debt Organization (Düyun-u Umumiye) formed by European financiers to absorb tax revenue after the empire's bankruptcy in 1875,[64] and ensure the construction of a thoroughly 'native' (that is, Turkish-Muslim) bourgeoisie, sovereign over capital accumulation and equipped to resist European imperialism.[65] Differences notwithstanding, both the Young Turks and the Kemalists took to heart proposals of the kind that Helphand offered, with the latter making use of the Greek–Turkish exchange to deepen and expand the anti-liberal economic policies launched by the former (Kemal himself would declare in 1936 that the Turkish revolution had always been developed in accordance with 'a system other than "liberalism" ').[66] After all,

[61] Zafer Toprak, *Türkiye'de 'Milli İktisat' (1908–1918)* (Ankara: Yurt Yayınları, 1982), 25–35.

[62] Şevket Pamuk, 'The Ottoman Economy in World War I', in *The Economics of World War I*, ed. Stephen Broadberry and Mark Harrison (Cambridge: Cambridge University Press, 2005), 112, at 119. See further Roman Szporluk, *Communism and Nationalism: Karl Marx versus Friedrich List* (New York: Oxford University Press, 1988), 228–9.

[63] On this see Z. A. B. Zeman and W. B. Scharlau, *The Merchant of Revolution: The Life of Alexander Israel Helphand (Parvus) 1867–1924* (London: Oxford University Press, 1965), ch. 6.

[64] See especially Donald C. Blaisdell, *European Financial Control in the Ottoman Empire: A Study of the Establishment, Activities, and Significance of the Administration of the Ottoman Public Debt* (New York: Columbia University Press, 1929). See further Herbert Feis, *Europe the World's Banker 1870–1914: An Account of European Foreign Investment and the Connection of World Finance with Diplomacy before the War* (New Haven: Yale University Press, 1930), 332–41; Roger Owen, *The Middle East in the World Economy 1800–1914* (London: Methuen, 1981), 191–200.

[65] For Helphand's writings from this period, see Parvus Efendi, *Türkiye'nin Malî Tutsaklığı*, ed. Muammer Sencer (İstanbul: May Yayınları, 1977). For analysis see M. Asım Karaömerlioğlu, 'Helphand-Parvus and His Impact on Turkish Intellectual Life', *Middle Eastern Studies* 40 (2004), 145; Hans-Lukas Kieser, 'World War and World Revolution: Alexander Helphand-Parvus in Germany and Turkey', *Kritika: Explorations in Russian and Eurasian History* 12 (2011), 387.

[66] Quoted in Donald E. Webster, 'State Control of Social Change in Republican Turkey', *American Sociological Review* 4 (1939), 247, at 247. For Kemal's most influential statement of economic policy see Mustafa Kemal, 'Gazi Mustafa Kemal Paşa Hazretlerinin İlk Türkiye İktisat Kongresindeki İftitahī Nutukları', in *İzmir İktisat Kongresi (17 Şubat–4 Mart 1923)*, ed. A. Afetinan (Ankara: Türk Tarih Kurumu Basımevi, 1982), 57.

once approximately one-sixth of the cultivable land in western Anatolia had been vacated, and the proportion of Christians to the total population had dropped from roughly one in five citizens (in 1913) to something on the order of one in forty (in 1923), it was no difficult business for the Kemalists to press ahead with the Young Turks' plan to institute a new property regime favouring a thoroughly 'indigenous' Turkish-Muslim bourgeoisie.[67] 'Land reform' of this sort was deemed essential to economic development, particularly as 80 per cent of Turks in the early republic belonged to the peasantry.[68]

That the Greek–Turkish exchange had been instigated in part by Greece's determination to realize the *Megali Idea* of an enlarged Hellenic state—a guiding principle of its foreign policy that was seen as key to its claim to modernity,[69] and that was frequently defended by Greek jurists[70]—was significant here as well. Of all the non-Muslim *millets*, Ottoman Greeks had benefited most visibly from the empire's incorporation into the world economy from the late eighteenth century onwards: they engaged in banking, were active in Ottoman political and diplomatic circles, and played a crucial role as intermediaries in international trade and investment.[71] Western states and corporations, the latter increasingly employing Istanbul as a regional distribution and marketing centre, preferred to work with Greeks and other Ottoman non-Muslims rather than with the empire's Muslim entrepreneurs.[72] During and after the Great War, at a time when Venizelos routinely called for 'the creation of a great and powerful Greece, constituting not an extension of the State by conquest, but a natural return to the limits within

[67] Çağlar Keyder, *The Definition of a Peripheral Economy: Turkey 1923–1929* (Cambridge: Cambridge University Press/Paris: Éditions de la Maison des sciences de l'homme, 1981), 23; Çağlar Keyder, 'The Consequences of the Exchange of Populations for Turkey', in *Crossing the Aegean: An Appraisal of the 1923 Compulsory Population Exchange between Greece and Turkey*, ed. Renée Hirschon (New York: Berghahn, 2003), 39, at 43.

[68] Gülten Kazgan, 'Millî Türk Devletinin Kuruluşu ve Göçler', *İstanbul Üniversitesi İktisat Fakültesi Mecmuası* 30 (1970–1), 311, at 323.

[69] Richard Clogg, *A Concise History of Greece*, 3rd ed. (Cambridge: Cambridge University Press, 2013), ch. 3.

[70] To take only one example, Neoklis Kazazis of the University of Athens argued that every state is entitled to pursue a course of national integration. For discussion see Anastasia Stouraiti and Alexander Kazamias, 'The Imaginary Topographies of the *Megali Idea*: National Territory as Utopia', in *Spatial Conceptions of the Nation: Modernizing Geographies in Greece and Turkey*, ed. Nikiforos Diamandouros, Thalia Dragonas, and Çağlar Keyder (London: Tauris, 2010), 11, at 19.

[71] The causal relations at work in such processes are not entirely clear, though, not least because nineteenth-century Ottoman Greeks could also be suspicious of Western capital, viewing foreigners as competitors rather than collaborators. On this see the work of Reşat Kasaba: 'Was There a Compradore Bourgeoisie in Mid-Nineteenth-Century Western Anatolia?', *Review* 11 (1988), 215; *The Ottoman Empire and the World Economy: The Nineteenth Century* (Albany: State University of New York Press, 1989), 58–60, 75–83, 85; and also 'A Time and a Place for the Nonstate: Social Change in the Ottoman Empire during the "Long Nineteenth Century"', in *State Power and Social Forces: Domination and Transformation in the Third World*, ed. Joel S. Migdal, Atul Kohli, and Vivienne Shue (Cambridge: Cambridge University Press, 1994), 207, at 213. On the complex relations of rivalry and patronage that ensued see Barkey, *Empire of Difference* (n 46), 280 ff.

[72] For a good case study see Yavuz Köse, 'Nestlé in the Ottoman Empire: Global Marketing with Local Flavour 1870–1927', *Enterprise and Society* 9 (2008), 724, at 733, 742.

which Hellenism has flourished ever since the prehistoric period',[73] nationalistic factions within the Greek *millet* saw an opportunity to achieve the *Megali Idea*. Predictably, they also bore the brunt of the Turkish-Muslim elite's xenophobic reaction when it came to feel that it had its proverbial back against the wall. The politico-economic ramifications of the resulting displacements were considerable. A sizable portion of those transferred to Greece through the population exchange and the immediately preceding expulsions were urban, literate, and commercially dynamic; they were often in command of a broad array of professional skills and in possession of a high degree of cosmopolitan social capital.[74] By contrast, the majority of those who found themselves transferred to Turkey were farmers, dependent upon the land and without substantial experience in lucrative trades and industries.[75]

The economic division between Muslim and non-Muslim, fundamental to the political economy of late Ottoman rule, fuelled the expulsion of Greeks from what remained of Turkey after the Greek–Turkish War, since the drive to forge a 'national economy' was deemed to necessitate the transfer of properties in the hands of non-Muslims to Muslims, particularly Turkish Muslims.[76] In 1857 *The Times* had been able to boast of London's financial and political domination of the Ottoman Empire: 'The Turks have a fine territory and no money, energy, or skill; we have all three, and they pour into Turkey as naturally as water finds its level'.[77] Similarly, the *Moniteur ottoman*, the Porte's quasi-official gazette, had lauded the capitulations as the key to Turkey's economic openness: 'In no part of the world does foreign merchandise pay so low an import duty as in Turkey', it had observed, suggesting that 'for the space of three hundred years the Sultans have realized an object which civilized Europe is now earnestly labouring to accomplish'.[78] No longer, it was believed, would such brash expressions of overconfidence by foreigners and overt avowals of co-option by local elites go unanswered.

[73] El. K. Venizelos, *Greece in Her True Light: Her Position in the World-Wide War*, trans. Socrates A. Xanthaky and Nicholas G. Sakellarios (New York: Socrates A. Xanthaky and Nicholas G. Sakellarios, 1916), 191–2.

[74] See, e.g., Ladas, *Exchange of Minorities* (n 22), 729; Dimitri Pentzopoulos, *The Balkan Exchange of Minorities and Its Impact upon Greece* (Paris: Mouton & Co., 1962), 101–2; and, more generally, Elisabeth Kontogiorgi, 'Economic Consequences following Refugee Settlement in Greek Macedonia, 1923–1932', in *Crossing the Aegean: An Appraisal of the 1923 Compulsory Population Exchange between Greece and Turkey*, ed. Renée Hirschon (New York: Berghahn, 2003), 63.

[75] See, e.g., Aktar, 'Nüfusun Homojenleştirilmesi' (n 19), 46–7; Kemal Arı, *Büyük Mübadele: Türkiye'ye Zorunlu Göç (1923–1925)* (İstanbul: Tarih Vakfı Yurt Yayınları, 1995), 177; and, for some statistics, see Mehmet Çanlı, 'Yunanistan'daki Türklerin Anadolu'ya Nakledilmesi I', *Tarih ve Toplum* 129 (1994), 54, at 59–60.

[76] Haldun Gülalp, 'Capitalism and the Modern Nation-State: Rethinking the Creation of the Turkish Republic', *Journal of Historical Sociology* 7 (1994), 155, at 158–9.

[77] Editorial, *The Times*, 20 February 1857, 7.

[78] 'On Freedom of Commerce in the Ottoman Empire', *Moniteur ottoman* [n.d.], reproduced in *Opinions of the European Press on the Eastern Question, Translated and Extracted from Turkish, German, French, and English Papers and Reviews*, ed. David Ross (London: James Ridgway & Sons, 1836), 1, at 4–5, 6.

III. Toward a Definitive Exchange Arrangement

Drawing out the broader legal implications of this rather messy sequence of events is no easy matter. Although it did not take root in general international law, the notion that the strength of a given claim to statehood is at least partly dependent upon a correlative claim to nationhood had received support from legal and political scholars for some time prior to the 1910s. At least as early as Vattel's *Le droit des gens*, one finds hints that the state is best conceived as a kind of outward expression of the nation: Vattel has a tendency to present the latter as logically, or perhaps even chronologically, prior to the former.[79] And the attempt to conjoin statehood tightly with nationhood was deployed with devastating force in the writings of political theorists and international lawyers during the late nineteenth and early twentieth centuries. Rudolph von Jhering wrote that an 'iron fist' is needed for nations to achieve the kind of 'state order' necessary for political stability;[80] Heinrich von Treitschke argued that '[i]n a single state the whole content of culture can never be realized';[81] and T. J. Lawrence proclaimed that *Staatenbunden* belong to a 'lower type of union' and are 'in a condition of unstable equilibrium', the only truly secure state being that which houses one and only one nation.[82] Such views exerted considerable influence over Ottoman jurists and statesmen, who received them as part of a convoluted process of appropriating and reinterpreting European legal thought: a variety of new codes with strong European traits were introduced into the empire throughout the course of the nineteenth century,[83] a faculty of law equipped to teach international law was established in Istanbul in 1870,[84] a number of European lawyers were appointed as counsellors in a considerably enlarged foreign ministry,[85] and widely circulated European treatises like Henri Bonfils' *Manuel de droit international public* were

[79] One example: 'The Sovereign represents his entire Nation, he combines in his person all its Majesty.' Emer de Vattel, *Le droit des gens, ou Principes de la loi naturelle, appliqués à la conduite et aux affaires des Nations et des Souverains*, vol. 1 (Londres: n.p., 1758), 285.

[80] Rudolph von Jhering, *Der Zweck im Recht*, vol. 1 (Leipzig: Druck und Verlag von Breitkopf & Härtel, 1877), 312.

[81] Heinrich von Treitschke, *Politik: Vorlesungen, gehalten an der Universität zu Berlin*, vol. 1 (Leipzig: Verlag von S. Hirzel, 1899), 29.

[82] T. J. Lawrence, *The Principles of International Law*, 4th ed. (Boston: D. C. Heath & Co., 1910), 70.

[83] For useful surveys see Gülnihâl Bozkurt, *Batı Hukukunun Türkiye'de Benimsenmesi: Osmanlı Devleti'nden Türkiye Cumhuriyeti'ne Resepsiyon Süreci (1839–1939)* (Ankara: Türk Tarih Kurumu Basımevi, 1996), pt. 2; Esin Örücü, 'The Impact of European Law on the Ottoman Empire and Turkey', in *European Expansion and Law: The Encounter of European and Indigenous Law in 19th- and 20th-Century Africa and Asia*, ed. W. J. Mommsen and J. A. de Moor (Oxford: Berg, 1992), 39.

[84] Fahri Çoker, '"Dârülfünûn-i Osmani" ve "Mekteb-i Hukuk"', *Tarih ve Toplum* 121 (1994), 26; and also Ali Arslan, *Darülfünun'dan Üniversite'ye* (İstanbul: Kitabevi Yayınları, 1995).

[85] For details see Sinan Kuneralp and Emre Öktem, eds., *Chambre des conseillers légistes de la Sublime Porte: Rapports, avis et consultations sur la condition juridique des ressortissants étrangers, le statut des communautés non musulmanes et les relations internationales de l'Empire ottoman (1864–1912)* (Istanbul: Les éditions Isis, 2012), 9–10.

translated into Ottoman Turkish.[86] By the 1910s the influence had become so palpable that Mahmut Esat, later to become Turkey's minister of justice, could structure the entirety of his doctoral dissertation around an argument to the effect that the Ottoman capitulations were incompatible with the national character of the modern state.[87]

Still, it was not until the late 1910s that there emerged a body of international treaty law capable of regulating and facilitating *en masse* migration with a view to achieving this mutual alignment of nation and state. If minority protection was nominally a norm in central and eastern Europe, enshrined in international treaties and incorporated into domestic legislation, then enforced movement of populations was this norm's exception in Europe's near abroad, the application of minority protection's goal of governing nationalism to conditions in which minority protection alone was deemed insufficient. In seeking to engineer a nationally integrated state, Turkey, like Greece, may have taken 'a leaf out of Western political conceptions'.[88] But it was also committing itself to a mechanism of nation-building that the West itself was not yet able to stomach for its own troubles.

[86] See Henri Bonfils, *Hukuk-i Umumiye-yi Düvel*, ed. Paul Fauchille, trans. Ahmet Selâhattin and Mehmet Cemil (İstanbul: Matbaa-i Jirayir-Keteon, 1325 [1907–8]).

[87] Mahmoud Essad, *Du régime des capitulations ottomanes: leur caractère juridique d'après l'histoire et les textes* (Stamboul: Fratelli Haim, 1928). The dissertation was defended in Fribourg in 1918. Esat's stance in regard to the capitulations fed his litigation strategy in the *Lotus* case, in which he acted as Turkey's agent; see *Case of the S.S. 'Lotus'* (*France v Turkey*) PCIJ Rep. Series A No 10 (1927).

[88] Winthrop D. Lane, 'Why Greeks and Turks Oppose Being "Exchanged"', *New York Times Current History* 18 (1923), 86, at 90.

3

'A Subject which Excites the Deepest Interest throughout the Civilised World': Legal Diplomacy at the Conference of Lausanne

Lausanne was a natural location for a conference to bring Turkey's involvement in the Great War to an end.[1] Switzerland's long-standing isolation from continental rivalry and close affiliation with the Red Cross promised a degree of neutrality. Lausanne had also been the site for the signature of the treaty that marked the end of the 1911–12 Italian–Turkish War, waged over Tripolitania, the last properly Ottoman province in Africa.[2] And then there was the fact that Ottoman reformers and Turkish nationalists had maintained a curiously close relationship with the city and its university. Many members of the Young Turk elite, and of the Kemalist intelligentsia that succeeded it, held degrees, often in law, from Swiss universities. Lausanne itself was a favourite destination, leading a Swiss jurist who would serve as adviser to the Turkish government after the peace conference to dub a faction of the new nationalist elite *les Lausannois*.[3] Even so, the conference that brought the 1919–22 Greek–Turkish War to an end has long been remembered for its duration: the proceedings commenced in November 1922 and none of the instruments save the convention regulating the exchange and a related agreement on the restitution of interned civilians and exchange of prisoners of war were signed until July 1923, the disagreements ranging widely and reaching at times a fevered pitch.

[1] The quotation in the title of this chapter derives from Lord Curzon's characterization of 'the question of the protection of minorities', which he, like others at Lausanne, linked to the issue of 'the great transference of populations'. Minutes of the Territorial and Military Commission's (TMC's) meeting on 12 December 1922, in *Lausanne Conference on Near Eastern Affairs (1922–1923): Records of Proceedings and Draft Terms of Peace* (Cmd 1814) (London: His Majesty's Stationery Office, 1923), 175–6.

[2] Traité de paix, signed at Lausanne, 18 October 1912, reproduced in G. Fr. de Martens, *Nouveau recueil général de traités et autres actes relatifs aux rapports de droit international*, 3rd series, ed. Heinrich Triepel, vol. 7 (Leipzig: Librairie Dieterich, 1913), 7.

[3] Georges Sauser-Hall, 'La réception des droits européens en Turquie', in *Recueil de travaux publié à l'occasion de l'Assemblée de la Société suisse des juristes à Genève, du 4 au 6 septembre 1938* (Genève: Imprimerie Albert Kundig, 1938), 323, at 345. For details see Masami Arai, *Turkish Nationalism in the Young Turk Era* (Leiden: Brill, 1992), 76–81; Hans-Lukas Kieser, *Vorkämpfer der 'Neuen Türkei': Revolutionäre Bildungseliten am Genfersee (1870–1939)* (Zürich: Chronos, 2005).

In this chapter I turn to two of the most illuminating aspects of Lausanne's preparatory work—the various delegations' views on the place of ethno-nationalism in the exchange process, and the exchange's design as a mechanism geared toward a specific region with a specific set of traditions and institutions. I first argue that debates regarding the exchange were informed by a profound ambiguity in respect to ethno-nationalism. On the one hand, the exchange was a technocratic exercise in conflict resolution. On the other hand, the exchange tethered the sovereignty of Greece and Turkey to the ethnicities of their 'founding peoples', recruiting—and legitimizing—the very ethno-nationalism that reliance upon 'technical' law was supposed to impede. I then argue that the exchange comprised a method of nation-building with a distinct range of spatial application. Although many doubted whether minority protection would be sufficient in central and eastern Europe, room for doubt was that much greater in the case of Greece and Turkey, where the need for a more muscular approach to nation-building was widely felt. Likewise, while the idea of an American mandate had won support among some Turks as a means of staving off a feared British occupation,[4] acquiescing in a mandate over predominantly Turkish territory had never been more than a remote possibility for Kemal and most members of his inner circle.[5] If the exchange proved as adept at curbing ethno-nationalism as it did, this was due mainly to the fact that it had been designed with the characteristics of a particular region in mind—a region whose semi-peripheral status demanded a mechanism that departed both from minority governance (in Europe) and from colonial or neo-colonial rule (throughout large parts of the extra-European world).

I. Between Technocracy and Ethno-Nationalism

The sub-commission tasked with negotiating the terms of the Greek–Turkish exchange met on more occasions than any other at Lausanne,[6] and its minutes testify to a concerted effort on the part of all delegates to put an end to the violence with which the Near East had come to be so closely associated. The exchange's

[4] See, e.g., Stanford J. Shaw, *From Empire to Republic: The Turkish War of National Liberation 1918–1923: A Documentary Study*, vol. 2 (Ankara: Türk Tarih Kurumu Basımevi, 2000), 429–37. For related proposals see Tarık Zafer Tunaya, *Türkiye'de Siyasal Partiler*, 2nd ed., vol. 2 (İstanbul: Hürriyet Vakfı Yayınları, 1986), 245–63.

[5] Thus, the first assembly of Turkish nationalists would adopt a resolution repudiating the possibility of a mandate or protectorate. See M. Fahrettin Kırzıoğlu, *Bütünüyle Erzurum Kongresi*, vol. 2 (Ankara: Kültür Ofset, 1993), 243–6. Radical Turkish reactions are captured accurately, albeit hyperbolically, in the words of a contemporaneous jurist and publicist: '[H]aving lived independently for a thousand years, the Turks cannot allow foreigners to so much as ride horses in their country under the pretence of a mandate or trusteeship.' Ahmet Selâhattin Bey, 'Vekâlet ve Müzaheret' [1919], reproduced as 'Mandat ve Yardım', in *Lozan'ın 50. Yıl Armağanı* (İstanbul: Fakülteler Matbaası, 1978), 3, at 6.

[6] A total of 24, the next closest sub-commissions being those responsible for issues of property and contract and for minority protection strictly understood. For a tabulation see *Lausanne Conference* (n 1), ii.

relationship to ethno-nationalism raised a complex array of issues that tended to be approached from two different but mutually reinforcing angles.

The first such angle elided ethno-nationalism altogether, and did so in the name of a need to 'unmix' the peoples of Greece and Turkey through the most rational, technically sophisticated means available. Frequently employed by the great powers, but also finding a home in some of Greece and Turkey's own demands, this was a strategy driven by a preponderantly managerial analysis of the territorial frontiers and demographic compositions of the two states that were to be reconstructed by the exchange. The argument on its behalf had as its major premise the conjecture that the exchange could be conceived and implemented *in abstracto*—as a fundamentally self-contained enterprise, fuelled by what one contemporaneous jurist deftly termed the 'constructive and practical idealism'[7] then being developed by League officials. This enterprise would, to be sure, bump up against ethno-nationalism. Yet, at root, it would retain an irreducibly 'scientific' core of intentional design, strong enough to impede, or at least defer, the international system's disintegration in the face of such nationalism.[8]

Thus, efforts to reconfigure the region did not imply an 'intention to attack the sovereignty of Turkey'—and even less a wish to intervene so as 'to create an *imperium in imperio* or a State within a State'.[9] Rather, as emphasized by Nansen, who inaugurated formal discussion of the exchange at Lausanne, the impetus behind moving hundreds of thousands of people from one end of the Aegean to the other was an overwhelmingly pragmatic one: 'the Great Powers are in favour of' an exchange, he declared, 'because they believe that to unmix the populations of the Near East will tend to secure the true pacification of the Near East', this being 'the quickest and most efficacious way of dealing with the grave economic results which must result from the great movement of populations which has already occurred'.[10] Among other things, an exchange would make space available in Macedonia and elsewhere for the settlement of those already expelled from Turkey, which, in turn, would go some way to ameliorating economic and political conditions on the ground. Lord Curzon, chief British delegate and former viceroy of India,[11] went out of his way to reassure the

[7] Arnold D. McNair, 'Equality in International Law', *Michigan Law Review* 26 (1927), 131, at 135.

[8] Cf. Nathaniel Berman, '"But the Alternative is Despair": European Nationalism and the Modernist Renewal of International Law', *Harvard Law Review* 106 (1993), 1792, at 1864 ff (analysing attempts to impede 'the cracking of the surface of the state system by nationalist desire').

[9] TMC minutes (9 January 1923), in *Lausanne Conference* (n 1), 299.

[10] TMC minutes (1 December 1922), in *Lausanne Conference* (n 1), 114. On this see further Roland Huntford, *Fridtjof Nansen and the Unmixing of Greeks and Turks in 1924* (Oslo: Norwegian Academy of Science and Letters, 1998), 8.

[11] Interestingly, during his tenure in India, he seems to have attempted to partition Bengal by separating Hindus and Muslims. Eric D. Weitz, 'From the Vienna to the Paris System: International Politics and the Entangled Histories of Human Rights, Forced Deportations, and Civilizing Missions', *American Historical Review* 113 (2008), 1313, at 1337. For materials pertaining to his time in India see George Nathaniel Curzon, *Lord Curzon in India, Being a Selection from His Speeches as Viceroy and Governor-General of India 1898–1905* (London: Macmillan, 1906). A contemporaneous assessment can be found in H. Caldwell Lipsett, *Lord Curzon in India 1898–1903* (London: R. A. Everett & Co., 1903).

Turks—to whom he was otherwise openly hostile[12]—that '[n]o one wanted to interfere with their independence or sovereignty'. On the contrary, 'everyone wanted to build up a sovereign independent Turkish State' in order to resolve the Near Eastern crisis, but felt that 'no solution would ever be reached if every statement made were to be met by Turkey wrapping herself up in her cloak and saying that [Allied proposals were] incompatible with her sovereign independence'.[13] Statements of this kind had the effect of rendering the exchange something of a sterile, mechanical exercise, one that lay at a significant distance from the dirty business of attending to particular ethno-national aspirations and grievances. The socio-historical context within which any exchange would need to take place was to be given short shrift, or at most no more consideration than was required to ensure that the process could be managed in such a way as to yield a successful outcome, one that addressed ongoing economic instability, satisfied humanitarian needs, and ensured regional security.

A second approach struck a different note. Most of those present in Lausanne were also inclined to see ethno-nationalism as deeply integral to the exchange, albeit for different reasons and with different degrees of demonstrated conviction. The Turkish delegation generally preferred to throw its weight behind the proposition that debates relating to the exchange's legal form could not be disconnected from questions concerning the ethnic composition of the future Turkish state. Turkey had experienced more than its share of violence—and by no means only in the context of the Armenian genocide. In the eyes of Turkish delegates, much of this violence had been linked to Western powers exploiting extraterritorial privileges afforded by consular jurisdiction or exercising treaty-based rights of guardianship over Christian communities.[14] For İsmet Paşa, the principal delegate, Turkey's support for a compulsory exchange followed from its 'legitimate desire to prevent minorities . . . becoming weapons in the hands of foreigners'.[15] So long as Turkey harboured sizable and resourceful non-Muslim communities, willing and able to assist Russia or Britain as fifth columnists, it would be unable to achieve internal security and contribute to international peace.

Statements from other participants can be read in similar terms—as attempts not to displace ethno-nationalist politics but to *harness* it to a project of legal nation-building. Portraying the exchange as a method of effecting Turkish

[12] As an American delegate wrote in his personal diary, 'Curzon seemed to have no understanding of the Turkish national aspirations; he did no good to the cause of the Allies by browbeating Ismet at the conference table as if the latter had been one of his "natives" in India'. Joseph C. Grew, *Turbulent Era: A Diplomatic Record of Forty Years, 1904–1945*, ed. Walter Johnson, vol. 1 (Boston: Houghton, Mifflin, & Co., 1952), 553. Similarly, the memoirs of Turkey's second-highest-ranking delegate speak of the Allies' lack of appreciation for the Turks' new 'mentality'. Rıza Nur, *Hayat ve Hatıratım*, vol. 3 (İstanbul: Altındağ Yayınevi, 1968), 992–3.

[13] TMC minutes (13 December 1922), in *Lausanne Conference* (n 1), 214.

[14] Russia's move in the nineteenth century to merge its 'humanitarian' interest in the Balkans with a distinctly post-Napoleonic appeal for national independence for Slavic peoples is a classic case in point. For legal analysis see Boris Mirkine-Guetzévitch, 'L'influence de la Révolution française sur le développement du droit international dans l'Europe orientale', *RCADI* 22 (1928-II), 295, at 424, ch. 7 generally.

[15] TMC minutes (13 December 1922), in *Lausanne Conference* (n 1), 207.

withdrawal from Europe, Curzon, for instance, would suggest that, with the exchange, '[i]n Europe the greater part, if not the whole, of the Turkish population in Greek territory . . . will cease to be a minority population because they will return to Turkey'.[16] As the only Muslims to whom this comment could apply were natives of the Balkans, the implication was clearly that Turkish presence in Europe remained—after nearly six centuries of Ottoman power in the Balkans and several centuries of earlier Turkic *Völkerwanderungen*—an essentially, irredeemably, alien one. The Turks, Curzon was suggesting, were a jarringly foreign presence, physically occupying European territory but religiously set apart from—or, at best, incidental to—'Europe'.[17] After all, even those episodes of apparent interpenetration between the 'public law of Europe' and the *dār al-Islām* spearheaded by the Ottomans, such as Turkey's controversial admission into the European state system in the 1856 Treaty of Paris, owed more to *raison d'état* than to any 'cultural' or 'civilizational' bond, Istanbul having acquired the attendant 'advantages' largely to maintain the continental balance of power. Unlike the first approach, then, a managerial, technocratic approach to the exchange, this second approach saw the exchange as a messy, even sinister, affair—something to be broached not only with 'scientific' acumen, as though entire nation-states might be created by sheer dint of will, but also, and at least equally, by attending to ethno-nationalism's lure.

Before considering in detail these two strands of argument—the one shirking direct, unmediated engagement with ethno-nationalism, the other geared precisely toward such engagement—it is worth underscoring the complexity of the diplomatic context within which the delegates at Lausanne worked. The exchange was negotiated against the background of a wide range of legal disputes—and this despite the fact that most delegates at Lausanne were career diplomats rather than trained lawyers. Most of these disputes involved questions that pitted Kemalist Turkey against Britain, France, several other great powers,[18] and even, in some cases, officials like Nansen from the League of Nations, an organization with which Turkey had yet to establish official relations.[19]

Relations between Turkey and the Allies, and also among the Allies themselves, underwent considerable change in the months leading up to the conference. Although efforts had been made to ensure that the great powers would act in concert, they were unable to maintain a unified stance on all issues. Curzon secured the position of the conference's president, and, wielding enormous symbolic

[16] TMC minutes (12 December 1922), in *Lausanne Conference* (n 1), 177.

[17] Curzon was given to making such statements; see, e.g., Shaw, *From Empire to Republic* (n 4), 400; Margaret MacMillan, *Paris 1919: Six Months That Changed the World* (New York: Random House, 2001), 373.

[18] The powers with a stake in the Lausanne negotiations were chiefly European. Japan, although present at the conference, had little direct interest in the Near East. The United States, also present, used the negotiations mainly to contest European hegemony over eastern Mediterranean trade. Soviet Russia, Georgia, and Ukraine, for their part, were allowed to participate actively only in those discussions that pertained to the status of the Turkish Straits.

[19] Turkey was not yet a member of the League; it would join comparatively late, in 1932.

power, would direct most discussions as *primus inter pares*. He had, as he himself put it, 'the art of getting on with Orientals',[20] and this 'art' was bolstered by the work of British code-breakers supplying him with a constant stream of intercepted telegrams between Ankara and Lausanne.[21] France had largely broken ranks with Britain, adhering to those portions of the Sykes–Picot Agreement that had dealt with the partition of predominantly Arab territories but otherwise lending support and war matériel to Turkish nationalists.[22] Italy had to drop its earlier demands for territorial compensation in Anatolia on account of Anglo-French indifference and Kemal's growing strength,[23] although Mussolini's personal presence at the conference assured Italian control over the strategically important Dodecanese.[24]

Although the British had supported the Greek occupation of western Anatolia, this support had not been unequivocal. In a classic illustration of multivectoral realpolitik, the Foreign Office had extended support to the Greek cause only to a degree, never so much that a failure would jeopardize Britain's broader geopolitical ambitions. Any number of reasons can be cited for this: a desire to maintain nominally cordial relations with the French, insufficient domestic support for another costly foreign adventure, divided domestic opinion on the merits of the Treaty of Sèvres, and others. Above all, though, it was a calculated assessment of the risks inherent in the Greek expedition that underpinned British ambivalence. The Ottoman state had often been presented as a *cordon sanitaire* on the road to India, both before and after the completion of the Suez Canal in 1869 and Britain's imposition of effective control over Egypt in the early 1880s.[25] Now that it had collapsed, part of the responsibility of shielding the 'Jewel of the Crown' was to be shifted to an appropriately enlarged Greece.[26] But this, naturally, was

[20] Quoted in Harold Nicolson, *Curzon: The Last Phase 1919–1925: A Study in Post-war Diplomacy* (London: Constable & Co., 1934), 298.

[21] G. H. Bennett, *British Foreign Policy during the Curzon Period, 1919–24* (London: St. Martin's Press, 1995), 91. Curzon had ample experience in this regard, having established a battery of intelligence agencies during his tenure in India. Richard J. Popplewell, *Intelligence and Imperial Defence: British Intelligence and the Defence of the Indian Empire 1904–1924* (London: Frank Cass, 1995), ch. 2.

[22] Michael Llewellyn Smith, *Ionian Vision: Greece in Asia Minor, 1919–1922*, 2nd ed. (London: C. Hurst & Co., 1998), 240. For the agreement concluded between France and the Ankara government, the first that Ankara concluded with a west European state, see Agreement with a View to Promoting Peace, with Protocol relating thereto, Protocol concerning Its Coming into Force, and Exchange of Notes, signed at Ankara, 20 October 1921, 54 LNTS 177.

[23] For these earlier demands, themselves typically ignored, see H. James Burgwyn, *Italian Foreign Policy in the Interwar Period 1918–1940* (Westport: Greenwood, 1997), 7–8, 11, 14.

[24] Dilek Barlas, 'Friends or Foes? Diplomatic Relations between Italy and Turkey, 1923–36', *International Journal of Middle East Studies* 36 (2004), 231, at 233. On the limited rights of Muslims in the Dodecanese after Lausanne, see Elçin Macar, 'Lozan'dan Günümüze Onikiada Türklerinin Sorunları', *İstanbul Üniversitesi Siyasal Bilgiler Fakültesi Dergisi* 34 (2006), 35.

[25] For a typical articulation see Valentine Chirol, 'Our Imperial Interests in Nearer and Further Asia', in *The Empire and the Century: A Series of Essays on Imperial Problems and Possibilities by Various Writers* (London: John Murray, 1905), 728.

[26] A memorandum circulated within the Foreign Office in 1920 was anything but evasive in this regard: 'The idea which prompted our support of Greece was . . . the natural expression of our historical policy—the protection of India and the Suez Canal. For a century we had supported Turkey as the first line of defence in the Eastern Mediterranean. Turkey had proven a broken reed and we fell back on the second line, the line from Salamis to Smyrna.' Quoted in Theo Karvounarakis,

a gamble, and not one to which the Foreign Office would commit itself blindly. Among other things, a conflict with Turkey could lead to full-blown rebellion in British India, where support for Kemal was strong, especially as his nationalists often portrayed themselves as committed to the caliphate.[27]

The Allies would try to weaken the Turkish camp even before negotiations began by extending two invitations, rather than simply one, to 'Turkey'—the first to Kemal's provisional government in Ankara, by then in effective control of most of Asia Minor, and the second to the sultan's court, so confined to Istanbul that Cemil Bilsel, an international lawyer and influential legal educator, would later describe it as having by then become 'a wholly municipal government'.[28] The ploy was not subtle. By opting for two invitations, the Allies hoped to split the Turks, lessening the bargaining power Ankara had amassed after repulsing Allied forces. The initiative came to nothing, though, as Ankara had already denounced the Ottoman court as collaborationist. It rejected the proposal, and the parties agreed that the conference would be convened with Kemal's government as the sole representative of 'Turkey'.[29] All of this strengthened Turkey's hand. Rather than arriving in Lausanne as representatives of a defeated Central Power, the Turks postured as the commanding force on most issues. Their strategy was dictated in most respects by the nationalist movement's founding charter, the 'National Pact'.[30] Prepared and circulated three years earlier, this document declared that the sovereignty of the Turkish nation was a *sine qua non* for any lasting resolution to the war, its sixth and final article stating that 'complete independence and liberty' constituted 'a fundamental condition' of this nation's 'life and continued existence'.[31]

'End of an Empire: Great Britain, Turkey and Greece from the Treaty of Sevres to the Treaty of Lausanne', *Balkan Studies* 41 (2000), 171, at 172 (de-emphasized from original).

[27] Azmi Özcan, *Pan-Islamism: Indian Muslims, the Ottomans and Britain (1877–1924)* (Leiden: Brill, 1997), ch. 6. Efforts to win support for Turkey among Muslims in India and elsewhere had been deployed by Abdülhamid II, the last sultan to wield effective authority. See especially Kemal H. Karpat, *The Politicization of Islam: Reconstructing Identity, State, Faith, and Community in the Late Ottoman State* (Oxford: Oxford University Press, 2001), esp. 15–18, 211–14, 233–9; and, for the link with Kemalist strategy, Engin Deniz Akarlı, 'The Tangled Ends of an Empire and Its Sultan', in *Modernity and Culture: From the Mediterranean to the Indian Ocean*, ed. Leila Tarazi Fawaz and C. A. Bayly (New York: Columbia University Press, 2002), 261, at 278–9.

[28] M. Cemil [Bilsel], *Lozan*, vol. 1 (İstanbul: Ahmet İhsan Matbaası, 1933), 444. A fervent advocate of Kemalist reform, he would serve as the first dean of the Ankara School of Law, established in 1925 as a key instrument of state ideology, and also as rector of the University of Istanbul after its reconstitution in 1933. See Hüseyin Boğaç Erozan, 'Producing Obedience: Law Professors and the Turkish State' (PhD dissertation, University of Minnesota, 2005), 83.

[29] Pointing to the invitation as illustrative of Istanbul's capitulation to the West, Kemal's Ankara-based assembly would go on to abolish the sultanate in November 1922. For the legal implications see Bülent Tanör, *Osmanlı-Türk Anayasal Gelişmeleri (1789–1980)* (İstanbul: Yapı Kredi Yayınları, 1998), 277–80.

[30] Baskın Oran, 'Lausanne Barış Antlaşması', in *Türk Dış Politikası: Kurtuluş Savaşından Bugüne Olgular, Belgeler, Yorumlar*, ed. Baskın Oran, vol. 1 (İstanbul: İletişim Yayınları, 2001), 215, at 219.

[31] 'National Pact', reproduced in Arnold J. Toynbee, *The Western Question in Greece and Turkey: A Study in the Contact of Civilisations* (London: Constable & Co., 1922), 207, at 210.

Fixed on this imperative, the Turkish delegation argued in favour of a strong interpretation of sovereign equality. State sovereignty, it maintained, was inviolable, an absolute point of reference conditioned solely by the need to conserve the structural integrity of the international system. In espousing this strong interpretation of sovereign equality—which has always attracted charges of positivism[32]—the Turks received support from the Bolsheviks, who had signed a 'treaty of friendship' with Ankara the year before[33] and who backed the principle of Turkish sovereignty over the Bosphorus and Dardanelles.[34] The Kemalists were highly ambivalent about proletarian revolution,[35] but the alliance, which owed much to the Bolsheviks' desire to avoid international isolation and shore up their southern flank, supplied Ankara with additional leverage and irked delegates from other parties,[36] perhaps none more so than Curzon, who had previously chaired a British governmental committee formed to combat Bolshevism in the Middle East.[37] Indeed, Bolshevik support for the 'new Turkey' was a key factor in allowing the Turkish delegation to treat Lausanne as a prolongation of war by other means. A large Greek army was, after all, positioned to march on Istanbul,[38] and İsmet, a general during the Greek–Turkish War, likened the conference to a military struggle 'which the Turkish delegation mobilized for and worked 24 hours around the clock'.[39]

[32] See, e.g., Alfred-Maurice de Zayas, 'International Law and Mass Population Transfers', *HILJ* 16 (1975), 207, at 224. For similar complaints see Berdal Aral, 'An Inquiry into the Turkish "School" of International Law', *EJIL* 16 (2005), 769.

[33] Treaty of Friendship between Russia and Turkey, signed at Moscow, 16 March 1921, 118 BFSP 990. For analysis see especially Bülent Gökay, *A Clash of Empires: Turkey between Russian Bolshevism and British Imperialism, 1918–1923* (London: Tauris, 1997), 109–12.

[34] See, e.g., TMC minutes (4 December 1922), in *Lausanne Conference* (n 1), 128–31; TMC minutes (6 December 1922), in *Lausanne Conference* (n 1), 148–9; TMC minutes (8 December 1922), in *Lausanne Conference* (n 1), 159–63. Cf. Antoine Rougier, 'La question des Détroits et la convention de Lausanne', *RGDIP* 31 (1924), 309; Ali Fuad, *La question des Détroits: ses origines, son évolution, sa solution à la Conférence de Lausanne* (Paris: Imprimerie du Montparnasse et de Persan-Beaumont, 1928), 135–43; Samy Kabbara, *Le régime des Détroits (Bosphore et Dardanelles) avant et depuis le traité de Lausanne* (Lyon: Imprimerie Bosc frères & Riou, 1929), 88–98. Even with Soviet support, the Turkish delegation was eventually forced to accept the demilitarization and internationalization of the Straits—a position that would remain unchanged until the 1936 Montreux Convention, which placed the Straits fully under the jurisdiction of Turkey.

[35] As some Bolsheviks were, of course, well aware; see, e.g., Sultan Galiev, 'The Social Revolution and the East' [1919], reproduced in *Muslim National Communism in the Soviet Union: A Revolutionary Strategy for the Colonial World*, ed. Alexandre S. Bennigsen and S. Enders Wimbush (Chicago: University of Chicago Press, 1979), 131, at 137.

[36] See, e.g., TMC minutes (4 December 1922), in *Lausanne Conference* (n 1), 133; TMC minutes (6 December 1922), in *Lausanne Conference* (n 1), 149–50.

[37] John Fisher, 'The Interdepartmental Committee on Eastern Unrest and British Responses to Bolshevik and Other Intrigues against the Empire during the 1920s', *Journal of Asian History* 34 (2000), 1, at 2.

[38] Douglas Dakin, 'The Importance of the Greek Army in Thrace during the Conference of Lausanne 1922–1923', in *Greece and Great Britain during World War I: First Symposium Organized in Thessaloniki (December 15–17, 1983) by the Institute for Balkan Studies in Thessaloniki and King's College in London* (Thessaloniki: Institute for Balkan Studies, 1985), 211.

[39] Quoted and translated in Fatma Müge Göçek, 'The Politics of History and Memory: A Multidimensional Analysis of the Lausanne Peace Conference, 1922–1923', in *Histories of the Modern Middle East: New Directions*, ed. Israel Gershoni, Hakan Erdem, and Ursula Woköck (Boulder: Lynne Rienner, 2002), 207, at 214. See also Nur, *Hayat ve Hatıratım* (n 12), 996 (speaking of a 'battlefield' on which 'both sides attacked and defended with all their might').

Consider the proceedings themselves. The Territorial and Military Commission, one of several such commissions into which the conference was divided, was, among other things, concerned with negotiating the terms of the population exchange. On 1 December 1922, less than two weeks into the negotiations, a lengthy statement by Nansen was read at the commission's eighth meeting, on the ground that Nansen 'had for some time been in negotiation with both Turkey and Greece on the subject'.[40] Amid what turned out to be a pointed call to action, Nansen's statement recounted his experiences and pressed for the immediate implementation of an exchange of minorities. Nansen stressed that the idea of an exchange had won support among elites in Greece and Turkey, as well as from the great powers. Hence, unlike the Mandate System, in which he was also invested,[41] the exchange would not be an exclusive outgrowth of Western diplomacy, but would instead involve all concerned actors.[42] Further, Nansen underscored his willingness to continue serving as a diplomatic go-between. Though he had already been able to 'bring some small relief with the funds placed at [his] disposal by the members of the League to the starving refugees of both nationalities',[43] far more needed to be done and he alone was not in a position to do it. Turkey was not a member of the League of Nations, but Nansen felt comfortable suggesting to his 'Turkish friends that they could confide their interests in this matter to the Council of the League with absolute confidence'.[44]

Ultimately, what was of greatest importance for Nansen was that all of the parties to the negotiations should get on with the business of organizing a coordinated exchange. On the table was not ethno-nationalism *in extremis*, but a 'matter',[45] a 'question' that demanded a 'quick and efficient' resolution with no more than 'a minimum of delay'.[46] Moreover, if this was a 'matter' that deserved 'immediate and earnest consideration', this was so first and foremost because of its 'real importance to the peace and economic stability of the Near East'.[47] That 'the economic aspect of the matter' was 'a most important aspect',[48] requiring in particular the immediate restoration of agricultural production, was indeed a fact that could not be overlooked:

More can be done by a prompt and efficient exchange of minority populations to prevent these disastrous economic results from coming about than by any other measure which

[40] TMC minutes (1 December 1922), in *Lausanne Conference* (n 1), 113.

[41] For discussion see Daniel Gorman, 'Liberal Internationalism, the League of Nations Union, and the Mandates System', *Canadian Journal of History* 40 (2005), 449, at 471.

[42] 'In addition to the support given to the proposal by the Great Powers, I understand that the two Governments principally interested both desire that an agreement should be made. The Turkish authorities have assured me on no fewer than four occasions that they are in favour of such an exchange. The Greek Government has given me the same assurance in a series of official documents.' TMC minutes (1 December 1922), in *Lausanne Conference* (n 1), 114.

[43] TMC minutes (1 December 1922), in *Lausanne Conference* (n 1), 113.

[44] TMC minutes (1 December 1922), in *Lausanne Conference* (n 1), 117.

[45] See, e.g., TMC minutes (1 December 1922), in *Lausanne Conference* (n 1), 113.

[46] TMC minutes (1 December 1922), in *Lausanne Conference* (n 1), 116–17.

[47] TMC minutes (1 December 1922), in *Lausanne Conference* (n 1), 113.

[48] TMC minutes (1 December 1922), in *Lausanne Conference* (n 1), 115.

can be taken. Such an exchange will provide Turkey immediately and in the best possible conditions with the population necessary to continue the exploitation of the cultivated lands which the departed Greek populations have abandoned. The departure from Greece of its Moslem citizens would create the possibility of rendering self-supporting a great proportion of the refugees now concentrated in the towns and in different parts of Greece.[49]

The associated 'difficulties' were 'immense'.[50] Among other things, 'the displacement of populations of many more than 1,000,000 people' necessitated 'uprooting these people from their homes, transferring them to a strange new country, . . . registering, valuing and liquidating their individual property which they abandon, and . . . securing to them the payment of their just claims to the value of this property'.[51] But these were 'technical difficulties—difficulties, that is to say, of securing the just, prompt and efficient application of any agreement that may be made'.[52] And they were 'not insuperable'.[53] Members of the commission responsible for seeing through the 1919 Greek–Bulgarian exchange agreement had already assured Nansen of as much.[54] The treaty that had governed this earlier exchange could, in fact, 'be taken as a model'.[55] That the Greek and Turkish delegations were 'in the fortunate position of having at their disposal experts in this question of exchange' would only make the drafting of such a treaty that much easier.[56]

It is striking that Nansen, anything but reticent on the exchange's organizational 'machinery' (a term of his own choosing),[57] had little of substance to say about the fact that it would involve the legalization and legitimation of a series of factual changes whose eventual outcome would be a large-scale reconfiguration of the Near East's ethno-confessional make-up. Obviously, any exchange would need to be a product of methodical calculation, and in highlighting the need for such caution Nansen was reiterating a point around which a rough-and-ready consensus had already formed. But the exchange would also need to wrestle with—and enlist—a considerable measure of *völkisch* romanticism, rendering it far less cut-and-dry an affair than the rather arid procedures on which he pinned his hopes. Nansen himself was not prepared to recognize as much publicly at Lausanne: one searches in vain in his transcribed speech for an indication that 'the economic aspect of the matter' was not for him of far and away the greatest significance.[58]

49 TMC minutes (1 December 1922), in *Lausanne Conference* (n 1), 115, also 116.
50 TMC minutes (1 December 1922), in *Lausanne Conference* (n 1), 114.
51 TMC minutes (1 December 1922), in *Lausanne Conference* (n 1), 114.
52 TMC minutes (1 December 1922), in *Lausanne Conference* (n 1), 115.
53 TMC minutes (1 December 1922), in *Lausanne Conference* (n 1), 115.
54 TMC minutes (1 December 1922), in *Lausanne Conference* (n 1), 115–16.
55 TMC minutes (1 December 1922), in *Lausanne Conference* (n 1), 116.
56 TMC minutes (1 December 1922), in *Lausanne Conference* (n 1), 116. It is not clear whom exactly Nansen had in mind here.
57 TMC minutes (1 December 1922), in *Lausanne Conference* (n 1), 116–17.
58 A search of the French minutes yields similar results; see 'Séance du vendredi 1er décembre 1922', in *Conférence de Lausanne sur les affaires du Proche-Orient (1922–1923). Recueil des Actes de la Conférence*, vol. 1 (Paris: Imprimerie nationale, 1923), 96–9.

None of this was lost on İsmet Paşa, the first to respond to Nansen's speech. Although Turkey was not a League member and could therefore attach no more than a 'personal character' to Nansen's statement,[59] it agreed that progress needed to be made on the exchange. From Ankara's vantage point, the exchange concerned a much wider set of issues than Nansen had suggested. The terms of the exchange could not be negotiated in the abstract; they were intertwined, at all levels, with the question of the legal status of minorities in the post-Ottoman Near East. Indeed, İsmet maintained, the problem of determining the form of the exchange could not be separated from the problem of determining what kind of legal arrangements would need to be made in order to manage majority–minority relations in Greece and Turkey.[60] And this, in turn, testified to the exchange's testy relationship with ethno-nationalism: as the question of the exchange was closely related to that of minority protection, the former could not be broached, let alone resolved, without determining which groups were to be moved and which were to be afforded protection as national minorities.

This meeting of the Territorial and Military Commission came to an end without İsmet having an opportunity to elaborate his delegation's position in any great detail, but in subsequent meetings it soon became apparent that his attempt to conjoin the issue of the exchange tightly with that of minorities had serious implications for Turkey's stance in regard to ethno-nationalism. İsmet had argued already, on 1 December, that the principal purpose of any exchange would have to be the definitive resolution of the 'minorities problem'. Ankara, he had explained, would insist that any exchange would need to include Greeks resident in Izmir and Istanbul—both cosmopolitan centres of vital importance to eastern Mediterranean commerce, and both lynchpins of the irredentist project of achieving a 'greater Greece'.[61] In a long memorandum he read on 12 December,[62] İsmet went further, running the gamut from Mehmed II's grant of privileges to non-Muslims after the conquest of Constantinople to the high-water mark of secessionist nationalism in the late nineteenth century and finally to 'the lamentable Armenian question'.[63] Studded with purposefully selected passages from Voltaire[64] and a litany of legal treatises,[65] the statement was intended to establish

[59] TMC minutes (1 December 1922), in *Lausanne Conference* (n 1), 117. This brought a sharp rebuke from Curzon, who insisted that Nansen's status was irrelevant, the only pertinent issue being the fact that the exchange concerned the material interests of Greece and Turkey. TMC minutes (1 December 1922), in *Lausanne Conference* (n 1), 118. Note that Nansen's humanitarian credentials appealed to many Western diplomats on account of their ability to draw 'the fire of public opinion'. Huntford, *Fridtjof Nansen* (n 10), 15.

[60] TMC minutes (1 December 1922), in *Lausanne Conference* (n 1), 117.

[61] TMC minutes (1 December 1922), in *Lausanne Conference* (n 1), 120.

[62] 'Statement read by Ismet Pasha', annex to TMC minutes (12 December 1922), in *Lausanne Conference* (n 1), 190.

[63] 'Statement read by Ismet Pasha', in *Lausanne Conference* (n 1), 197.

[64] 'Statement read by Ismet Pasha', in *Lausanne Conference* (n 1), 191.

[65] Chief among them Philip Marshall Brown's *Foreigners in Turkey; Their Juridical Status* (Princeton: Princeton University Press, 1914). Brown's book—a slim study growing out of his time in the American embassy in Istanbul—lent support to İsmet's position; see, e.g., 23–4, 118. For İsmet's reference see 'Statement read by Ismet Pasha', in *Lausanne Conference* (n 1), 190–1.

that '[i]ntervention in the name of the Christian religion' had marked Turkey's relations with the West for centuries.[66] While the Ottomans had 'never failed to acknowledge the rights of the non-Moslem elements so long as the latter did not abuse the generosity of the country in which they lived in comfort' (a claim purportedly evidenced by the fact that Jews had only seldom complained of Turkish rule),[67] they had been forced to quell uprisings among subject nationalities collaborating with Russia and other powers when the empire went into decline.[68]

For İsmet, a compulsory exchange guaranteed stability and development, curbing external interference and securing internal order. Ankara, he explained, believed that 'the amelioration of the lot of the minorities in Turkey depend[ed] above all on the exclusion of every kind of foreign intervention and of the possibility of provocation coming from outside'.[69] It was convinced that this objective was achievable only through a comprehensive exchange, and that 'the best guarantees for the security and development of the minorities remaining after the application of the measures for reciprocal exchange would be those supplied both by the laws of the country and by the liberal policy of Turkey with regard to all communities whose members have not deviated from their duty as Turkish citizens'.[70] A compulsory exchange was also useful as a response to the recent displacement of large numbers of Turks and Muslims; 'there were', in any event, 'over a million Turks without food or shelter in countries in which neither Europe nor America took nor was willing to take any interest'.[71] Only an exchange could relieve the region of its plight, and in the process neutralize sectarian conflict.[72] Turkey's earlier experiences with transfers and exchanges, which served as 'valuable precedents' in this regard,[73] had already confirmed as much, if largely in a negative fashion on account of their not having gone far enough.

Curzon would also link the issue of minorities to that of the population exchange. And he would also see this link as suggestive of a nervy relationship

[66] 'Statement read by Ismet Pasha', in *Lausanne Conference* (n 1), 192.

[67] 'Statement read by Ismet Pasha', in *Lausanne Conference* (n 1), 201, and similarly 203–4 ('As for the Jewish community, the spirit of loyalty which it has always shown to the Turkish Government leads to the presumption that its members will continue peacefully to collaborate with their Turkish fellow-citizens for the betterment and prosperity of the country'). See also TMC minutes (13 December 1922), in *Lausanne Conference* (n 1), 208 ('[T]his hard-working and intelligent element . . . deserved to be held up to all other sections of the population as a pattern of quiet unruffled conduct').

[68] Note, though, that such claims were often exaggerated, not least because Russian authorities do not always seem to have had a consistent policy regarding Anatolian Armenians (and also Anatolian Kurds). See Peter Holquist, 'The Politics and Practice of the Russian Occupation of Armenia, 1915–February 1917', in *A Question of Genocide: Armenians and Turks at the End of the Ottoman Empire*, ed. Ronald Grigor Suny, Fatma Müge Göçek, and Norman M. Naimark (Oxford: Oxford University Press, 2011), 151; and also Michael A. Reynolds, *Shattering Empires: The Clash and Collapse of the Ottoman and Russian Empires, 1908–1918* (Cambridge: Cambridge University Press, 2011), esp. chs. 2, 5.

[69] 'Statement read by Ismet Pasha', in *Lausanne Conference* (n 1), 204.

[70] 'Statement read by Ismet Pasha', in *Lausanne Conference* (n 1), 204.

[71] TMC minutes (12 December 1922), in *Lausanne Conference* (n 1), 189.

[72] 'Statement read by Ismet Pasha', in *Lausanne Conference* (n 1), 202.

[73] 'Statement read by Ismet Pasha', in *Lausanne Conference* (n 1), 203.

with ethno-nationalism. On the one hand, the exchange was 'a thoroughly bad and vicious solution, for which the world would pay a heavy penalty for a hundred years to come'.[74] He 'deeply regretted' it,[75] underscored 'the suffering [it] entailed',[76] and sought to minimize Western responsibility by explaining that the Allied Powers 'had attempted to do no more than to act in the rôle of mediators', intervening only after the exchange had become unavoidable so as 'to secure the conclusion of an agreement capable of practical application and of a character to reduce the inevitable suffering'.[77] On the other hand, Curzon was also at pains to note that should the exchange be implemented under the terms of a formal treaty, it would almost certainly result in 'the question of the minorities' being 'to a certain extent simplified'.[78] Even as he voiced discomfort with the exchange mechanism, particularly its roots in an unruly ethno-nationalism, Curzon felt compelled to underscore its necessity, even desirability.

Statements made by other delegations displayed a structurally analogous ambivalence about ethno-nationalism. In a report to Curzon, Giulio Cesare Montagna, the Italian chair of the sub-commission on the exchange, noted that 'the compulsory solution was regarded by everyone with repugnance'—only to follow it with the unabashedly technocratic claim that '[t]aking the statistics of the Turkish delegation as a basis, we were able to prove mathematically that it was not necessary for Turkey to remove the Greeks of Constantinople in order to establish the Moslems of Greece on her territory'.[79] Camille Barrère, chief negotiator for France, emphasized that the conflict in the Near East could not be resolved without taking seriously the politico-economic consequences of the proposed exchange: 'commercial, industrial and agricultural activity' was 'necessary to every country for repairing damages due to a long series of wars and for exploiting undeveloped wealth', and Turkey could not 'fail to recognise how vitally important it is for it to preserve certain educated, industrious and hard-working elements of the population'.[80] However, he also voiced sympathy for Turkey's attempt 'to develop itself as a nation, . . . to assert its independent political existence, to reconcile all the requirements of progress with its own national tradition'.[81] The ethno-nationalist modernization project of which the exchange was so integral an element was not one that could simply be tossed aside.

Considered as a totality, Lausanne's *travaux* reveal a significant degree of vacillation in regard to the nature and purpose of ethno-nationalism in the exchange's design and implementation. Whether the exchange was to be understood as a

[74] TMC minutes (13 December 1922), in *Lausanne Conference* (n 1), 212.
[75] TMC minutes (13 December 1922), in *Lausanne Conference* (n 1), 212.
[76] TMC minutes (27 January 1923), in *Lausanne Conference* (n 1), 412.
[77] TMC minutes (27 January 1923), in *Lausanne Conference* (n 1), 412.
[78] TMC minutes (12 December 1922), in *Lausanne Conference* (n 1), 177.
[79] 'Report addressed to Lord Curzon, President of the First Commission, by M. Montagna, President of the Sub-Commission on the Exchange of Populations', annex to TMC minutes (10 January 1923), in *Lausanne Conference* (n 1), 330–1.
[80] TMC minutes (12 December 1922), in *Lausanne Conference* (n 1), 181.
[81] TMC minutes (12 December 1922), in *Lausanne Conference* (n 1), 181.

submission to the ethno-nationalist movements that had led to *en masse* migration and expulsion, or instead as a technocratic response to a potentially overwhelming economic, humanitarian, and security-related crisis—at Lausanne, this was not a question to be answered so much as an ambiguity to be formalized. Technocracy and ethno-nationalism bled into each other, congealing in the form of a confused amalgam of competing pressures that ultimately yielded agreement on a legally mediated population exchange.

II. An Enterprise neither European nor Non-European

The notion that the exchange mechanism marked a significant departure from intra-European practices of nation-building, minority protection chief among them, was brought to the fore with especial force in two, closely related positions that İsmet adopted during the Lausanne negotiations. Both concerned questions at the heart of Turkey's attempt to reconstitute itself as a national state, but each was supported with a distinct line of reasoning.

The first such position stemmed from the belief—exceedingly common among Turkish nationalists after Sèvres—that minority protection would not be up to the task of ensuring peace in Greece and Turkey. The League's protective mechanisms aimed to shield minority groups *in situ*, ensuring a modicum of security without uprooting peoples from their 'ancestral homes'. While the Turkish delegation saw the question of the exchange as linked closely to that of minorities, and while it was willing to concede that some protective instruments would need to be installed, it was adamant on limiting their application to non-Muslims, refusing to countenance the kind of nominally robust regime of minority protection that had become pro forma in central and eastern Europe following the Paris Peace Conference. In line with the Ottoman *millet* system, minority protection was to be extended solely to Turkey's non-Muslim citizens; non-Turkish Muslims simply would not be recognized as members of minorities. Further diluting the force of whichever protective instruments would ultimately be introduced was the fact that the total number of non-Muslims in Turkey had fallen sharply during the decade beginning with the Balkan Wars and closing with the Greek–Turkish War, and was fated to fall even further with the completion of the formal exchange. With the exchange, there simply would not be minorities of sufficient number or political weight to warrant a genuinely vigorous minority-protection regime. If protective mechanisms were to be transmitted to Turkey from one or another member of the European 'belt of minority states', this could not but be a highly attenuated and circumscribed process.

The second position concerned the ambit of Turkey's sovereignty—or, to be more precise, the felt need to eradicate all forms of extraterritoriality so as to acquire and safeguard 'the same rights as every nation that was sovereign, independent and master of its destinies'.[82] İsmet's position with regard to the

[82] Minutes of the Commission on the Régime of Foreigners' (CRF's) meeting on 2 December 1922, in *Lausanne Conference* (n 1), 469.

numerous issues raised by this general problematic of sovereignty—first and foremost, those concerning the conditions under which civil and criminal jurisdiction could be asserted over aliens and 'privileged' Ottoman nationals—was rooted firmly in history. In addition to according a significant degree of autonomy to its non-Muslim minorities through the *millet* system, the Ottoman Empire had granted wide-ranging privileges to subjects of foreign sovereigns resident on Ottoman territory via an elaborate system of capitulations.[83] The soon to be established Turkish Republic could not adhere to anything that smacked of these privileges; Turkish and non-Turkish jurists had long regarded them as anomalous and exceptional,[84] and an uncompromising, across-the-board abrogation of the extraterritorial regime they made possible was required to consolidate national statehood. Crucially, this objective was connected to the population exchange. For once the exchange was finalized, and a fully 'national' state was established, most of the material conditions that had justified the conservation of the capitulatory regime would have disappeared: because the commercial 'colonies'[85] set up by European merchants and maintained partly by local non-Muslims, particularly Greeks and Armenians, would have been dissolved, the capitulations would have come to be stripped of their material foundations, with Turkey ceasing to be the 'open and free market' it had been for centuries.[86]

Consider the first position. In principle, İsmet was not opposed to minority protection, at least so long as it did not entail 'exceptional treatment more rigorous than that applied to other countries'[87] and Turkish authorities remained free to adapt the relevant 'provisions to the local needs and special position of the

[83] As noted in the first chapter, the two systems—the one designed for the *zimmi* (the non-Muslim subject of an Islamic sovereign), the other for the *müstemin* (the non-Muslim foreigner resident on Islamic soil)—ran parallel in some ways, meshing to form complex jurisdictional arrangements; see, e.g., Lauren Benton, *Law and Colonial Cultures: Legal Regimes in World History, 1400–1900* (Cambridge: Cambridge University Press, 2002), 108–9. Still, their relation is open to interpretation and not entirely clear; see Maurits H. van den Boogert, *The Capitulations and the Ottoman Legal System: Qadis, Consuls, and* Beratlıs *in the 18th Century* (Leiden: Brill, 2005), 30–1, 55–6.

[84] From a vast literature see, e.g., James Lorimer, *The Institutes of the Law of Nations: A Treatise of the Jural Relations of Separate Political Communities*, vol. 1 (Edinburgh: William Blackwood & Sons, 1883), 313–14; John Westlake, *Chapters on the Principles of International Law* (Cambridge: Cambridge University Press, 1894), 101–3; Elihu Root, 'The Basis of Protection to Citizens Residing Abroad', *ASIL Pd.* 4 (1910), 16, at 20; L. Oppenheim, *International Law: A Treatise*, 3rd ed., ed. Ronald F. Roxburgh, vol. 1 (London: Longmans, 1920), 34.

[85] The term was employed loosely by Allied delegates in reference to commercial establishments, a feature of eastern Mediterranean trade at least as far back as the *fondachi* operated for trading and tax-farming purposes by Genoese, Venetian, and other merchants during the Renaissance. For references to such 'colonies' see, e.g., CRF minutes (28 December 1922), in *Lausanne Conference* (n 1), 483–4, 496; CRF minutes (6 January 1923), in *Lausanne Conference* (n 1), 511. On their proto-history see Kate Fleet, *European and Islamic Trade in the Early Ottoman State: The Merchants of Genoa and Turkey* (Cambridge: Cambridge University Press, 1999), esp. 134–41.

[86] Thomas Naff, 'The Ottoman Empire and the European States System', in *The Expansion of International Society*, ed. Hedley Bull and Adam Watson (Oxford: Clarendon Press, 1984), 143, at 158.

[87] TMC minutes (13 December 1922), in *Lausanne Conference* (n 1), 210. See also TMC minutes (9 January 1923), in *Lausanne Conference* (n 1), 301.

minorities in Turkey'.[88] Turkey was, he reminded his fellow delegates, 'acutely sensitive' when it came to questions concerning its sovereignty and independence, as 'up to the present day Turkish sovereignty had always been infringed on the plea of humanitarian considerations'.[89] It was willing to recognize 'the rights of non-Moslem minorities in accordance with the principles accepted by various European States and embodied in treaties'.[90] But it could not grant minority status to its non-Turkish Muslims. There simply 'were no Moslem minorities in Turkey', as 'no distinction was made either in theory or in practice between the various elements of the Moslem population'.[91]

Moreover, İsmet was convinced that minority protection, in and of itself, would never be enough to keep Muslims and Christians from 'tear[ing] themselves to pieces for nothing but the advantage of political interests'.[92] If the Allies insisted on minority protection alone, post-Ottoman Turkey would find itself in much the same situation as its imperial predecessor: just as the sultan's court had tried to fend off attempts to weaken or splinter the empire, so too would Ankara need to counter efforts on the part of Western powers or League authorities to exploit the issue for political ends. The Turks had come to Lausanne prepared to give some ground on minority protection but committed above all to the exchange. İsmet's delegation was, in fact, under orders that the exchange was to be its 'main objective' in regard to the issue of minorities.[93]

It is revealing that, in staking out this position, İsmet took note of Clemenceau's letter to Polish officials on the occasion of the finalization of the Polish Minority Treaty. İsmet pointed in particular to Clemenceau's assurance that the League would take greater care when managing majority–minority relations than had the Concert of Europe. For İsmet, the policies Clemenceau articulated were predicated on the view that minority protection was applicable to some, but not all, states.[94] İsmet was also unconvinced by promises of impartial supervision on the part of the League: 'The present organisation of the League of Nations does not, in spite of the opinion of the French statesman, appear to be such as to avoid this serious defect.'[95] This much had become clear, he added sharply, from 'the

[88] TMC minutes (9 January 1923), in *Lausanne Conference* (n 1), 292.

[89] TMC minutes (14 December 1922), in *Lausanne Conference* (n 1), 219.

[90] TMC minutes (14 December 1922), in *Lausanne Conference* (n 1), 221.

[91] TMC minutes (9 January 1923), in *Lausanne Conference* (n 1), 301.

[92] 'Statement read by Ismet Pasha', in *Lausanne Conference* (n 1), 203.

[93] Bilâl N. Şimşir, ed., *Lozan Telgrafları: Türk Diplomatik Belgelerinde Lozan Barış Konferansı*, vol. 1 (Ankara: Türk Tarih Kurumu Basımevi, 1990), xiv. On this see Ayhan Aktar, 'Türk–Yunan Nüfus Mübadelesi ve Diplomasi', in Ayhan Aktar, *Türk Milliyetçiliği, Gayrimüslimler ve Ekonomik Dönüşüm* (İstanbul: İletişim Yayınları, 2006), 99, at 107–9.

[94] Bilsel's commentary on the negotiations makes the point starkly. With the institution of new mechanisms of minority protection after 1919, 'powerful states were held to one standard, while other states were held to another'. This demanded a decision: 'Europe must choose between two paths: either everyone within a state must be as much a subject of the nation as a subject of the state, or else borders must be redrawn and population exchanges undertaken in accordance with nations in order to remedy the situation. There can be no state within a state.' M. Cemil [Bilsel], *Lozan*, vol. 2 (İstanbul: Ahmet İhsan Matbaası, 1933), 266, 269.

[95] 'Statement read by Ismet Pasha', in *Lausanne Conference* (n 1), 202.

aggressive designs of Greece on Turkish Asia Minor', in his view an exemplary 'campaign of devastation and carnage intermingled with all kinds of abominable crimes'.[96] The only way forward, then, was to take concrete steps to render 'certain minorities inaccessible to provocations from outside'[97]—that is, to implement a population exchange, 'the most radical and humane remedy' of all.[98] Once the exchange was completed, neither foreign powers nor the League would be able to undermine Turkey's national sovereignty, at least not with the kind of impunity that had been possible under Ottoman rule and which newly installed regimes in central and eastern Europe invited. At root, it was 'to the unity and indivisibility of Turkey' that Ankara bound itself most firmly.[99] If all relevant 'rights, duties, advantages and obligations' were now 'to be shared by all Turkish citizens alike', this was so because the situation on the ground was to be altered with a view to 'bringing about perfect understanding between all Turkish citizens'.[100]

Although they too supported an exchange, Allied delegates often tried to persuade İsmet that Turkey should align itself more closely with minority protection. Some delegates pointed to Ottoman traditions of legal pluralism to underscore the need for strong entitlements for non-Muslims. Curzon himself took time in one session to recount the myriad privileges which the *millet* system had extended to non-Muslim subjects of the sultan and which had been bolstered by a variety of decrees and treaties in the nineteenth century. Indeed, he suggested, even when the Ottoman Empire initiated its first full-scale modernization efforts, it did not strip its non-Muslim subjects of these privileges, but instead reinforced and formalized them. These privileges ought to be enshrined in the new laws of the republic that would be founded after Lausanne. It would also be preferable if the observance and implementation of such laws were placed under League authority. This would provide an effective means of ensuring Turkey's compliance with its international obligations.[101]

Interestingly, a similar argument came from a Balkan delegate. İsmet had laid stress on external pressures when sketching the dissolution of Ottoman authority in south-east Europe, playing up Russia's role and marginalizing nationalist forces endogenous to the region itself. In response, Miroslav Spalaikovitch, representing

[96] 'Statement read by Ismet Pasha', in *Lausanne Conference* (n 1), 202–3. Turkey did not maintain official relations with the League, and İsmet made a point of highlighting this after Nansen's introductory speech. However, Turkey would eventually 'come around' on this issue. As İsmet explained later in the conference, Turkey had always regarded the League 'with all due respect and consideration' (TMC minutes (13 December 1922), in *Lausanne Conference* (n 1), 209), and would take steps to join it once the terms of peace had been settled, although it still rejected Allied proposals to have a League representative stationed in Turkey in the interim (TMC minutes (9 January 1923), in *Lausanne Conference* (n 1), 301 (İsmet 'could not see any utility in it')).

[97] 'Statement read by Ismet Pasha', in *Lausanne Conference* (n 1), 202, and similarly 203 (speaking of 'agitations from outside').

[98] 'Statement read by Ismet Pasha', in *Lausanne Conference* (n 1), 203.

[99] TMC minutes (9 January 1923), in *Lausanne Conference* (n 1), 302.

[100] TMC minutes (9 January 1923), in *Lausanne Conference* (n 1), 302.

[101] For the argument in full see TMC minutes (14 December 1922), in *Lausanne Conference* (n 1), 222–3.

the Serb-Croat-Slovene state, turned İsmet's analysis on its head by insisting that he ignored a 'second factor', namely 'the feeling of the Christian nationalities in the Balkans, who were unable to forget their national ideals'.[102] It was 'this national feeling', Spalaikovitch argued, that had 'played a decisive rôle in the creation of all modern States', those of central and eastern Europe included.[103] And it was this same 'national feeling' that drove 'the present birth of a new, Kemalist, national Turkey'.[104] The implications were obvious: just as minority protection had been accepted by the newly formed or reformed states of central and eastern Europe, at least nominally, so Turkey would now have to submit to the 'practical system' that had 'been adopted by all civilised nations'.[105] Turkey should not be worried that compliance with this new order would injure its sovereignty. There had been an 'evolution' in 'the legal ideas and institutions of Europe as regards the international problem of minorities', and '[t]he days of individual or collective intervention' were 'over'.[106] Turkey could not 'exclude herself from' this order, this 'new régime of universal international law', so long as 'she really desire[d] to take her place among modern States'.[107]

İsmet was happy to concede that Turkey would need to undertake reforms to 'take her place among modern States', but he was not willing to go so far as to claim that it needed to bring its legal and administrative institutions entirely in line with central and east European practices. Again, the issue of minorities was linked closely to that of the exchange, and minority protection was to be extended to the few non-Muslim communities that were to remain in Turkey after the exchange. But it was this exchange, and not minority protection itself, that would do most of the difficult work in curbing violence in the region: physical segregation of Greeks and Turks would yield functional stability, reining in an ethno-nationalism to which a certain deference was to be extended but which could not be permitted to run amok; minority protection would serve as an ancillary mechanism, minimizing whatever majority–minority tensions might still remain after the exchange had been completed. And in a piercing turn, İsmet warned that any breakdown in the negotiations resulting from protracted disagreement on this question would likely help, rather than hinder, Ankara's hand: 'Should a rupture take place . . ., and should the minorities problem be regarded as a convenient pretext for it, the Turkish delegation were convinced that, once these truths were known, the voices raised in favour of the Turkish delegation would come not only from Angora, but also from the conscience of all peoples.'[108] That İsmet had in mind potential revolts in the colonial world, particularly in India, where support for Kemal had yet to wane, is not difficult to surmise.

102 TMC minutes (12 December 1922), in *Lausanne Conference* (n 1), 187.
103 TMC minutes (12 December 1922), in *Lausanne Conference* (n 1), 187.
104 TMC minutes (12 December 1922), in *Lausanne Conference* (n 1), 187.
105 TMC minutes (12 December 1922), in *Lausanne Conference* (n 1), 188.
106 TMC minutes (12 December 1922), in *Lausanne Conference* (n 1), 188.
107 TMC minutes (12 December 1922), in *Lausanne Conference* (n 1), 188.
108 TMC minutes (14 December 1922), in *Lausanne Conference* (n 1), 220.

Second, and as something of a supplement to this first argument, experience with the Ottoman capitulatory regime had, İsmet argued, taught the Turks to be highly suspicious of decentralization. In a long-winded and heavily historical memorandum, this one read before the Commission on the Régime of Foreigners on 2 December, ten days before his statement on minorities in Turkey before the Territorial and Military Commission, İsmet maintained that the abrogation of the capitulations was permitted to Turkey under international law.[109] To begin with, a careful analysis of the documentary record supported the decades-old Turkish argument that the capitulations were 'essentially unilateral acts'.[110] Some European jurists may have interpreted the capitulations, anomalous though they were, as international treaties,[111] but, in truth, they could not be characterized as such, at least if 'treaty' was understood strictly to mean an instrument imposing legally binding obligations on all state parties. They had instead to be understood as decree-like grants of privileges by the sultan of a limited and essentially revocable nature. That Turkey was now going ahead and exercising its right to revoke them could not, therefore, be held against it.[112] Further, even if the capitulations were to be characterized as treaties, instruments that were reciprocally binding rather than unilaterally granted and unilaterally revocable, the circumstances that had given rise to them had been subject to fundamental change. Hence, in this instance, *rebus sic stantibus* trumped the otherwise general rule of *pacta sunt servanda*, releasing Turkey from its capitulatory obligations without breaching international public law's basic principles.[113] Both lines of reasoning, particularly the latter, were supported by a third, more sweeping argument: if the capitulations were to be situated within their historical contexts, approached as legal artefacts

[109] 'Memorandum read by the Turkish Delegate at the Meeting of December 2, 1922, of the Commission on the Régime of Foreigners', annex to CRF minutes (2 December 1922), in *Lausanne Conference* (n 1), 471.

[110] 'Memorandum read by the Turkish Delegate', in *Lausanne Conference* (n 1), 478. See also CRF minutes (2 December 1922), in *Lausanne Conference* (n 1), 469.

[111] This position would be affirmed by Allied delegates during the course of the Lausanne negotiations. See, e.g., CRF minutes (2 December 1922), in *Lausanne Conference* (n 1), 470 (the Italian delegate remarking that 'the Capitulations were based on treaties'); CRF minutes (6 January 1923), in *Lausanne Conference* (n 1), 516 (the same delegate suggesting that 'the Capitulations were nothing more nor less than conventions concluded between the parties thereto in their mutual interest').

[112] Ottoman elites had long maintained this position, although it should also be noted that they sometimes characterized the capitulations as 'treaties'. Compare, for instance, 'Projet de note verbale presénté au grand-vézir Haqqî Pacha, le 29 avril 1910', with 'Avant-projet de protocole pour le règlement des conflits capitulaires en matière judiciaire presénté à Nedjmeddîn Bey, ministre de la justice, le 23 février 1911', both reproduced in Léon Ostroróg, *Pour la réforme de la justice ottomane* (Paris: Pedone, 1912), 319 and 323 respectively, at 321 and 332. For contemporaneous discussion of the question, never resolved satisfactorily, see Shih Shun Liu, *Extraterritoriality: Its Rise and Its Decline* (New York: Columbia University Press, 1925), ch. 9.

[113] 'Memorandum read by the Turkish Delegate', in *Lausanne Conference* (n 1), 478–9. This, interestingly, was a doctrine that had begun to come into its own in the late nineteenth century partly through great-power involvement in the 'Eastern Question'. See, e.g., György Haraszti, 'Treaties and the Fundamental Change of Circumstances', *RCADI* 146 (1975-III), 1, at 16–21; David J. Bederman, 'The 1871 London Declaration, Rebus Sic Stantibus and a Primitivist View of the Law of Nations', *AJIL* 82 (1988), 1, at 4–22. See further L. H. Woolsey, 'The Unilateral Termination of Treaties', *AJIL* 20 (1926), 346, at 349–50.

intelligible only within the specific temporal and spatial circumstances that had produced them, one could only conclude that they were informed by a conception of personal law that had long since become 'an anomaly and an anachronism'.[114] In other words, since 'modern legal conceptions' mandated that 'each State, in order to be considered as an independent State, must enjoy, within the limits of its frontiers, a complete and full independence', Ankara could 'in no wise agree to the re-establishment of the Capitulations, which are in direct conflict with the modern conception of a State and with the principles of public law'.[115] Once again, İsmet was on direct orders from Ankara to stand his ground on this issue—and to walk out of the negotiations should this prove necessary.[116]

In railing against the capitulations, İsmet took note that 'no such régime exists in any of the other European countries, not even in Greece and the other Balkan States'[117] (although it also bears reminding that extraterritorial regimes of various kinds had been in place in China, Japan, Siam, and a number of other non-European states for some time).[118] For İsmet, the war to which an end was to be put had been 'carried on contrary to all rules'; time after time, 'the Turkish nation had been completely disarmed and deprived of the resources which international law placed at the disposal of nations desirous of peace'.[119] As 'the Turkish people, like all other peoples, was . . . obliged to be extremely jealous in all that concerned its existence, independence and rights',[120] it now sought to make full use of the resources made available to it by modern international law to bolster its sovereign power. A key component in this struggle was the abolition of the capitulations. They had long been regarded by Ottoman reformists and Turkish

[114] 'Memorandum read by the Turkish Delegate', in *Lausanne Conference* (n 1), 479.

[115] 'Memorandum read by the Turkish Delegate', in *Lausanne Conference* (n 1), 479.

[116] Şimşir, *Lozan Telgrafları* (n 93), xiv.

[117] 'Memorandum read by the Turkish Delegate', in *Lausanne Conference* (n 1), 479. He would make the same point even more strongly elsewhere: 'Not only have the Balkan States been free from all capitulatory restrictions ever since they came into existence, but also no such régime has been set up in the States created after the great war, for instance Poland, Czechoslovakia, Lithuania, Esthonia, &c. Such a régime does not even exist in Greece.' CRF minutes (28 December 1922), in *Lausanne Conference* (n 1), 491–2. See also CRF minutes (6 January 1923), in *Lausanne Conference* (n 1), 511, 514.

[118] Indeed, the resemblances were anything but passing. Even as late as the mid-nineteenth century, by which time the 'standard of civilization' had begun to circulate, some British jurists seem not to have drawn sharp distinctions between the kind of extraterritorial powers British officials enjoyed over large swaths of Africa and the Pacific and the more formal extraterritorial jurisdiction they were authorized to exercise in China and the Ottoman Empire. W. Ross Johnston, *Sovereignty and Protection: A Study of British Jurisdictional Imperialism in the Late Nineteenth Century* (Durham: Duke University Press, 1973), 29. From a large literature on China and Japan, the most thoroughly analysed analogues, see especially Francis C. Jones, *Extraterritoriality in Japan and the Diplomatic Relations Resulting in Its Abolition, 1853–1899* (New Haven: Yale University Press, 1931); G. W. Keeton, *The Development of Extraterritoriality in China*, 2 vols. (London: Longmans, Green, & Co., 1928); Pär Kristoffer Cassel, *Grounds of Judgment: Extraterritoriality and Imperial Power in Nineteenth-Century China and Japan* (Oxford: Oxford University Press, 2012); and Teemu Ruskola, *Legal Orientalism: China, the United States, and Modern Law* (Cambridge: Harvard University Press, 2013).

[119] TMC minutes (13 December 1922), in *Lausanne Conference* (n 1), 206, 207.

[120] TMC minutes (13 December 1922), in *Lausanne Conference* (n 1), 207.

nationalists alike as deeply inimical to Turkey's independence, running counter to attempts on the part of leading Ottoman diplomats from the mid-nineteenth century onwards to reframe the empire's relations with Western powers on the basis of general principles of sovereign equality and reciprocity.[121] The Committee of Union and Progress—regarded by many British authorities as substantially indistinguishable from the Kemalists on hand at Lausanne[122]—had moved to abrogate them unilaterally in 1914,[123] at a time when Turkish-Muslim publicists regularly encouraged their readers to adopt *Weltpolitik* with exhortations like '[w]e must now fully realize that our honor and our people's integrity cannot be preserved by those old books of international law, but only by war'.[124] But this had fallen on deaf ears, securing formal recognition from none of the relevant Western states save for Germany and Austria–Hungary.[125] They were now to be done away with once and for all, in line with the Turkish delegation's insistence on concluding 'treaties of commerce, settlement and extradition, and consular conventions, on the basis of reciprocity and the principles of general international law'.[126] That the population exchange would effectively liquidate the 'colonies' whose operation the capitulations facilitated made the realization of this goal much easier than would otherwise have been the case.

[121] Thus, Gabriel Noradounghian, a prominent Ottoman jurist who would rise to the rank of foreign minister before turning to Armenian nationalism, would, for example, write against a Belgian push to enforce those clauses of an 1838 treaty that seemed to place criminal prosecution of Belgian subjects accused of crimes against Ottoman subjects within the jurisdiction of Belgian consular courts. Gabriel Noradounghian, 'Le traité turco–belge de 1838 et la compétence en matière pénale des autorités ottomanes envers les étrangers', *RDILC* 8 (1906), 119.

[122] G. R. Berridge, *Gerald Fitzmaurice (1865–1939), Chief Dragoman of the British Embassy in Turkey* (Leiden: Nijhoff, 2007), 238.

[123] 'Ottoman Circular Announcing the Abrogation of the Capitulations, 9 September 1914', reproduced in *Diplomacy in the Near and Middle East: A Documentary Record: 1535–1956*, ed. J. C. Hurewitz, vol. 2 (New York: Octagon, 1972), 2. The French original is reproduced in *RGDIP* 21 (1914), 488.

[124] Quoted in Mustafa Aksakal, *The Ottoman Road to War in 1914: The Ottoman Empire and the First World War* (Cambridge: Cambridge University Press, 2008), 21.

[125] Nasim Sousa, *The Capitulatory Régime of Turkey: Its History, Origin, and Nature* (Baltimore: The Johns Hopkins Press, 1933), 195–6; Jean Albert Mazard, *Le régime des capitulations en Turquie pendant la guerre de 1914* (Alger: Imprimerie Jean Gaudet, 1923); Ahmed Rechid, 'La condition des étrangers dans la République de Turquie', *RCADI* 46 (1933-IV), 165, at 180–2. Germany had been dangling the carrot of a termination of its capitulations for some time already. Reader Bullard, *Large and Loving Privileges: The Capitulations in the Middle East and North Africa* (Glasgow: Jackson, Son, & Co., 1960), 32; Halil İnalcık, 'Imtiyāzāt', in *The Encyclopaedia of Islam: New Edition*, vol. 3, ed. Bernard Lewis et al. (Leiden: Brill, 1986), 1179, at 1188. This was contemporaneous with the *Drang nach Osten*, a long-term strategy of expansion aimed in part at gaining control over Near Eastern markets that would culminate in the Berlin-to-Baghdad railway project. See Sean McMeekin, *The Berlin–Baghdad Express: The Ottoman Empire and Germany's Bid for World Power* (Cambridge: Harvard University Press, 2012). The scale and depth of German ambition should not be underestimated: between 1888 and 1914, Berlin's share in direct foreign investment in the Ottoman Empire is estimated to have grown from 1 to 27 per cent. Donald Quataert, 'The Age of Reforms, 1812–1914', in *An Economic and Social History of the Ottoman Empire*, ed. Halil İnalcık and Donald Quataert, vol. 2 (Cambridge: Cambridge University Press, 1994), 759, at 774; and also Şevket Pamuk, *The Ottoman Empire and European Capitalism, 1820–1913: Trade, Investment and Production* (Cambridge: Cambridge University Press, 1987), 68–72, 79–81.

[126] 'Memorandum read by the Turkish Delegate', in *Lausanne Conference* (n 1), 480.

Neither İsmet nor his interlocutors sought explicitly and consistently to link the question of the capitulations to that of the population exchange. Nevertheless, it was evident that the exchange, once concluded, would alter the territorial distribution of powers and peoples in the Near East so totally and irreversibly as to render the continuation of the capitulatory regime impossible. The commercial 'colonies' that European nationals had operated on Ottoman territory with the help of local protégés had diminished dramatically, both in size and in strength, during the preceding years. Even the Jews, a British delegate noted with alarm, 'members of a non-Moslem community of which the Turkish delegation themselves admit that Turkey has never had reason to complain, are liquidating their property and leaving Smyrna'.[127] As a result, the putative rationale for the capitulations had lost much of its bite: there were far fewer European merchants in the empire, far fewer local non-Muslims to assist them, and so far less need for a capitulatory regime.

The Allies were willing to recognize the formal abrogation of the capitulations, if only grudgingly. In return for this recognition, though, they insisted that Turkey launch a series of reforms. Among other things, the Allies demanded that Turkey staff courts presiding over civil and criminal suits involving foreigners with foreign judges, 'recommended to the Turkish Government by the Permanent International Tribunal [sic] of The Hague' but 'appointed by the Turkish Government without any interference on the part of foreign Powers'.[128] Since its 'machinery of justice' was fundamentally 'defective',[129] Turkey needed to provide 'such guarantees as regards legislation and the administration of justice as will inspire confidence in all those who will be obliged to have recourse thereto'.[130]

None of this was novel. Nor, for that matter, was it limited to the Turkish case. Incremental reductions in extraterritorial jurisdiction in other states where capitulatory and unequal treaty regimes were operative had nearly always been conditioned on the ability and willingness of local elites to ensure that contracts were enforced, property rights respected, and pro-Western reforms undertaken. If Turkey were permitted to do away with the capitulations for good, it would need to bind itself to similar commitments, putting at ease those who had 'established themselves in Turkey and built up important enterprises there in reliance on the guarantees offered to them by the [capitulatory] treaties'.[131] It had taken some time for comparable programmes to reach maturity in Japan, where, as its own chief delegate put it, '[i]t was only after hard work . . ., lasting more than twenty years, that the Powers were able to agree to the Capitulations being brought to an end'.[132]

[127] CRF minutes (28 December 1922), in *Lausanne Conference* (n 1), 487, and similarly 488.

[128] CRF minutes (28 December 1922), in *Lausanne Conference* (n 1), 482.

[129] CRF minutes (28 December 1922), in *Lausanne Conference* (n 1), 497.

[130] CRF minutes (2 December 1922), in *Lausanne Conference* (n 1), 467. A British delegate put this even more forcefully, speaking of the Turks' 'duty . . . to do their utmost to reassure foreigners'. CRF minutes (28 December 1922), in *Lausanne Conference* (n 1), 487.

[131] CRF minutes (2 December 1922), in *Lausanne Conference* (n 1), 467.

[132] CRF minutes (2 December 1922), in *Lausanne Conference* (n 1), 470. See also CRF minutes (28 December 1922), in *Lausanne Conference* (n 1), 483, 495.

A similar 'transitory period'[133] was needed for Turkey to suppress *Kadijustiz*, promulgate new codes, and cultivate a well-trained judiciary not beholden to *Sharī'a*.[134] Any attempt to nationalize its economy in one fell swoop would undermine investor confidence and generate unprecedented capital flight, doing irreparable damage to the '[g]reat business houses' of Istanbul and Izmir and reducing Turkey 'to the condition, not of a great and prosperous nation, but of a little country lost in the wastes of Asia'.[135]

The Turkish delegation feared that these demands were ruses with which to preserve, or even bolster, the substance of the capitulations while doing away with their form.[136] Turkey, İsmet stressed, had 'been at work on reorganisation and reform for half a century . . ., and ha[d] thus succeeded in creating institutions which are entirely consonant with modern needs'.[137] Under no circumstances could it accept 'outside interference' with 'the drafting of Turkish internal legislation'.[138] Crucially, this was a position to which he remained wedded on account of his commitment to press ahead with a compulsory exchange. The 'principle of nationalities', however exactly it was to be understood, had to receive 'equal application everywhere' if it was to be applied anywhere: 'Just as the Greeks established at Marseilles could not reasonably think of creating there an independent Greek State or of annexing it to their mother-country', so too, İsmet argued,

[133] CRF minutes (28 December 1922), in *Lausanne Conference* (n 1), 483. See further CRF minutes (6 January 1923), in *Lausanne Conference* (n 1), 516.

[134] The Japanese analogue had particularly deep roots: Cemil Aydın, *The Politics of Anti-Westernism in Asia: Visions of World Order in Pan-Islamic and Pan-Asian Thought* (New York: Columbia University Press, 2007), ch. 4; and also Renée Worringer, '"Sick Man of Europe" or "Japan of the Near East"?: Constructing Ottoman Modernity in the Hamidian and Young Turk Eras', *International Journal of Middle East Studies* 36 (2004), 207. For a state that succeeded in persuading Western powers to revise their unequal treaties in the 1920s through non-confrontational means, see Stefan Hell, *Siam and the League of Nations: Modernisation, Sovereignty and Multilateral Diplomacy, 1920–1940* (Bangkok: River Books, 2010), esp. 35–7, 42–3, 240.

[135] CRF minutes (28 December 1922), in *Lausanne Conference* (n 1), 497–8. Such sentiments were common. Nansen warned that 'the flight of the Greek and Armenian populations from Constantinople' would result in the 'complete commercial and financial suicide' of the country, stripping it of its 'richest asset'. Fridtjof Nansen, 'Reciprocal Exchange of Racial Minorities between Greece and Turkey', LN Doc. C.736.M.447.1922, *LNOJ* 4 (1923), 126, at 129. Similarly, Toynbee argued that 'if western enterprise is alarmed and outraged by Turkey's new policy towards foreigners . . ., it will boycott Turkey and prefer to invest its energies in China, Mexico or any other field where the risks and difficulties are even slightly less great than in the dominions of Angora'. Arnold J. Toynbee, 'The East after Lausanne', *Foreign Affairs* 2 (1923), 84, at 95. There was, of course, something to these predictions: Turkey's per capita gross domestic product in 1923, the year of the republic's formal establishment, stood approximately 40 per cent below its level in 1914, a drop explicable only if one takes into account the fact that Turkey had experienced a full decade of war, and that this decade had been marked by the flight of non-Muslim capital and concomitant loss of commercial skills and contacts. Şevket Pamuk, 'Economic Change in Twentieth-Century Turkey: Is the Glass More Than Half Full?', in *The Cambridge History of Turkey*, vol. 4, ed. Reşat Kasaba (Cambridge: Cambridge University Press, 2008), 266, at 276.

[136] CRF minutes (2 December 1922), in *Lausanne Conference* (n 1), 468. As a journalist would later note, the fear was linked closely to Allied strategy: 'The Allies deemed it profitable to try to rescue all that could be rescued from the sinking ship of the capitulatory regime.' Ali Naci Karacan, *Lozan Konferansı ve İsmet Paşa* (İstanbul: Maarif Matbaası, 1943), 106.

[137] CRF minutes (6 January 1923), in *Lausanne Conference* (n 1), 510.

[138] TMC minutes (14 December 1922), in *Lausanne Conference* (n 1), 226.

'the Greeks or Armenians in Turkey could not legitimately desire the same thing in Turkey'.[139] İsmet was willing to make certain concessions, such as obliging Turkish authorities to draw upon the expertise of European legal advisers and allowing certain issues of personal status involving Allied nationals to be decided by courts of Allied states.[140] But he could go no further. The exchange and the capitulations' formal abolition would make it possible for 'Turkey to have a judicial system' which would 'be one and the same for all people in her territory—foreign and Turkish alike'.[141]

In combination, both of these positions—the one concerned with minority protection, the other with the capitulations—situated the exchange at a considerable distance from the more familiar European practices of the time. In the one case just as much as in the other, İsmet's aim was to bolster Turkey's sovereignty to the greatest extent possible, and to do so in a way that accorded with the distinctive features of the context at hand. Curzon would chide İsmet for being 'highly sensitive respecting questions of supervision'[142] on a number of occasions, exasperated at having to respond time and again to 'the old argument regarding the infringement of Turkish sovereignty'.[143] 'I do implore Ismet Pasha', he declared at one point, 'to abandon this argument, to wrap up and put away in a cupboard this phantom of Turkish sovereignty which none of us wants to injure'.[144] İsmet's rejoinder, as recorded in summary form by the minutes' compiler, was tellingly blunt: 'The integrity of Turkey had', he declared, 'been guaranteed by means of promises from the highest authorities and also by solemn treaties, and yet Turkish sovereignty had repeatedly been violated and Turkey had been dismembered again and again. How could Turkey help having misgivings?'[145] Given the firmness of this stance, it is not surprising that Turkey should have succeeded in resisting efforts to impose the kind of regime that had been crafted for central and east European states after 1919. What is striking, though, is that it should have been by way of an atypical mechanism, one whose legal status had yet to be settled conclusively, whose scope of application was limited at the time to the Near East, and whose precedential force under international law was highly ambiguous,[146] that Turkey should have made the transition from empire to republic.

[139] 'Statement read by Ismet Pasha', in *Lausanne Conference* (n 1), 203.

[140] CRF minutes (28 December 1922), in *Lausanne Conference* (n 1), 485; CRF minutes (27 January 1923), in *Lausanne Conference* (n 1), 523.

[141] CRF minutes (27 January 1923), in *Lausanne Conference* (n 1), 523.

[142] TMC minutes (14 December 1922), in *Lausanne Conference* (n 1), 219.

[143] CRF minutes (28 December 1922), in *Lausanne Conference* (n 1), 496.

[144] CRF minutes (28 December 1922), in *Lausanne Conference* (n 1), 496.

[145] TMC minutes (14 December 1922), in *Lausanne Conference* (n 1), 219.

[146] Richard Child, an American delegate, raised this thorny issue explicitly when he warned that 'new precedents which tend to establish the right of nations to expel large bodies of their citizens to become burdens upon other nations must be carefully considered before countenance is given them, lest a new and unwholesome principle find foothold to vex international law and justice'. TMC minutes (12 December 1922), in *Lausanne Conference* (n 1), 187.

III. Two Tensions Enshrined: The Legal Form of the Exchange

The package of international legal instruments ultimately produced by the Conference of Lausanne reflected the tensions inherent in these negotiations—that concerning the place of ethno-nationalism in the exchange's design and execution, and that relating to the regionally specific character of the exchange mechanism. The Convention concerning the Exchange of Greek and Turkish Populations (and a related agreement on the restitution of interned civilians and exchange of prisoners of war) was annexed to the Peace Treaty when it and 14 other instruments were finally signed in July 1923 to form the complete peace settlement with Turkey. The fact that it had been signed in January, some six months prior to all but the restitution and prisoner exchange agreement, testifies to its centrality for the peace settlement.[147]

In line with Ottoman tradition, the Lausanne Peace Treaty contained no stipulation that Turkey recognize Kurds, Arabs, or any of its other non-Turkish Muslim communities as national minorities. Nor did it make allowance, as had the Treaty of Sèvres, for Kurdish autonomy or an Armenian 'national home', regarded by many at Versailles a few years earlier as a virtual certainty.[148] The Turks had remained firm in the face of half-hearted Allied demands of this sort, meeting 'all the questions put to them' on these matters 'with an absolute and clear refusal'.[149] The Peace Treaty restricted the application of minority status to those non-Muslim groups that had commanded dominant positions within the *millet* system but that had recently seen their numbers reduced drastically: the Greek, Armenian, and Jewish communities.[150] A number of issue-specific provisions of the treaty—the already mentioned Articles 37 to 44[151]—fixed the parameters within which Turkey would henceforth address minority protection: in order to ensure observance of the general right to equality enshrined in Article 39,

[147] Cf. Baskın Oran, 'The Story of Those who Stayed: Lessons from Articles 1 and 2 of the 1923 Convention', in *Crossing the Aegean: An Appraisal of the 1923 Compulsory Population Exchange between Greece and Turkey*, ed. Renée Hirschon (New York: Berghahn, 2003), 97, at 97.

[148] The Armenian delegation to the Paris Peace Conference had maintained that it was 'quite certain that the major portion of [Armenian] emigrants will return to their liberated fatherland'; see *The Armenian Question Before the Peace Conference: A Memorandum Presented Officially by the Representatives of Armenia to the Peace Conference at Versailles, on February 26th, 1919* (Paris: Imprimerie P. Dumont, 1919), 7.

[149] TMC minutes (9 January 1923), in *Lausanne Conference* (n 1), 308. As Grew would observe, '[t]here is no subject upon which the Turks are more fixed in obstinacy'. Grew, *Turbulent Era* (n 12), 531. This stance was naturally opposed by an increasingly vocal Armenian diaspora; see in particular the documents reprinted in the American Committee Opposed to the Lausanne Treaty, *The Lausanne Treaty, Turkey and Armenia* (New York: n. p., 1926).

[150] Curzon glossed the decision with apprehension: 'The sub-commission originally pressed for the inclusion of all racial minorities, Moslem and non-Moslem—for instance, the Kurds, Circassians and Arabs. The Turkish delegation insisted that these minorities required no protection, and were quite satisfied with their lot under Turkish rule. I hope that this will be the case.' TMC minutes (9 January 1923), in *Lausanne Conference* (n 1), 296.

[151] Treaty of Peace, signed at Lausanne, 24 July 1923, 28 LNTS 11 ('Lausanne Peace Treaty'), at 31–7.

it was provided that non-Muslims could practise their religion freely (Article 38), make full use of their native languages in private and in public (Article 39), maintain educational and charitable foundations without undue state interference (Article 40), and so on.[152] Minority protection was thus introduced into Turkey. But it came in a highly constricted and problematic form. Not only was its application restricted to demographically negligible groups of non-Muslims, thereby underscoring the primacy of a specifically Turkish-Muslim *ethnos*, but this restricted application followed directly from the population exchange and other displacements, which made it factually impossible for a genuinely robust minority-protection regime to be put into effect.

Importantly, Turkey could comply with these treaty obligations if and only if it promulgated newer, more 'modern' laws (which, in turn, would provide a measure of 'compensation' to the Western powers for the capitulations' abolition).[153] This much the Kemalists were prepared to undertake, as it coincided with their own commitment to part with Ottoman traditions of pluralism and adopt many of the West's legal and administrative innovations.[154] So much so that they agreed to permit 'a number of European legal counsellors' selected from a list drafted by the Permanent Court to be posted on a temporary basis in Izmir and Istanbul for the sake of participating in legislative commissions, observing the operation of Turkish courts, and preparing reports for the Turkish minister of justice when needed—all 'with a view to the institution of such reforms as may be rendered advisable by the development of manners and civilisation'.[155] What the Kemalists were *not* willing to do, though, was to allow the most visible elements of the extraterritorial regime enshrined in the capitulations to be preserved.

To be sure, some aspects of the Lausanne settlement betrayed the ongoing influence of the capitulations. In addition to the European legal advisers, there was, for instance, the apportionment of the Ottoman public debt,[156] the limitation of tariffs and related measures for a number of years,[157] and the placing of matters of personal status and family law involving non-Muslim nationals of the Allied Powers within the jurisdiction of their respective countries' courts.[158]

[152] Lausanne Peace Treaty (n 151), 31–3.

[153] A quid pro quo appreciated well in Edgar Turlington, 'The Settlement of Lausanne', *AJIL* 18 (1924), 696, at 697–9, 706.

[154] See, e.g., Mustafa Kemal, 'Ankara Hukuk Fakültesinin Açılışında (5.XI.1925)', in *Türkiye'de Siyasal Kültürün Resmî Kaynakları*, ed. Taha Parla, vol. 3 (İstanbul: İletişim Yayınları, 1992), 292.

[155] Declaration relating to the Administration of Justice, signed at Lausanne, 24 July 1923, 36 LNTS 161, at 163. The four men to be selected as advisers were Georges Sauser-Hall (Switzerland), Goeman Borgesius (Netherlands), Fritz Sterzel (Sweden), and Luis Folache de Orozco (Spain)—two judges and two professors of law. That these 'counsellors' were selected from states that had been neutral during the Great War irked some Allied jurists; see, e.g., Achille Mestre, *L'étranger en Turquie d'après le Traité de Lausanne* (Paris: Revue politique et parlementaire, 1923), 22 (complaining that such officials would not represent 'directly the French point of view').

[156] Lausanne Peace Treaty (n 151), Arts 46–57, at 37–51.

[157] Commercial Convention, signed at Lausanne, 24 July 1923, 28 LNTS 171.

[158] Convention respecting Conditions of Residence and Business and Jurisdiction, signed at Lausanne, 24 July 1923, 28 LNTS 151, Art 16, at 163. For consideration of these and related concessions see Philip Marshall Brown, 'The Capitulations', *Foreign Affairs* 1 (1922–3), 71, at 79–81; Philip Marshall Brown, 'From Sèvres to Lausanne', *AJIL* 18 (1924), 113, at 114; Marcel

However, while certainly not negligible,[159] none of this alters the fact that Article 28 of the Peace Treaty, which formalized 'the complete abolition of the Capitulations in Turkey in every respect', eliminated the most noticeable features of the regime.[160] If the capacity to enact and enforce legislation freely is, as the Permanent Court would observe in a few years' time, 'one of the most obvious forms of the exercise of sovereign power',[161] the abolition of the capitulations—tied closely to the drive towards ethnic homogeneity and territorial sovereignty that underpinned the population exchange—marked a key moment in the augmentation of Turkey's capacity to exercise this power. As Manley Hudson noted, it was fundamental to Turkish elites' desire to achieve 'two main objectives'—'to create a Turkish nation of Turkish people living on Turkish territory, and to win for this nation a place of equality among the nations of the Western World'.[162]

The text of the Exchange Convention is equally revealing. Its first two articles called for the institution of a compulsory exchange between 'Turkish nationals of the Greek Orthodox religion' and 'Greek nationals of the Moslem religion', but also allowed exceptions to this rule in the case of Greeks 'established' in Istanbul and Muslims 'established' in western Thrace (and, when read in conjunction with Article 14 of the Peace Treaty, Greeks resident on two Aegean islands assigned to Turkey).[163] By any account, this was a rather murky attempt to align ethnicity and religion with territory: it was often unclear which of the two state parties ought to be assigned control over a given community, these being notoriously ill-defined,[164] and the

Ogier, 'L'élaboration des clauses économiques du Traité de Lausanne', *Revue de droit international* 1 (1927), 301; and Jean Teyssaire, 'Les concessions et le Traité de Lausanne', *RGDIP* 35 (1928), 447.

[159] Indeed, it has been maintained that, despite having secured its political independence, Turkey was in some respects 'one of the few countries where "Open Door" conditions actually held', at least for a limited period after 1923. Çağlar Keyder, *The Definition of a Peripheral Economy: Turkey 1923–1929* (Cambridge: Cambridge University Press/Éditions de la Maison des sciences de l'homme, 1981), 9, 69–71 for details. On these short-term limitations on protectionism, see Korkut Boratav, *Türkiye'de Devletçilik*, 2nd ed. (Ankara: İmge Kitabevi Yayınları, 2006), 33–5.

[160] Lausanne Peace Treaty (n 151), 27.

[161] *Legal Status of Eastern Greenland* (*Denmark v Norway*) PCIJ Rep. Series A/B No 53 (1933), 48.

[162] Manley O. Hudson, 'Law Reform in Turkey', *American Bar Association Journal* 13 (1927), 5, at 5.

[163] Convention concerning the Exchange of Greek and Turkish Populations, and Protocol, signed at Lausanne, 30 January 1923, 32 LNTS 75 ('Exchange Convention'), at 77; Lausanne Peace Treaty (n 151), 23. The islands in question were Imbros/Gökçeada and Tenedos/Bozcaada.

[164] The most famous illustrations are the Karamanlides/Karamanlılar, Turkish-speaking Orthodox Christians from central Anatolia, and the Muslims of Crete, who did not always self-identify as 'Turks'. In both cases, the religious criterion ultimately helped to settle the issue: the Greek Orthodox of central Anatolia found themselves in Greece, while the Muslims of Crete were transferred to Turkey. See Richard Clogg, 'A Millet Within a Millet: The Karamanlides', in *Ottoman Greeks in the Age of Nationalism: Politics, Economy, and Society in the Nineteenth Century*, ed. Dimitri Gondicas and Charles Issawi (Princeton: Darwin Press, 1999), 115, at 115, 131–2; Renk Özdemir, 'Borders of Belonging in the "Exchanged" Generations of Karamanlis', in *Land of Diverse Migrations: Challenges of Emigration and Immigration in Turkey*, ed. Ahmet İçduygu and Kemal Kirişci (İstanbul: İstanbul Bilgi University Press, 2009), 29; Elektra Kostopoulou, 'The Art of Being Replaced: The Last of the Cretan Muslims Between the Empire and the Nation-State', in *Religion, Ethnicity and Contested Nationhood in the Former Ottoman Space*, ed. Jørgen Nielsen (Leiden: Brill, 2012), 129; Ioannis N. Grigoriadis, *Instilling Religion in Greek and Turkish Nationalism: A 'Sacred*

availability of exceptions, however limited, allowed for the creation of dangerously vulnerable enclaves. Articles 8 through 17 explained that the exchange procedure was to be coordinated by a mixed commission, an international organization funded by all of 'the States concerned'.[165] Article 7 stipulated that those subject to the exchange would be stripped of their previous citizenship and transformed into nationals of the state to which they had been transferred.[166] This was to be an automatic process of renationalization, and, as such, a far cry from other ways of dealing with problems of citizenship arising from situations of state succession. For instance, no plebiscite—a mechanism of limited application even in Europe[167]—was organized for the resolution of conflict between Greece and Turkey. Turkey pressed for a plebiscite in western Thrace,[168] and also in the oil-rich former Ottoman province of Mosul,[169] but both requests were denied. The only exception was the ethnically mixed border province of Alexandretta (Hatay), incorporated into France's Syrian mandate in the 1920s but annexed by Turkey after a controversial plebiscite in 1938.[170] The right of option, enabling individuals to choose their citizenship after state dissolution, had been popularized in post-Versailles Europe, and enjoyed some traction in post-Ottoman

Synthesis' (New York: Palgrave Macmillan, 2013), 37–42. For the experiences of the Dönme, Ottoman Jews who professed Islam in public, see Marc David Baer, *The Dönme: Jewish Converts, Muslim Revolutionaries, and Secular Turks* (Stanford: Stanford University Press, 2010), ch. 6. For religion as a criterion of differentiation see Emile Kolodny, 'Primauté de l'identité religieuse sur la citoyenneté: le cas des échanges obligatoires de population entre la Grèce et la Turquie (1923)', in *Religion et identité. Actes du colloque d'Aix-en-Provence, octobre 1996*, ed. Gabriel Audisio (Aix-en-Provence: Publications de l'Université de Provence, 1998), 134.

165 Exchange Convention (n 163), 79–85. 166 Exchange Convention (n 163), 79.

167 Sarah Wambaugh, *Plebiscites since the World War, with a Collection of Official Documents*, vol. 1 (Washington: Carnegie Endowment for International Peace, 1933), 42 (noting that 'the Allies avoided a plebiscite in every region of first importance save that of Upper Silesia, and that when they resorted to a plebiscite it was as a method of compromise, to escape from a dilemma rather than as a deliberate choice').

168 Samim Akgönül, *Une communauté, deux États: la minorité turco-musulmane de Thrace occidentale* (Istanbul: Les éditions Isis, 1999), 24–6 ff.

169 Mosul's status—more complex and economically urgent than that of western Thrace—was not resolved at Lausanne. A 1924 investigation by a League expedition resulted in a report underscoring the logistical challenges of holding a plebiscite and the inevitability of placing Mosul under the same mandate as Baghdad and Basra. Although resistance within Turkey was strong, the Kemalists eventually agreed to recognize Britain's mandate south of the boundary the expedition recommended (the so-called 'Brussels line') in exchange for a 10 per cent per annum cut of Iraq's oil royalties for a period of 25 years. For the PCIJ's crucial opinion on the League Council's powers in the matter, see *Interpretation of Article 3, Paragraph 2, of the Treaty of Lausanne (Frontier between Turkey and Iraq)*, Advisory Opinion, PCIJ Rep. Series B No 12 (1925). For analysis see Quincy Wright, 'The Mosul Dispute', *AJIL* 20 (1926), 453; A. Berriedale Keith, 'The League of Nations and Mosul', *Journal of Comparative Legislation and International Law* 8 (1926), 38; Wambaugh, *Plebiscites* (n 167), 538–44; Abdul-Malik Salim Al-Zaibag, 'The Mosul Boundary Question' (MA thesis, Tufts College, 1948); David Cuthell, 'A Kemalist Gambit: A View of the Political Negotiations in the Determination of the Turkish–Iraqi Border', in *The Creation of Iraq, 1914–1921*, ed. Reeva Spector Simon and Eleanor H. Tejirian (New York: Columbia University Press, 2004), 80.

170 Significantly, the evidence suggests that Turkey's successful annexation owed more to French reluctance to become embroiled in another Levantine conflict than to the actual number of votes cast. For details see Majid Khadduri, 'The Alexandretta Dispute', *AJIL* 39 (1945), 406; Sarah D. Shields, *Fezzes in the River: Identity Politics and European Diplomacy in the Middle East on the Eve of World War II* (New York: Oxford University Press, 2011).

territories: Articles 31 through 35 of the Lausanne Peace Treaty provided a two-year right of option for certain persons resident in territories detached from Turkey and administered as League mandates, conditional upon the consent of the receiving state.[171] But once again, expulsions and other displacements had already segregated the region's constituent communities to a significant degree, and were to segregate them even further with the completion of the compulsory exchange of minorities between Greece and Turkey. This diluted the efficacy of any residual right of option that was made available.[172] Even more to the point, no right of option was deployed to resolve the Greek–Turkish conflict itself. In this case, nothing less than a compulsory exchange was deemed sufficient.

The population exchange, as formalized at Lausanne, offered a unique method of resolving conflict, one that was driven both by ethno-nationalism and by its putative antithesis—a technocratic effort to bring new modes of legal administration to bear upon a given territory and population. The exchange was also positioned at a considerable distance from minority protection and related intra-European mechanisms of nation-building, underscoring its roots in a specific region with a specific set of embedded legal and political practices. In order to gain an appreciation of how these and related tensions fuelled the actual implementation of the exchange, I turn now to the Permanent Court of International Justice's opinion in a case arising from conflicting interpretations of the Exchange Convention. As with other actors and institutions involved in the exchange's design and implementation, the Permanent Court sought to regulate ethno-nationalism in a regional context characterized by distinct traditions and institutions.

[171] Lausanne Peace Treaty (n 151), 29–31.

[172] Cf. Norman Bentwich, 'Nationality in Mandated Territories Detached from Turkey', *BYIL* 7 (1926), 97, at 98.

4

Humanitarianism, the World Court, and the Relation between Domestic and International Law

In 1934, more than a decade after the Ottoman Empire's formal dissolution, the Greek–Turkish mixed commission for the exchange of minority populations sat down to take stock of its record. Supported by the League, staffed partly by international civil servants, and deriving its authority from the Exchange Convention, the commission had been entrusted with the unenviable task of supervising this procedure, coordinating the movement of displaced persons, valuing and liquidating both movable and immovable property, and overseeing the distribution of compensation for resulting losses. Over the years it had been deluged with all manner of cases, confronting issues of Greek and Ottoman property and inheritance law in addition to questions of conflict of laws and public international law. Interestingly, though, it was the population exchange's juridical and geographic distinctiveness that members of the commission felt compelled to underscore in their final report. For the commission, the exchange was a fundamentally juridical enterprise, one in which each of the concerned states, not to mention the commission itself, sought to act—or at least to style their actions—'in harmony with the letter and spirit of the Convention of Lausanne'.[1] What is more, as a 'theatre of exodus and migration', Asia Minor and the Balkans displayed, 'in connection with the problem of minorities, an appearance different from the rest of Europe', an approach that lay at a significant distance from more conventional European techniques of minority protection.[2] Only in the 'Near East' could the notion of a compulsory population exchange—'an event without precedent in the life of states'—take root as 'a radical solution' to 'the problem of minorities' with as much intensity as it had.[3]

This chapter provides a contextual analysis of the 1925 advisory opinion in *Exchange of Greek and Turkish Populations*. Highly neglected, the opinion is

[1] Commission mixte pour l'échange des populations grecques et turques, 'Rapport final', annex to *Actes, décisions, sentences arbitrales relatifs à l'échange des populations grecques et turques*, vol. 2 (n.p.: Imprimerie Tsitouris frères, n.d.), 1, at 48.

[2] Commission mixte, 'Rapport final' (n 1), 9.

[3] Commission mixte, 'Rapport final' (n 1), 10–12.

remarkable for its forthright and unrestrained engagement with an international treaty whose purpose was nothing less than the regulation of a compulsory exchange of minorities between two states determined to reconstitute themselves along fully national lines.[4] I begin with a discussion of the relief organizations that were involved in resettlement and reconstruction efforts before and during the Greek–Turkish exchange's formal implementation. I then consider the Permanent Court's opinion on its own terms, focusing on the Court's attempt to grapple with the issue of Istanbul's *établis*, Greek residents of the city who were deemed to be exempt from the exchange. Here I examine the way in which the Court—in the eyes of many internationalists an agent for 'the rule of public right in lieu of impulse and selfishness and brutal force'[5]—articulated the distinction between domestic and international law, bypassing Turkish concerns about the exchange's implementation so as to shield as many of Istanbul's Greeks as possible from the exchange. I argue that this interpretation of the treaty-based rights of Istanbul's Greek community cannot be appreciated without grasping the context within which its status came to be an object of concern, especially the commitment of many humanitarian organizations to protect the few minority communities that remained in Greece and Turkey by controlling and deflecting ethno-nationalist claims to sovereign power. International law was essential to the Near East's stabilization, and was recognized as such by the Court no less than the humanitarian organizations involved in the region. The exercise of interpreting the agreement that formalized the population transfer—the juridically distinct and regionally specific mechanism through which such stabilization was to be achieved—was crucial in this regard.

I. 'The Embodiment of Internal Disorder and Cruelty'

Although nineteenth-century jurists fond of the Concert of Europe's balance of power had been wont to speak of non-intervention as 'the first and highest interest of the great commonwealth of States',[6] many had also been inclined to recognize the legality of intervention, particularly though not exclusively on behalf of 'humanity' in cases of despotic or tyrannical rule.[7] Nowhere had this inconsistency manifested itself with greater force than in the case of Turkey: even as most great powers saw it in their interest to preserve its integrity and independence, the Ottoman Empire came to serve as a testing-ground for new modes of intervention,

[4] *Exchange of Greek and Turkish Populations (Lausanne Convention VI, January 30th, 1923, Article 2)*, Advisory Opinion, PCIJ Rep. Series B No 10 (1925).

[5] Elihu Root, 'The Permanent Court of International Justice', *ASIL Pd.* 17 (1923), 1, at 6.

[6] Mountague Bernard, *On the Principle of Non-Intervention: A Lecture Delivered in the Hall of All Souls' College* (Oxford: J. H. and Jas. Parker, 1860), 24.

[7] T. J. Lawrence, for example, listed multiple exceptions to the norm of non-intervention, only one of which was 'humanitarian' intervention; see T. J. Lawrence, *The Principles of International Law* (London: Macmillan, 1895), 115–35.

from the constitution of an independent Greek kingdom in the 1830s through the pacification of inter-confessional strife in Lebanon in the early 1860s to the resolution of competing Greek and Ottoman claims to Crete in the late 1890s. Indeed, humanitarian intervention's emergence as a staple of international legal discourse is incapable of being understood without reference to great-power involvement in the ethno-confessional strife and counter-insurgent police action that characterized Ottoman life in the late nineteenth and early twentieth centuries.[8] Nevertheless, after 1914, and even more so after the war's conclusion in 1918, wholesale, often indiscriminate, destruction and displacement, both of persons and of properties, transformed what remained of the Ottoman Empire into a *cause célèbre* for an astonishingly wide range of actors. Just as Antoine Rougier, one of the first jurists to subject humanitarian intervention to sustained legal examination, could argue even before the 1912–13 Balkan Wars that '[t]he origin and development of the idea of humanitarian intervention appear to be linked in some measure to the history of the Eastern question',[9] so too could a Cambridge lawyer writing in 1924, with the Armenian genocide and Greek–Turkish exchange behind him, suggest that it was Turkey that had always been '[t]he particular case thinly concealed behind most of the generalities concerning humanitarian intervention'.[10] Such views echoed and amplified statements made by jurists to the effect that Turkey was in need of far-reaching legal and administrative reforms, and that only when such reforms had been implemented might it succeed in securing acceptance as a properly modern state adhering to the rule of law with sufficient consistency to render the capitulations unnecessary.

Unsurprisingly, the Ottoman Empire's centrality for humanitarian activism found expression in the work of missionary and philanthropic groups of various stripes. Active throughout the long nineteenth century,[11] during which they had been protected by the Ottoman capitulatory regime, many such organizations redoubled their efforts in the wake of Versailles, positioning themselves as contributors to the empire's transformation into a stable component of the evolving

[8] For the most comprehensive treatment to date see Davide Rodogno, *Against Massacre: Humanitarian Interventions in the Ottoman Empire 1815–1914* (Princeton: Princeton University Press, 2012).

[9] Antoine Rougier, 'La théorie de l'intervention d'humanité', *RGDIP* 17 (1910), 468, at 472.

[10] P. H. Winfield, 'The Grounds of Intervention in International Law', *BYIL* 5 (1924), 149, at 161. Such sentiments were exceedingly common at the time; see, e.g., Ellery C. Stowell, *Intervention in International Law* (Washington: John Byrne & Co., 1921), 80 ff (discussing the Armenian genocide as a case in which the United States 'felt constrained by the obligations of a common humanity to intervene diplomatically'); André Mandelstam, 'La protection des minorités', *RCADI* 1 (1923-I), 363, at 373 (arguing that '[t]he principal cause of the Great Powers' constant intervention in Turkey was the despotic character of the Ottoman Empire').

[11] Ussama Makdisi, *Artillery of Heaven: American Missionaries and the Failed Conversion of the Middle East* (Ithaca: Cornell University Press, 2008); Hans-Lukas Kieser, *Nearest East: American Millennialism and Mission to the Middle East* (Philadelphia: Temple University Press, 2010); Mehmet Ali Doğan and Heather J. Sharkey, eds., *American Missionaries and the Middle East: Foundational Encounters* (Salt Lake City: University of Utah Press, 2011); Eleanor H. Tejirian and Reeva Spector Simon, *Conflict, Conquest, and Conversion: Two Thousand Years of Christian Missions in the Middle East* (New York: Columbia University Press, 2012), chs. 6–7.

'family of nations'. Frequently accompanying this was a belief in the need to reorganize the region along ethnic and religious lines, with Greeks and Turks being segregated and independent states or 'national homes' being created for Arabs, Armenians, and others, perhaps in the form of a federated Ottoman state reinforced by British or American power. This, it was thought, would go a long way to anchor the region in an international order that was itself undergoing systemic reconfiguration and institutionalization, partly due to the ubiquity of the suggestive but juridically imprecise rhetoric of self-determination.

James Barton, chief representative of Near East Relief, a US-based philanthropic organization founded in 1915 to assist Armenians fleeing genocide, offers a fine example of this phenomenon. For Barton, the German-sponsored call for *jihād* against the Allied Powers that the sultan-caliph had issued in 1914 had succeeded in rallying neither Arab nor Indian Muslims. 'Mohammedans are beginning to realize that their solidarity is broken, that their hope of universal Mohammedan rule over the world is shattered forever', wrote Barton, adding with more than a touch of glee that there had 'never been a time since Christianity came into open conflict with Islam when conditions seemed so favorable for a wise, judicious, united approach to the Mohammedan world with the message of Christianity'.[12] Facilitating the Ottoman Empire's transformation into a modern state governing itself under international law and embedded in the League of Nations would allow Western powers 'to bring upon Turkey the pressure of moral force', compelling 'Turkey to set her house in order, to revise her court procedure, the relation of the official classes to the minority populations, her educational system, her moral standards, so that she may become a worthy member of the great sisterhood [of nations]'.[13] After all, though '[p]hysical force' had 'failed to coerce Turkey', it was still possible to 'mobilize the moral forces of the world and bring them to bear through the League upon that country which has so long stood before the world as the embodiment of internal disorder and cruelty'.[14] Championing proposals to institute an American mandate over Armenia within a federally restructured Ottoman Empire,[15] Barton served as foreign secretary of the American Board of Commissioners for Foreign Missions, an umbrella organization for a resourceful Protestant missionary movement which positioned itself in transnational terms[16]

[12] James L. Barton, 'The Effect of the War on Protestant Missions', *Harvard Theological Review* 12 (1919), 1, at 17–18.

[13] James L. Barton, 'A Program for the Near East', *Annals of the American Academy of Political and Social Science* 108 (1923), 153, at 158–9.

[14] Barton, 'A Program for the Near East' (n 13), 159.

[15] Joseph L. Grabill, *Protestant Diplomacy and the Near East: Missionary Influence on American Policy, 1810–1927* (Minneapolis: University of Minnesota Press, 1971), 102–4, 124–6, also 171–2.

[16] Protestant missionaries appear to have begun deploying the quasi-legal notion of 'supranationality' toward the end of the First World War in an effort to counter internment, repatriation, and other forms of hostility. John Stuart, 'Beyond Sovereignty?: Protestant Missions, Empire and Transnationalism, 1890–1950', in *Beyond Sovereignty: Britain, Empire and Transnationalism, c. 1880–1950*, ed. Kevin Grant, Philippa Levine, and Frank Trentmann (Houndmills: Palgrave Macmillan, 2007), 103, at 109.

and upon which even diplomats could be found relying for accurate information.[17] And Near East Relief—a group which (as the 'Near East Foundation') still touts itself as the 'first true international development organization', having 'pioneered international humanitarian assistance' and much of the accompanying culture industry[18]—was the largest and most sophisticated humanitarian outfit of its kind in the region. Funded by the Rockefeller Foundation and enjoying the support of the Wilson administration,[19] its central task, as articulated in its congressional act of incorporation, was 'to provide relief and to assist in the repatriation, rehabilitation, and reestablishment of suffering and dependent people of the Near East and adjacent areas'.[20]

Barton's views were anything but uncommon. During the Balkan Wars, Anglican clergy called for the eradication of 'the immoral system of unmitigated force applied by the Turks in their travesty of government to all the common relationships of life'.[21] The Great War saw missionaries and relief workers make similar appeals, as when a Red Cross official operating in the famine-stricken Levant encouraged American authorities to 'make common cause with the forces of justice against the demons of cruelty'.[22] Even as it remained silent on the Armenian genocide, partly because of its tradition of deference to state authorities, the International Committee of the Red Cross, which would oversee the exchange of prisoners of war between Greece and Turkey after the Lausanne negotiations, eventually felt compelled to add internal conflict to its mandate in the face of turmoil within the Ottoman Empire and elsewhere.[23] For their part, governmental authorities generally refrained from adopting theologically charged language only

[17] G. R. Berridge, *British Diplomacy in Turkey, 1583 to the Present: A Study in the Evolution of the Resident Embassy* (Leiden: Nijhoff, 2009), 135.

[18] Near East Foundation, 'Near East Foundation Celebrates 90th Year; First U.S. International Development Organization; Pioneer of American Philanthropy Abroad' (2005), <http://www.neareast.org/images/uploads/90th_Anniversary.pdf>, 1–2. Such claims would not, of course, go uncontested; see, e.g., Harald Fischer-Tiné, 'Global Civil Society and the Forces of Empire: The Salvation Army, British Imperialism, and the "Prehistory" of NGOs (ca. 1880–1920)', in *Competing Visions of World Order: Global Moments and Movements, 1880s–1930s*, ed. Sebastian Conrad and Dominic Sachsenmaier (New York: Palgrave Macmillan, 2007), 29, at 52.

[19] Wilson would go so far as to proclaim 'Near East Relief Days'. Robert L. Daniel, *American Philanthropy in the Near East, 1820–1960* (Athens: Ohio University Press, 1970), 153, 163–5. The Rockefeller family was particularly active in health-related philanthropy, often working in conjunction with the League; see Daniel Gorman, *The Emergence of International Society in the 1920s* (Cambridge: Cambridge University Press, 2012), 184.

[20] James L. Barton, *Story of Near East Relief (1915–1930): An Interpretation* (New York: Macmillan, 1930), 432.

[21] W. L. Grane, quoted in Albert Marrin, *The Last Crusade: The Church of England in the First World War* (Durham: Duke University Press, 1974), 239.

[22] J. H. Finley, quoted in Tejirian and Simon, *Conflict, Conquest, and Conversion* (n 11), 175.

[23] André Durand, *From Sarajevo to Hiroshima: History of the International Committee of the Red Cross* (Geneva: Henry Dunant Institute, 1984), 197–200; David P. Forsythe, *The Humanitarians: The International Committee of the Red Cross* (Cambridge: Cambridge University Press, 2005), 33, 298. The Red Cross involved itself in the repatriation of prisoners of war in a variety of locales, including Russia; see Francesca Piana, 'L'humanitaire d'après-guerre: prisonniers de guerre et réfugiés russes dans la politique du Comité international de la Croix-Rouge et de la Société des Nations', *Relations internationales* 151 (2012), 63.

for reasons of political expedience, as when the British and French, fearing rebellion in India and Africa, opposed a Russian draft of a diplomatic note in respect to the deportation and massacre of Armenians that would have condemned crimes 'against Christianity and civilization' (the wording was altered to crimes 'against humanity and civilization' and would eventually find its way into positive international law as 'crimes against humanity').[24] Even comparatively progressive policy-makers could be found asking themselves whether 'a revived Turkey [would] conform to the standards of the world in regard to economic development and the welfare of the subject races', given that there seemed to be 'some quality . . . present in the Turkish mind which marks it as lacking the political instinct needed for sovereignty'.[25]

Barton and his various rivals and colleagues, most of whom were themselves relief workers associated with the Red Cross and groups like the newly formed Save the Children Fund, pressed hard to realize their vision of a reformed Near East, assisting with repatriation and resettlement efforts and supplying food, clothing, and medical aid to the region's refugees. From 1915 to 1929, Near East Relief itself was reported to have devoted over US$75 million to relief and related work in a range of locales, from Greece and Bulgaria in the west to Syria and Iraq in the east.[26] As the principal American delegate to the Lausanne negotiations, Richard Child quoted the same figure for humanitarian aid by US nationals before remarking that his country's citizens demanded 'no return for this expenditure unless it be assurance that this conference . . . will find means to wipe away at once the causes for this waste of human life and human suffering'.[27] A Near East Relief official appears to have been the first American national not in the

[24] Sharp, US ambassador to France, to Bryan, US secretary of state, 28 May 1915, reproduced in *Papers Relating to the Foreign Relations of the United States: 1915 Supplement* (Washington: United States Government Printing Office, 1928), 981. The Allies were generally willing to countenance the possibility of 'crimes against humanity' after the First World War, although dissenting US members of the 1919 Commission on the Responsibility of the Authors of the War and on Enforcement of Penalties insisted that 'no fixed and universal standard of humanity' is available: *Violation of the Laws and Customs of War: Reports of Majority and Dissenting Reports of American and Japanese Members of the Commission of Responsibilities, Conference of Paris 1919* (Oxford: Clarendon Press, 1919), 73. See further Egon Schwelb, 'Crimes against Humanity', *BYIL* 23 (1946), 178, at 180–3; M. Cherif Bassiouni, *Crimes against Humanity in International Criminal Law*, 2nd ed. (The Hague: Kluwer, 1999), 62–9; Antonio Cassese, 'Crimes Against Humanity: Comments on Some Problematical Aspects', in Antonio Cassese, *The Human Dimension of International Law: Selected Papers* (Oxford: Oxford University Press, 2008), 457, at 458; Sévane Garibian, 'From the 1915 Allied Joint Declaration to the 1920 Treaty of Sèvres: Back to an International Criminal Law in Progress', *Armenian Review* 52 (2010), 87; and also Michelle Tusan, '"Crimes Against Humanity": Human Rights, the British Empire, and the Origins of the Response to the Armenian Genocide', *American Historical Review* 119 (2014), 47. But for a different appraisal of 'crimes against humanity', one that links it to the criminalization of the slave trade in the nineteenth century, see Jenny S. Martinez, *The Slave Trade and the Origins of International Human Rights Law* (New York: Oxford University Press, 2012), 115–16 ff.

[25] Noel Buxton and T. P. Conwil-Evans, *Oppressed Peoples and the League of Nations* (London: J. M. Dent & Sons, 1922), 135, 165.

[26] Barton, *Story* (n 20), 439.

[27] Minutes of the Territorial and Military Commission's (TMC's) meeting on 12 December 1922, in *Lausanne Conference on Near Eastern Affairs (1922–1923): Records of Proceedings and Draft Terms of Peace* (Cmd 1814) (London: His Majesty's Stationery Office, 1923), 185.

direct employment of the US government to receive accreditation from Mustafa Kemal's Ankara-based parliament.[28] An agreement between the organization and the nationalist government was concluded shortly thereafter,[29] and much of the formal exchange would unfold under its watch, with its personnel and associates assuming responsibility for a good portion of the nuts-and-bolts work of resettlement and aid provision. In fact, as Barton pointed out proudly, '[t]he first transfer of Moslem and Greek populations under the terms of the Treaty of Lausanne was made under the authority and supervision of the Near East Relief',[30] with both states supporting its involvement even before the mixed commission had been constituted.[31]

Such efforts reinforced the loans and logistical assistance that the League of Nations and a number of Western governments made available to Greece. Receiving the lion's share of refugees and therefore having to allocate significantly more resources to resettlement programmes than Turkey, Greece drew heavily upon international funds to undertake relief operations and organize the transfer in tandem with a broad-based project of land reform, partly by way of the League-sponsored Greek Refugee Settlement Commission.[32] But unquestionably the most effective force behind the population exchange's design and implementation was Nansen, who, as League of Nations High Commissioner for Refugees, shaped general policy in respect to the movements and provided logistical support throughout the process. This was part of a broader programme of employing the League—despite complaints that it had 'little real power', and then mostly of 'an advisory or ministerial character',[33] a veritable 'system of world-services' in the eyes of many advocates[34]—as a vehicle for forging a new legal regime for displaced persons. Although the term 'refugee' was already in circulation,[35] it

[28] Barton, *Story* (n 20), 142; and also Dzovinar Kévonian, *Réfugiés et diplomatie humanitaire: Les acteurs européens et la scène proche-orientale pendant l'entre-deux-guerres* (Paris: Publications de la Sorbonne, 2004), 292.

[29] For the text see Barton, *Story* (n 20), 149–50.

[30] Barton, *Story* (n 20), 165.

[31] Barton, *Story* (n 20), 166–7; Daniel, *American Philanthropy* (n 19), 167; Near East Relief, *Report to Congress for 1923* (New York: Near East Relief, 1924), 20–1.

[32] Louis P. Cassimatis, *American Influence in Greece 1917–1929* (Kent: Kent State University Press, 1988), chs. 8–11; Mark Mazower, *Greece and the Inter-war Economic Crisis* (Oxford: Clarendon Press, 1991), 74–9; Elisabeth Kontogiorgi, *Population Exchange in Greek Macedonia: The Rural Settlement of Refugees 1922–1930* (Oxford: Clarendon Press, 2006); Mihri Belli, *Türkiye–Yunanistan Nüfus Mübadelesi: Ekonomik Açıdan Bir Bakış*, trans. Müfide Pekin (İstanbul: Belge, 2006), pt. 3, also 94–5; Patricia Clavin, *Securing the World Economy: The Reinvention of the League of Nations, 1920–1946* (Oxford: Oxford University Press, 2013), 31–2. For corresponding details on resettlement programmes in Turkey, where neither the League nor foreign governments enjoyed as much influence, see Kemal Arı, *Büyük Mübadele: Türkiye'ye Zorunlu Göç (1923–1925)* (İstanbul: Tarih Vakfı Yurt Yayınları, 1995). For the instrument establishing the commission see Declaration relating to the Settlement of Refugees in Greece and the Creation for this Purpose of a Refugees Settlement Commission, signed on behalf of Great Britain, France, and Italy at Geneva, 29 September 1923, 20 LNTS 41.

[33] Edwin DeWitt Dickinson, *The Equality of States in International Law* (Cambridge: Harvard University Press, 1920), 371, 374.

[34] Alfred Zimmern, *The League of Nations and the Rule of Law, 1918–1935* (London: Macmillan, 1936), 310.

[35] Peter Gatrell, *The Making of the Modern Refugee* (Oxford: Oxford University Press, 2013), 64.

was largely through the Office of the High Commissioner and its successor, the Nansen International Office for Refugees, that displaced persons came to enjoy widespread recognition as 'refugees'.[36] It was also on account of this office that protection was made available to such persons, mainly through the popularization of the 'Nansen passport'[37] and the entry into force of the 1933 Refugee Convention, both of which were important for Russian, Greek, Armenian, Assyrian, and other refugees.[38] The Great War had inaugurated a period of increased surveillance of citizens and non-citizens alike, with immigration being restricted, passport controls being introduced or augmented, domestic systems of documentary identification gaining wider currency, and non-nationals coming to be subjected to intensive reporting regimes.[39] After 1919, though, the coordinated resettlement of whole peoples emerged as a full-fledged 'problem', with League officials in Geneva manoeuvring to position themselves at the head of the new movement.

In 1922, roughly a year after being provided with his official commission, Nansen established an 'advisory committee of voluntary organizations' to provide assistance to refugees, originally counting as members a total of 16 organizations, including Near East Relief, the International Committee of the Red Cross, and the YMCA World's Committee.[40] In addition to being the principal intermediary between Athens and Ankara in the weeks preceding Lausanne, and the first to propose an exchange of minorities at the conference itself, Nansen was a touchstone for nearly all matters relating to its macro-level planning and execution after the conclusion of the Exchange Convention. Especially useful was his ability to win the support of each of the state parties without sacrificing his own reputation for moral rectitude. Turkish nationalists might simply have branded him *persona non grata* due to his closeness to the great powers. This would have sat well with the Turkish delegation's refusal to accord anything more than a private character

[36] Nevzat Soguk, *States and Strangers: Refugees and Displacements of Statecraft* (Minneapolis: University of Minnesota Press, 1999), ch. 3.

[37] On the extension of the passport see Claudena M. Skran, *Refugees in Inter-war Europe: The Emergence of a Regime* (Oxford: Clarendon Press, 1995), 104–9, 113–22; and also John Torpey, *The Invention of the Passport: Surveillance, Citizenship and the State* (Cambridge: Cambridge University Press, 2000), 127–9.

[38] Convention relating to the International Status of Refugees, signed at Geneva, 28 October 1933, 159 LNTS 199. For discussion see Louise W. Holborn, 'The Legal Status of Political Refugees, 1920–1938', *AJIL* 32 (1938), 680, at 689–90; John Hope Simpson, *The Refugee Problem: Report of a Survey* (London: Oxford University Press, 1939), ch. 11; Elemér Balogh, 'World Peace and the Refugee Problem', *RCADI* 75 (1949-II), 363, at 392–412. For more recent analysis see Skran, *Refugees in Inter-war Europe* (n 37), 124–30; James C. Hathaway, *The Rights of Refugees under International Law* (Cambridge: Cambridge University Press, 2005), 87–91. Note that the 1933 Refugee Convention would be supplemented five years later by an additional treaty; see Convention concerning the Status of Refugees Coming from Germany, with Annex, signed at Geneva, 10 February 1938, 192 LNTS 59.

[39] Torpey, *Invention of the Passport* (n 37), 111–17; Michael R. Marrus, *The Unwanted: European Refugees from the First World War through the Cold War* (Philadelphia: Temple University Press, 1985), 92–3; Skran, *Refugees in Inter-war Europe* (n 37), 21–9.

[40] By 1936 its membership had expanded to no less than 40 such organizations. For details see Kévonian, *Réfugiés et diplomatie humanitaire* (n 28), 343–53; Skran, *Refugees in Inter-war Europe* (n 37), 78–83.

to the statements that Nansen made on behalf of an exchange at Lausanne.[41] And it would also have been in keeping with the manner in which Turkish authorities tended to engage with League officials during the 1920s.[42] Nansen would, after all, play a pivotal role in the Armenian relief and resettlement effort,[43] and even Turkish nationalists (like Kemal) who had initially been willing to condemn as criminals those responsible for ordering and implementing the genocide had proven reluctant to press ahead with their prosecution by Turkish or foreign authorities once the Allies threw their weight behind the Greek occupation of western Anatolia.[44] Still, the Kemalists cooperated with Nansen when negotiating and carrying out the exchange, drawing on his professional know-how for a variety of purposes.

In line with a characteristically semi-peripheral strategy, late Ottoman policy-makers had generally regarded missionary activity as a threat to the empire's integrity, even where the missionaries with whom they dealt made a point of adopting conciliatory postures so as to stand a better chance of operating unimpeded.[45] In some cases, the Ottomans had established their own relief organizations in response: the Ottoman Red Crescent, the first body of its kind in the extra-European world, had, for instance, been bolstered significantly during the Balkan Wars and First World War, and would assume responsibility for providing assistance to large numbers of refugees during the empire's final decade.[46] The Kemalists were similarly suspicious of missionary groups, particularly of the influence they wielded over matters of education.[47] The Lausanne

[41] See TMC minutes (1 December 1922), in *Lausanne Conference* (n 27), 117.

[42] For a powerful illustration see Keith David Watenpaugh, 'The League of Nations' Rescue of Armenian Genocide Survivors and the Making of Modern Humanitarianism, 1920–1927', *American Historical Review* 115 (2010), 1315, at 1333–6.

[43] Nansen's most ambitious project involved the resettlement of Armenians in (then Soviet) Yerevan, a scheme that ultimately fell through for want of funds; see 'Report by Dr. Fridtjof Nansen of an Enquiry by a Committee of Experts Made in Armenia under the Auspices of the International Labour Office (July 1925)', in *Scheme for the Settlement of Armenian Refugees: General Survey and Principal Documents*, LN Doc. C.699.M.264.1926.IV (Geneva: League of Nations, 1927), 65. His thoughts on the Armenians are recorded in Fridtjof Nansen, *Armenia and the Near East* (London: George Allen & Unwin, 1928).

[44] Vahakn N. Dadrian, 'Genocide as a Problem of National and International Law: The World War I Armenian Case and Its Contemporary Legal Ramifications', *Yale Journal of International Law* 14 (1989), 221, at 278, 291–317; Taner Akçam, *A Shameful Act: The Armenian Genocide and the Question of Turkish Responsibility*, trans. Paul Bessemer (New York: Metropolitan Books, 2006), 217, 294–302, 371; Vahakn N. Dadrian and Taner Akçam, *Judgment at Istanbul: The Armenian Genocide Trials* (New York: Berghahn, 2011).

[45] The ideological implications are analysed well in Selim Deringil, *The Well-Protected Domains: Ideology and the Legitimation of Power in the Ottoman Empire 1876–1909* (London: Tauris, 1998), ch. 5.

[46] Cf. Nadir Özbek, *Osmanlı İmparatorluğu'nda Sosyal Devlet: Siyaset, İktidar ve Meşruiyet 1876–1914* (İstanbul: İletişim Yayınları, 2002), 323 (suggesting that the Red Crescent was 'the association that made the most important contribution to the "nationalization" and "militarization" of the [Ottoman] public sphere' during this period).

[47] According to a 1929 study, all American schools in Turkey but one had been established by mission boards. Frank A. Ross, C. Luther Fry, and Elbridge Sibley, *The Near East and American Philanthropy: A Survey Conducted under the Guidance of the General Committee of the Near East Survey* (New York: Columbia University Press, 1929), 156. For their original mandate and conditions of operation see Uygur Kocabaşoğlu, *Anadolu'daki Amerika: Kendi Belgeleriyle 19. Yüzyılda Osmanlı İmparatorluğu'ndaki Amerikan Misyoner Okulları* (İstanbul: İmge Kitabevi Yayınları, 2000).

settlement did not introduce any significant legal constraints on foreign-funded schools in Turkey, providing instead for a nominal right to public education in native languages for members of non-Muslim minorities.[48] But the government in Ankara would soon promulgate a series of new laws designed to maximize the state's supervisory powers over education, bringing schools run by or for foreigners under the authority of a newly established ministry of education, doing away with the use of religious symbols, and introducing restrictions on religious instruction.[49]

When the Permanent Court of International Justice sat down to prepare its opinion on the proper interpretation of the Exchange Convention, it was operating against the background of a widely felt desire to constrain or reorient ethno-nationalist claims with a view to resolving outstanding conflicts in the Near East within an international framework. Part and parcel of an internationalist drive to which the League of Nations and a host of affiliated humanitarian organizations had pledged themselves, the World Court pressed hard to ensure that the exchange procedure was managed in accordance with a strict interpretation of the two states' international treaty obligations. This would bring the exchange fully within the fold of international law and ensure that ethno-nationalism was regulated through a League-sponsored programme of demographic engineering.

II. 'National Sovereignty is not Affected by the Convention in Question'

The Permanent Court's advisory opinion in *Exchange of Greek and Turkish Populations* is analysed only infrequently. And when analysis is offered, it tends to be oblique and rather elliptical. Thus, a typical interwar survey of the Permanent Court's jurisprudence notes that the opinion's significance lay primarily in the fact that it testified to the flexibility of the advisory procedure, and secondarily in the fact that one of the parties to the dispute—Turkey—was not a member of the League,[50] a situation that had earlier threatened to undermine the Court's

[48] Treaty of Peace, signed at Lausanne, 24 July 1923, 28 LNTS 11, Art 41, at 33–5.

[49] See Ayten Sezer, *Atatürk Döneminde Yabancı Okullar (1923–1938)* (Ankara: Türk Tarih Kurumu Basımevi, 1999), 15–35. This was broadly in line with recommendations made by John Dewey in his capacity as educational adviser to the early republican establishment; see, e.g., John Dewey, 'Foreign Schools in Turkey', *The New Republic* 41 (1924), 40, at 41 (arguing that remaining American schools needed to adopt 'secular social and scientific methods', and that 'the success or failure of this experiment, in view of the consequences both in the Near East and in the Moslem world, is of immense import to the future peace of the world').

[50] Alexander P. Fachiri, *The Permanent Court of International Justice: Its Constitution, Procedure and Work*, 2nd ed. (London: Oxford University Press, 1932), 209. Other examples include J. W. Wheeler-Bennett and Maurice Fanshawe, *Information on the World Court, 1918–1928* (London: George Allen & Unwin, 1929), 124–6; Manley O. Hudson, *The World Court, 1921–1938: A Handbook of the Permanent Court of International Justice*, 5th ed. (Boston: World Peace Foundation, 1938), 186–9. Much the same can be said about the Court's closely related opinion in *Interpretation of the Greco–Turkish Agreement of December 1st, 1926*. After offering little of

legitimacy.[51] What has attracted exceedingly little attention, though, is the way in which the Court's opinion jostled with many of the same questions of internationalism that undergirded the humanitarian effort to 'regenerate' the Near East in the 1910s and 1920s. The Court distinguished sharply between domestic and international law in rejecting a Turkish claim to the effect that the status of Istanbul's Greeks ought to be determined in light of Turkish law. This led it to relate national sovereignty to international order in a manner that mirrored the commitment of many humanitarian organizations to stabilize Anatolia and the Balkans by facilitating the consolidation of new states through international law. For the Court, as for these humanitarians, nationalism was something to be reined in and regulated in accordance with international law and organization. Sound interpretation and implementation of the exchange agreement—the legal form of a regionally and juridically distinct method of conflict resolution—was vital to the achievement of this end.

At root, the case turned on the interpretation of Article 2 of the Exchange Convention, which, as already mentioned, provided exceptions to the exchange between 'Turkish nationals of the Greek Orthodox religion' and 'Greek nationals of the Moslem religion' for Muslims 'established' in western Thrace and Greeks 'established' in Istanbul.[52] Of course, both of these general categories, as well as their exceptions, were quite nebulous: as with the 'voluntary' Greek–Bulgarian exchange, ethnic and even religious identity was notoriously fluid, and the parameters of the special zones the convention generated were not always precise, resulting in the kind of question with which the Permanent Court was forced to grapple in *Exchange of Greek and Turkish Populations*.[53] Article 2 stipulated that '[a]ll Greeks who were already established before the October 30, 1918, within the areas under the Prefecture of the City of Constantinople, as defined by the law of

substance about *Exchange of Greek and Turkish Populations*, J. H. W. Verzijl, for instance, claims flatly that, in the accompanying *Interpretation of the Greco–Turkish Agreement* opinion, '[t]he legal situation under the relevant instruments was . . . so clear and the reasoning of the Opinion so convincing that it cannot create a surprise that the Court was unanimous'. For the opinion itself see *Interpretation of the Greco–Turkish Agreement of December 1st, 1926 (Final Protocol, Article IV)*, Advisory Opinion, PCIJ Rep. Series B No 16 (1928). For the commentary see J. H. W. Verzijl, *The Jurisprudence of the World Court: A Case by Case Commentary*, vol. 1 (Leiden: Sijthoff, 1965), 144, and more generally 66–9, 140–4.

[51] The Soviet Union had declined to participate in advisory proceedings regarding the legal status of eastern Karelia in 1923, when it was neither a member of the League nor a party to the Statute of the PCIJ. See *Status of Eastern Carelia*, Advisory Opinion, PCIJ Rep. Series B No 5 (1923).

[52] Convention concerning the Exchange of Greek and Turkish Populations, and Protocol, signed at Lausanne, 30 January 1923, 32 LNTS 75 ('Exchange Convention'), at 77.

[53] These were common problems at the time. Like so many others, Isaiah Bowman, geographer and territorial adviser to the American delegation at the Paris Peace Conference, complained of the proliferation of 'statistical and cartographical tricks' after the First World War. Isaiah Bowman, 'Constantinople and the Balkans', in *What Really Happened at Paris: The Story of the Peace Conference, 1918–1919*, ed. Edward Mandell House and Charles Seymour (New York: Charles Scribner's Sons, 1921), 140, at 142. For more on Bowman see Neil Smith, *American Empire: Roosevelt's Geographer and the Prelude to Globalization* (Berkeley: University of California Press, 2003).

1912, shall be considered as Greek inhabitants of Constantinople'.[54] But among those 'Turkish nationals of the Greek Orthodox religion' who might have fallen under this category were a considerable number whom Turkish authorities would later deem ineligible to benefit from the exemption.

While their delegates at Lausanne had conceded that Greeks properly 'established' in Istanbul would be exempted from the exchange,[55] Turkish political elites were determined to keep the relevant numbers to a minimum so as to further their project of constructing an ethno-nationally homogeneous state.[56] For Turkish authorities, Article 2 of the Exchange Convention was best read with an eye to two Turkish laws. These two pieces of legislation, promulgated in 1902 and 1914 respectively, set out the conditions for individuals to be domiciled in Turkey. If the category of the *établis*, as it appeared in the convention, were defined by reference to these Turkish laws, Article 2 would be applicable to a much smaller class of individuals than would otherwise be the case. According to Turkish officials, any other interpretation of Article 2 would violate Turkey's sovereignty and independence. Indeed, argued Tevfik Rüştü, a former Young Turk with close ties to Moscow who served as the Turkish government's representative before the Permanent Court, suspending the application of domestic law for one segment of Turkey's citizenry would extend to it a special privilege and thereby destabilize relations between the country's majority and minorities.[57] Regulated exceptions aside, he stressed, 'any decision or act involving non-compliance by the citizens of a country with the laws of that country leads to administrative anarchy, and can harm the internal peace of the concerned nation'.[58] A point of sensitivity for Rüştü was the fact that Turkish delegates at Lausanne had acquiesced in the adoption of the term 'établis' over the term 'domiciliés' only after having received assurances that its meaning would be determined by tribunals in the event of dispute.[59]

Greek authorities supported the opposing interpretation of Article 2, arguing that it needed to be taken on its own terms rather than by reference, express or implied, to an external source of legal obligation, such as the Turkish legislation respecting domicile. As framed by Nicolas Politis, Greece's usual agent before the Permanent Court, the Greek position in respect to Article 2 amounted to the

[54] Exchange Convention (n 52), 77. 30 October 1918 was the date on which Allied and Ottoman forces agreed to cease hostilities; for the text see Armistice Convention between Great Britain and the Allied Powers, and Turkey, signed at Mudros, 30 October 1918, 224 CTS 169.

[55] For a précis of the debate see TMC minutes (10 January 1923), in *Lausanne Conference* (n 27), 313.

[56] Their Greek counterparts often shared similar concerns, particularly concerning the question whether Muslim Albanians in Greece ought to be exempted from the exchange; see Konstantinos Tsitselikis, *Old and New Islam in Greece: From Historical Minorities to Immigrant Newcomers* (Leiden: Nijhoff, 2012), 74–9.

[57] 'Mémoire du Gouvernement turc', in *Exchange of Greek and Turkish Populations*, PCIJ Rep. Series C No 7-I (1925), 222, at 223.

[58] 'Mémoire du Gouvernement turc' (n 57), 223.

[59] On this see 'Mémoire du Gouvernement turc' (n 57), 223, 225–6. For contemporaneous examination of the extent to which *travaux préparatoires* and related diplomatic correspondence can be considered for purposes of treaty interpretation, see Quincy Wright, 'The Interpretation of Multilateral Treaties', *AJIL* 23 (1929), 94.

claim that 'the word "établis"' meant simply 'inhabitants of Constantinople who had begun living there before 30 October 1918 with the intention of residing there habitually'.[60] In addition to being anxious about the possibility of an additional influx of displaced persons, Greece was concerned about the status of the Istanbul-based Ecumenical Patriarchate, nominally the spiritual and institutional head of Eastern Orthodoxy. Turkish authorities were suspicious of the patriarchate, particularly of the *imperium in imperio* it had enjoyed under Ottoman rule,[61] and often insisted that the question of its legal status was internal to Turkish law, so that Greece had no basis upon which to 'intervene in the constitution and administration' of a 'Turkish domestic institution'.[62] The Greeks generally countered such arguments by pointing to the fact that İsmet Paşa had sought to have the patriarchate removed from Istanbul at Lausanne, that this proposal had been rejected after proving highly controversial, and that it was only on the basis of a shared understanding that the patriarchate was to be excluded from the exchange that the convention had been concluded.[63] Politis was alive to the 'multiple humanitarian, economic and political interests' that were involved,[64] and argued the point energetically before the Court, emphasizing that, for Greece, 'the case of the Patriarchate is . . . a question not of internal order, but an international question'.[65] Not only had the matter been discussed and resolved during the Lausanne negotiations, but the patriarchate's status had been formalized through successive Ottoman grants, a community of *établis* Greeks without religious representation would be impractical, and there was, at any rate, no textual basis upon

[60] 'Discours prononcé par S. Exc. M. Politis (représentant le Gouvernement hellénique) à la séance publique du 16 janvier 1925', in *Exchange of Greek and Turkish Populations*, PCIJ Rep. Series C No 7-I (1925), 19, at 33.

[61] For a particularly vociferous example see A. Rustem Bey, 'The Future of the Oecumenical Patriarchate', *Foreign Affairs* 3 (1925), 604, at 605 ff. Such suspicions were widely shared at the time; see, e.g., John Riddell, ed., *Toward the United Front: Proceedings of the Fourth Congress of the Communist International, 1922* (Chicago: Haymarket, 2011), 660 (a Dutch delegate to the Comintern condemning the patriarchate's 'horrendous and bestial role' in the Greek–Turkish War and calling for solidarity with Kemal's forces). Feeding such animosity was the patriarchate's support for a 'greater Greece' and its tendency to appeal to Western powers for assistance; see, e.g., 'Note to the Great Powers', in Greek Patriarchate, *Persecution of the Greeks in Turkey, 1914–1918* (Constantinople, London: The Hesperia Press, 1919), 147.

[62] 'Expulsion of the Œcumenical Patriarch from Constantinople—Letter from the Turkish Government to the Secretary-General of the League', LN Doc. C.160.1925.VII, *LNOJ* 6 (1925), 579, at 580.

[63] See, e.g., 'Question of the Expulsion of the Œcumenical Patriarch—Letter and Memorandum from the Greek Government to the Secretary-General of the League', LN Doc. C.211.M.70.1925. VII, *LNOJ* 6 (1925), 637, at 638. Lord Curzon had been of the view that if the patriarchate's 'spiritual and ecclesiastical prerogatives were to be destroyed and the seat of the Patriarchate removed from Constantinople, a shock would be delivered to the conscience of the whole civilised world'. A representative of the Serb-Croat-Slovene state had been even more effusive, claiming that '[i]ts disappearance would create so great a moral void that a part of civilisation would seem to disappear with it'. TMC minutes (10 January 1923), in *Lausanne Conference* (n 27), 319, 321.

[64] 'Discours prononcé par S. Exc. M. Politis' (n 60), 19.

[65] 'Réplique de S. Exc. M. Politis (représentant le Gouvernement hellénique) à la séance publique du 16 janvier 1925', in *Exchange of Greek and Turkish Populations*, PCIJ Rep. Series C No 7-I (1925), 49, at 50.

which to exclude the patriarchate or its organs from the Article 2 exception.[66] Interestingly, Politis displayed much the same commitment to constraining state power when arguing that wholly arbitrary expulsion of non-nationals ran counter to norms of international law in his course at the Hague Academy of International Law that same year.[67]

As is so often the case, the dispute unfolded in a number of fora prior to being considered by the Permanent Court. The dispute was initiated after the Exchange Convention entered into force and the mixed commission commenced its liquidation and compensation work. Unable to agree on the proper interpretation of Article 2, the Greek and Turkish delegates to the commission prepared independent memoranda on the question. The dispute was not resolved when the commission convened in September 1924, and after several additional meetings, the Greeks exercised their right under Articles 11 and 14 of the League Covenant[68] to refer the matter of the *établis* to the League Council in October, Turkish authorities having seized some 4,500 Greeks for purposes of deportation in the meantime.[69] In December the Council requested that the Court offer its opinion on how the matter should be settled, presenting it with the question of the meaning and scope of the term 'established' in the Exchange Convention, as well as the closely related question of which conditions a given individual would need to satisfy in order to qualify as so 'established' in Istanbul.[70]

In response to the first of these two questions, the Court began by stating that the issue of the patriarchate's status was irrelevant, as the League Council had not requested an opinion on it,[71] and then noted that the term 'established' was not to be understood *in abstracto* but within the context of its usage in Article 2. As such, the dispute at hand was one that turned on the most appropriate interpretation of

[66] 'Discours prononcé par S. Exc. M. Politis' (n 60), 31–3.

[67] Nicolas Politis, 'Le problème des limitations de la souveraineté et la théorie de l'abus des droits dans les rapports internationaux', *RCADI* 6 (1925-I), 1, at 101–8.

[68] Covenant of the League of Nations Adopted by the Peace Conference at Plenary Session, 28 April 1919, *AJIL Sup.* 13 (1919), 128, at 132–3.

[69] *Exchange* (n 4), 12–13. For details see Stephen P. Ladas, *The Exchange of Minorities: Bulgaria, Greece and Turkey* (New York: Macmillan, 1932), 404–5; Onur Yıldırım, *Diplomacy and Displacement: Reconsidering the Turco–Greek Exchange of Populations, 1922–1934* (New York: Routledge, 2006), 114; Harry J. Psomiades, *The Eastern Question: The Last Phase—A Study in Greek–Turkish Diplomacy*, 2nd ed. (New York: Pella, 2000), 68. It should be noted that Turkey often applied pressure to the Greeks of Istanbul in retaliation for Greece's restriction of the rights of western Thrace's Turks; see Dimitris Kamouzis, 'Reciprocity or International Intervention? Greek and Turkish Minority Policy, 1923–1930', in *Reciprocity: Greek and Turkish Minorities—Law, Religion and Politics*, ed. Samim Akgönül (İstanbul: İstanbul Bilgi University Press, 2008), 49, at 59–65.

[70] 'Requète pour avis consultatif', in *Exchange of Greek and Turkish Populations*, PCIJ Rep. Series C No 7-I (1925), 54.

[71] *Exchange* (n 4), 17. The Council would request an opinion concerning its competence in regard to the issue of the patriarchate in March 1925, but this request would be withdrawn after Greece and Turkey settled their dispute about the issue. For details regarding the request see *Expulsion of the Œcumenical Patriarch*, PCIJ Rep. Series C No 9-II (1925). For the terms of the settlement see Alexis P. Alexandris, 'The Expulsion of Constantine VI: The Ecumenical Patriarchate and Greek–Turkish Relations, 1924–1925', *Balkan Studies* 22 (1981), 333; Elçin Macar, *Cumhuriyet Döneminde İstanbul Rum Patrikhanesi* (İstanbul: İletişim Yayınları, 2003), 133–6.

a treaty, involving a proper question of international law rather than 'a question of domestic concern between the administration and the inhabitants' of a particular territory.[72] Since the French version of the convention's text was authoritative, consideration had to be given to the fact that the French *établissement* denoted both residence and stability—that is, 'an intention to continue the residence in a particular place for an extended period'.[73] The Court admitted that this might be understood to beg the question as to whether the conception of 'establishment' that underlay Article 2 was identical to the doctrine of domicile, but it ultimately held that the convention could not be said to warrant such an interpretation, as its text simply did not evidence any explicit or implicit reference to national legislation.[74] Further, reading Article 2 on the basis of national legislation would lead 'to the division of the population being carried out in a different manner in Turkey and in Greece', which would not be 'in accordance with the spirit of the Convention, the intention of which is undoubtedly to ensure, by means of the application of identical and reciprocal measures in the territory of the two States, that the same treatment is accorded to the Greek and Turkish populations'.[75] Among the various subsidiary points made by the Court was one stemming from a rather bold claim that only Turkish courts were competent to determine who was and was not 'established' in Istanbul under Article 2. In response to this claim, the Court pointed out that Article 12 granted 'full power' over the execution of the Exchange Convention and the resolution of questions arising from it to the mixed commission.[76] For the Court, this could only mean that the commission—an international organization—was endowed with the authority to decide whether the conditions set out in Article 2 for being 'established' in Istanbul had been met in a particular instance.[77] Thus, the Court concluded, the 'Greek inhabitants of Constantinople' to which Article 2 referred meant all those who resided within the city's boundaries, as defined by the relevant 1912 law, had arrived there at some time prior to the critical date of 30 October 1918, and had demonstrated an intention to reside there for an extended period.[78] This was its

[72] *Exchange* (n 4), 17. [73] *Exchange* (n 4), 18. [74] *Exchange* (n 4), 19 ff.

[75] *Exchange* (n 4), 20, also 22. [76] Exchange Convention (n 52), 83.

[77] *Exchange* (n 4), 22. Illuminating comparisons may be drawn with other disputes. In 1928, for instance, the Franco–Turkish Mixed Arbitral Tribunal considered an interesting question: a former Turkish national had acquired French citizenship, and Turkey contested the tribunal's jurisdiction over his claim by pointing to the 1869 Ottoman Law on Nationality, which declared null and void any attempt on the part of an Ottoman subject to seek naturalization in another state absent approval from Ottoman authorities. Rejecting this argument, the tribunal held that while Turkey was entitled to demand prior authorization for changes of nationality, a failure to comply with this requirement would not bind other states. For the case see *Apostolidis c Gouvernement turc, Recueil des décisions des tribunaux arbitraux mixtes* 8 (1929), 373. For the law see 'Loi de nationalité, 19 janvier 1869', reproduced in *Corps de droit ottoman: Recueil des codes, lois, règlements, ordonnances et actes les plus importants du droit intérieur, et d'études sur le droit coutumier de l'Empire ottoman*, ed. George Young, vol. 2 (Oxford: Clarendon Press, 1905), 226, esp. Art 5, at 227. Note that Turkey had long been given to withholding permission for expatriation; see Edwin M. Borchard, 'Basic Elements of Diplomatic Protection of Citizens Abroad', *AJIL* 7 (1913), 497, at 509.

[78] *Exchange* (n 4), 26.

'natural meaning'.[79] Anything more would make for an unjustified and cumbersome reading of the convention.

The Court adopted a similarly curt stance in respect to the second question, once again drawing a hard distinction between those who were and were not to be subjected to the compulsory exchange. For an individual to belong to the latter class, her residence in Istanbul must, first, have preceded 30 October 1918, and, second, have been 'of a lasting nature'.[80] As a result, 'mere visitors' to the city, for instance, were strictly excluded from the category of the *établis*.[81] The Court naturally admitted that the 'degree of stability' needed for this standard residence requirement was 'incapable of exact definition',[82] but it stressed that this 'character of stability' comprised 'the condition necessary to constitute "establishment"' under Article 2.[83] It also underscored the fact that it was in no position to assess, let alone resolve, the 'complex problems' that arose from attempts to apply this standard of residence in certain circumstances, such as those in which one member of a family was found to have satisfied it whereas another was not.[84] The Court did not possess enough expertise or information to complete a task that only the mixed commission was authorized to finalize. Finally, it stressed, an essential objective of Article 2 was to provide exceptions to an otherwise comprehensive population exchange, and limiting the ambit of the exception for Istanbul's *établis* to the degree envisioned by the Turkish proposal would frustrate its basic purpose and render it ineffective.[85]

Interestingly, the Court was not entirely unwilling to speculate on the motivations behind Turkey's claims. Hesitant though it was to engage directly with Turkey's nationalistic aspirations, the 'reasons' for which were not of specifically legal concern,[86] the Court observed that Turkey's insistence on tethering Article 2 to domestic law was inspired by the need it felt to buttress its sovereignty and

[79] *Exchange* (n 4), 20. 'Natural meaning' and its various cognates (e.g. 'plain meaning', 'clear meaning') was an integral, if highly amorphous, element in the Court's analytical lexicon. For a technical breakdown see J. P. Fockema Andreæ, *An Important Chapter from the History of Legal Interpretation: The Jurisdiction of the First Permanent Court of International Justice (1922–1940)* (Leiden: Sijthoff, 1948), esp. chs. 3–4.

[80] *Exchange* (n 4), 23, also 26.

[81] *Exchange* (n 4), 23.

[82] *Exchange* (n 4), 23.

[83] *Exchange* (n 4), 24.

[84] *Exchange* (n 4), 24. Such situations were anything but uncommon, presenting themselves before the mixed commission for years to come. For a typical case see no 37201, box 198, folder 1, Collection of the Mixed Commission for the Exchange of Greek and Turkish Populations, League of Nations Archives, United Nations Library, Geneva.

[85] *Exchange* (n 4), 25. Hersch Lauterpacht tended to see such arguments from effectiveness as a key to treaty interpretation, albeit a problematic and often misunderstood one: 'The Pact of Paris and the Budapest Articles of Interpretation', *TGS* 20 (1934), 178, at 187; 'Restrictive Interpretation and the Principle of Effectiveness in the Interpretation of Treaties', *BYIL* 26 (1949), 48; and also *The Development of International Law by the International Court*, 2nd ed. (London: Stevens & Sons, 1958), pt. 4.

[86] See *Exchange* (n 4), 18 ('As, however, Turkey, *for reasons which do not concern the Court*, did not wish to be compelled to retain at Constantinople Greeks who had migrated there after the date of the armistice of Mudros, the Convention refers not to the whole of the Greek population of Constantinople as it exists at present, but only to those members of it who were such also on October 30th, 1918' (emphasis added)).

independence.[87] This, it stated, was misguided. Since Turkey had entered into the Exchange Convention freely and with full knowledge of its consequences, it was now obliged to discharge the duties it had incurred. Although Turkish officials had maintained 'the theory of an implicit reference to local legislation' on the ground that 'a contrary solution would involve consequences affecting Turkey's sovereign rights', this was unpersuasive, as the two states' obligations were 'absolutely equal and reciprocal' and it was 'impossible to admit that a convention which creates obligations of this kind, construed according to its "natural meaning", infringes the sovereign rights of the High Contracting Parties'.[88] Indeed, in the words of Huber, who would eventually complement his legal career by chairing the Nansen International Office's administrative council and serving as president of the International Committee of the Red Cross, it was clear that 'national sovereignty is not affected by the Convention in question'.[89] As an international act, the convention was an expression, and not an infringement, of sovereignty.[90]

Considered in its entirety, the Court's handling of the two questions with which it was presented is remarkable for its attempt to check what it regarded as unfounded Turkish assertions of national sovereignty in order to preserve the international legal regime established to coordinate the population exchange. Every Turkish attempt to restrict the number of persons to whom the *établi* exemption would apply—a typically semi-peripheral reaction to actual or perceived intervention—was countered by the Court's commitment to a strict interpretation of Article 2—a characteristically internationalist move to rein in chauvinism and further the consolidation of states with firm international boundaries and settled constitutional arrangements. The substantive outcome, presented as derived from faithful adherence to the Exchange Convention's letter and spirit, facilitated the segregation of those who were to be subjected to the procedure from those who were to be permitted to remain in Istanbul. The Court delineated the boundary between international and domestic law as crisply as possible. On the one hand, it reasoned, there were questions falling within the competence of the mixed commission as an international institution constituted pursuant to an international treaty. On the other hand, there was domestic Turkish law and the Turkish courts authorized to adjudicate disputes in accordance with it. Although it did not rule

[87] Rüştü had been quite vocal in this regard; see, e.g., 'Discours prononcé par Tevfik Rouchdy Bey (représentant le Gouvernement turc) à la séance publique du 16 janvier 1925', in *Exchange of Greek and Turkish Populations*, PCIJ Rep. Series C No 7-I (1925), 35, at 45 (stressing the importance of 'national sovereignty' and 'the independence of our courts and applicable laws, which are not contrary to the convention').

[88] *Exchange* (n 4), 21.

[89] *Exchange* (n 4), 22. On Huber's influence over the drafting committee in this case see Ole Spiermann, 'Judge Max Huber at the Permanent Court of International Justice', *EJIL* 18 (2007), 115, at 128–9.

[90] Tellingly, the Court recalled (at *Exchange* (n 4), 21) its statement that 'the right of entering into international engagements is an attribute of State sovereignty' in *Case of the S. S. 'Wimbledon' (Britain et al. v Germany)* PCIJ Rep. Series A No 1 (1923), 25. For contemporaneous discussion of the jurisprudential context see Ludwik Ehrlich, 'L'interprétation des traités', *RCADI* 24 (1928-IV), 1, at 133–5.

out the possibility of engaging with municipal law in other cases,[91] the Court held that the term 'established' needed to be understood on its own terms rather than by reference to domestic legislation, placing the matter squarely within the realm of international public law and elevating what might otherwise have been a dispute about public administration within a particular state to the status of a true question of international law.

III. Interpretation as Internationalism

It is significant that the Permanent Court's marginalization of Turkish national legislation did not follow unequivocally from its own jurisprudence. In fact, the Court's case law is somewhat ambiguous in situations where national laws were—or were claimed to be—at issue. Its decision in *Upper Silesia*, for instance, is often cited for the proposition that '[f]rom the standpoint of International Law and of the Court which is its organ, municipal laws are merely facts which express the will and constitute the activities of States, in the same manner as do legal decisions or administrative measures'.[92] But other cases, such as *Brazilian Federal Loans*,[93] are referenced for their explicit engagement with the question as to whether the Court was mandated, or at least permitted, to consider domestic jurisprudence in cases that involved or touched upon municipal law.[94] In that case the Court explained that, when obliged to apply municipal law, it had no choice but to 'pay the utmost regard to the decisions of the municipal courts of a country, for it is with the aid of their jurisprudence that it will be enabled to decide what are the rules which, in actual fact, are applied in the country the law of which is recognized as applicable in a given case'.[95] As 'a tribunal of international law', it was thoroughly acquainted with international law, but was 'not obliged also to know the municipal law of the various countries', and ought consequently to 'endeavour to make a just appreciation of the jurisprudence of municipal courts' whenever necessary.[96] This position would receive support a decade later in Manley Hudson's separate opinion in *The*

[91] Wilfred Jenks later took note of this, arguing that '[t]he decision must therefore be regarded as an *arrêt d'espèce* which does not preclude the possibility that in some future case the Court may hold that some other treaty is to be interpreted in the light of the conceptions of some particular legal system'. C. Wilfred Jenks, *The Prospects of International Adjudication* (London: Stevens & Sons, 1964), 578.

[92] *Case concerning Certain German Interests in Polish Upper Silesia (The Merits)* (*Germany v Poland*) PCIJ Rep. Series A No 7 (1926), 19. On this see Ole Spiermann, *International Legal Argument in the Permanent Court of International Justice: The Rise of the International Judiciary* (Cambridge: Cambridge University Press, 2005), 277–80.

[93] *Case concerning the Payment in Gold of Brazilian Federal Loans Contracted in France* (*France v Brazil*) PCIJ Rep. Series A No 21 (1929).

[94] See, e.g., Fockema Andreæ, *An Important Chapter* (n 79), 26; Rosalyn Higgins, 'The Role of National Courts in the International Legal Process', in Rosalyn Higgins, *Problems and Process: International Law and How We Use It* (Oxford: Clarendon Press, 1994), 205, at 205; André Nollkaemper, *National Courts and the International Rule of Law* (Oxford: Oxford University Press, 2011), 226–7.

[95] *Brazilian Federal Loans* (n 93), 124.

[96] *Brazilian Federal Loans* (n 93), 124.

'*Société Commerciale de Belgique*'. For Hudson, the Court was obliged to examine municipal law when a party to a dispute sought relief on its basis and provided the Court with the requisite materials.[97] Interestingly, Antonio Sánchez de Bustamante had written a dissenting opinion in *Brazilian Federal Loans*, arguing, among other things, that the rule articulated by the majority ought to be modified. De Bustamante had maintained that, where consideration of municipal laws proved necessary, the Court was duty-bound to 'weigh the meaning and scope of such municipal laws in the light of its own particular views without allowing itself to be guided or influenced by the decisions of the national courts of the Parties'.[98] In effect, this dissent called for a significantly greater level of invasiveness than the majority's judgment: while the latter required the Court to consider the case law of municipal courts, a clear sign of deference to national sovereignty, the dissent would have had the Court interpret municipal law without recourse to such case law, recruiting a more explicitly internationalist vision of its jurisdiction and competence.

Such divergence is telling. In the *Exchange* opinion, the Court did not seek to determine the most adequate technique for interpreting and applying domestic law. Rather, it sought to determine the relevance, if any, of such law for treaty interpretation, itself regarded by many at the time as 'one of the most confused subjects in international law'.[99] Nevertheless, the less-than-univocal stance in respect to domestic case law one encounters in *Brazilian Federal Loans* casts a certain degree of doubt on the Court's outright disavowal of municipal law in the *Exchange* opinion. After all, if the Court's position on the interpretation of municipal law was not entirely settled, with the majority and dissenting opinions in *Brazilian Federal Loans* disagreeing on whether to heed the jurisprudence of domestic courts, the Court's decision to bracket municipal law in the *Exchange* opinion, where plausible arguments could be made for integrating such law into the process of treaty interpretation, would also seem to be open to a measure of critical scrutiny. It is true that the Court generally held firm to the view that restrictions derived from treaties to which states have bound themselves cannot be regarded as violations of their sovereignty,[100] with Dionisio Anzilotti famously declaring that 'a government should bear the consequences of the wording of a document for which it is responsible'.[101] But it is also true that interwar jurists often admitted that invocations of 'natural meaning' such as the one that drove

[97] *The 'Société Commerciale de Belgique' (Belgium v Greece)* PCIJ Rep. Series A/B No 78 (1939), 184.

[98] *Brazilian Federal Loans* (n 93), 135. Epitácio Lindolfo da Silva Pessôa had expressed similar sentiments in his own dissenting opinion; see *Brazilian Federal Loans* (n 93), 151 (suggesting that 'the Court is bound to set on one side the decisions of international tribunals and itself to give that interpretation of the legal provisions which may seem most just in the particular case').

[99] Yi-ting Chang, *The Interpretation of Treaties by Judicial Tribunals* (New York: Columbia University Press, 1933), 19.

[100] For a typical articulation see *Jurisdiction of the European Commission of the Danube between Galatz and Braila*, Advisory Opinion, PCIJ Rep. Series B No 14 (1927), 36.

[101] *Case concerning the Polish Agrarian Reform and the German Minority (Interim Measures of Protection) (Germany v Poland)* PCIJ Rep. Series A/B No 58 (1933), 182.

the *Exchange* opinion were anything but infallible, such 'meaning' frequently being imprecise, context-dependent, or resistant to determination through rote application of this or that analytical mechanism.[102]

To be sure, no 'duplicitous' intent to prime the pump of progressive internationalism need be 'exposed' here: one has little reason to believe that the Court was acting in 'bad faith' when holding that treaty interpretation demands rigorous attention to what is specific to international law. The point, rather, is that the Court's rejection of Turkey's effort to amplify its sovereign powers under Lausanne bore a structural analogy to the way in which humanitarians like Barton and Nansen sought to channel ethno-national conflict into an internationally directed process of nation- and state-formation. It was Turkey's international obligations, as enshrined in a strictly construed Article 2, and not its domestic arrangements, as embedded in the two domicile laws it took to the Court, that were at issue. Put differently, what was of central importance was not Turkey's desire to augment its national sovereignty through unilateral application of domestic law, but its commitment to a new inter-state order buttressed by treaty law and premised upon a League-backed project of demographic engineering. Neither Turkey's specific motivations for attempting to limit the class of *établis* persons nor its general concerns about sovereignty and independence were pertinent: Turkey's nationalistic 'reasons' simply did 'not concern the Court', and 'national sovereignty' was 'not affected by the Convention in question'. Not unlike the humanitarianism that inspired the League and organizations like Near East Relief, the World Court pushed for international rather than national management of the exchange procedure, funnelling ethno-nationalism into a multilateral programme for constructing new states and preserving the few minorities that remained.

On the few occasions when it is remembered today, the *Exchange* opinion is dismissed as a mundane case of treaty interpretation involving a nasty but relatively obscure episode in interwar history. Contextual analysis yields a more complex and illuminating story. Remarkable for the fact that the World Court engaged directly with the exchange agreement rather than questioning its legal validity, the opinion stressed the need to remain faithful to its terms by interpreting them in strict accordance with international law. The Court's reluctance to

[102] See, e.g., Tsune-Chi Yü, *The Interpretation of Treaties* (New York: Columbia University Press, 1927), 28; Charles Cheney Hyde, 'The Interpretation of Treaties by the Permanent Court of International Justice', *AJIL* 24 (1930), 1, at 19; Harvard Research in International Law, 'Law of Treaties', *AJIL Sup.* 29 (1935), 653, at 939–47; Robert R. Wilson, 'Some Aspects of Treaty Interpretation', *AJIL* 33 (1939), 541, at 542. Such anxieties were not unrelated to concerns regarding the formal variability of treaties and other instruments; see, e.g., Jules Basdevant, 'La conclusion et la rédaction des traités et des instruments diplomatiques autres que les traités', *RCADI* 15 (1926-V), 535 (arguing, inter alia, that 'the drafting of diplomatic instruments other than treaties is uncertain, hesitant and contradictory' (641)). It was precisely from such concerns that Lord McNair sought to liberate international lawyers when he recommended that they ought to distance themselves 'from the traditional notion that the instrument known as the treaty is governed by a single set of rules' and focus instead on the task of 'study[ing] the greatly differing legal character of the several kinds of treaties'. Arnold D. McNair, 'The Functions and Differing Legal Character of Treaties', *BYIL* 11 (1930), 100, at 118.

take domestic law into account underscored the fact that the exchange procedure was structured as an international endeavour—as an attempt to cast a formal net over ethno-nationalism and ensure that nation-building was allowed to proceed without disruption. Indeed, when considered in light of the engagement of humanitarian organizations with the Ottoman Empire and the states formed from its protracted dissolution, the opinion reveals itself to be less an illustration of run-of-the-mill treaty interpretation and more an exercise in fixing the boundary between state power and international authority in the context of a large and legally formalized transfer of populations.

In the case of Greek–Turkish relations, minority protection had come to be regarded as insufficient and the neo-colonial Mandate System was generally viewed as inapplicable, not only to Greece but also to predominantly Turkish territory. Until recently at the helm of an imperial power and still disposed to accord themselves much the same clout, albeit now in a mainly 'anti-imperialist' register, Turkish elites were therefore able to see to it that their preferred 'solution'—the compulsory exchange of minority populations—was selected and implemented. Nevertheless, Rüştü and others were clearly not capable of arguing from a position of strength in The Hague. However vague the relevant rules of treaty interpretation may have been, the weight of legal opinion, not to mention that of political sympathy, was on Greece's side. Accordingly, Turkey pursued a characteristically semi-peripheral strategy, seeking to read down its international legal obligations and broaden the jurisdictional reach of its domestic laws and courts.[103] This strategy of resistance, indexed as it was to an expansive conception of national sovereignty, is difficult to explain without an appreciation of the history of activism and intervention in the Ottoman Empire over the preceding decades.

Non-binding though it was, both Greece and Turkey complied with the World Court's opinion and eventually resolved outstanding compensatory questions through treaty,[104] encouraging commentators to argue that, if nothing else, this was one case in which the advisory mechanism, itself one of the League's innovations,[105] had demonstrated its worth.[106] At long last, the world would

[103] Turkey was given to arguing that treaties to which it was signatory were misunderstood by other parties at the time—a tendency famously demonstrated in the *Lotus* case (*Case of the S. S. 'Lotus'* (*France v Turkey*) PCIJ Rep. Series A No 10 (1927)) and also in the Court's less widely known opinion on the determination of the Iraqi border, which ultimately brought wrangling between Britain and Turkey over the status of Mosul province largely to an end (*Interpretation of Article 3, Paragraph 2, of the Treaty of Lausanne (Frontier between Turkey and Iraq)*, Advisory Opinion, PCIJ Rep. Series B No 12 (1925)). On this see Charles Fairman, 'The Interpretation of Treaties', *TGS* 20 (1934), 123, at 128.

[104] See Convention regarding the Final Settlement of the Questions resulting from the Application of the Treaty of Lausanne and of the Agreement of Athens relating to the Exchange of Populations, signed at Ankara, 10 June 1930, 108 LNTS 233.

[105] Cf. Marika Giles Samson and Douglas Guilfoyle, 'The Permanent Court of International Justice and the "Invention" of International Advisory Jurisdiction', in *Legacies of the Permanent Court of International Justice*, ed. Christian J. Tams and Malgosia Fitzmaurice (Leiden: Nijhoff, 2013), 41, esp. at 42–4.

[106] 'The advice of the Court has been unquestioningly adopted by the parties. In this replanting of the population of the Near East, the machinery of the League has worked helpfully and constructively.' Norman Bentwich, 'The League of Nations and Refugees', *BYIL* 16 (1935), 114, at 124.

be rid of the ethno-confessional pluralism that Ottoman decentralization had made possible and that Ernest Renan had lamented as early as 1882 as having brought about 'the ruin of the East'.[107] A Greek enclave would exist in Istanbul. But as with Turkey's other non-Muslim communities, its legal authority would be circumscribed and its socio-economic sustainability would be highly tenuous.

If the delimitation and administration of disputed or 'anomalous' zones tend to crystallize assertions of sovereignty with particular lucidity,[108] the World Court's engagement with competing claims to the legal status of Istanbul—central to the political economy of the Near East and a key object of Greek irredentism and Turkish chauvinism alike—showcased the determination of international lawyers and institutions to police the boundaries of domestic jurisdiction. As the first legally structured compulsory exchange of its magnitude, the Greek–Turkish endeavour was the crucible within which population transfer arose as a distinct mode of nation-building through modern international law. Perhaps it is fitting that many of the struggles by which this process of stabilization unfolded were centred in Istanbul, a cosmopolitan city that enjoyed pride of place in the legal and political imaginations of regional elites and whose internationalization Lorimer had proposed long ago as a means of furthering 'international government'.[109]

[107] Ernest Renan, *Qu'est-ce qu'une nation? Conférence faite en Sorbonne, le 11 mars 1882*, 2nd ed. (Paris: Ancienne maison Michel Lévy frères, 1882), 9.

[108] See Lauren Benton, *A Search for Sovereignty: Law and Geography in European Empires, 1400–1900* (Cambridge: Cambridge University Press, 2010), esp. chs. 1, 5.

[109] Lorimer's proposal was nothing if not ambitious: through internationalization, Istanbul was to establish itself as a 'fulcrum' of '[i]nternational government', with great and small powers alike sending delegations to the city annually in order to create and codify new international law. James Lorimer, 'Of the Denationalisation of Constantinople and Its Devotion to International Purposes' [1876], in James Lorimer, *Studies National and International, Being Occasional Lectures Delivered in the University of Edinburgh 1864–1889* (Edinburgh: William Green & Sons, 1890), 121, at 128–9. Lorimer was not alone in making such proposals; no less a figure than Venizelos would suggest that the city be internationalized when presenting the Greek case at the Paris Peace Conference; see Eleutherios Venizelos, *La Grèce devant le Congrès de la Paix* (Paris: Imprimerie Chaix, 1919), 14.

Conclusion

It is impossible to know with certainty what Nansen might have been thinking when he set off for Istanbul in 1922. It is equally impossible to determine conclusively how much of the population exchange that subsequently unfolded grew out of his own preferences. What is clear, though, is that Nansen's mission encapsulates nearly all of what made the Greek–Turkish exchange as structurally idiosyncratic—and as devastatingly effective—as it was. The pervasive desire among European lawyers and diplomats to 'pacify' a region wracked by violence with an instrument tailored to its history and actual conditions; the odd mixture of arrogance and deference with which such lawyers and diplomats strained to adapt the tradition of minority protection they had inherited from their nineteenth-century forerunners, bringing its commitment to govern ethno-nationalism to bear on a context in which it had only limited application; their willingness to work with, and in many cases simply submit to the demands of, local elites determined to realize their own nationalist ambitions—as though in miniature, each of these features found a home in Nansen's mission.

Although it had its roots in Anatolia and the Balkans, legally mediated population transfer and related forms of demographic engineering travelled to other regions before long, experiencing something of a successive 'globalization' in the process. In the late 1930s and early 1940s, by which time Stalin had begun resorting to internal deportations in an effort to consolidate his nationalities policy but most of those displaced by First World War-related hostilities had either been resettled or repatriated,[1] Nazi diplomats concluded numerous transfer treaties with the Soviet Union and other east European states in the name of the Reich's 'protective right' over its ethnic kin.[2] Ethnic Germans in Latvia or Romania, Estonia or Croatia, were to be given the right to 'opt' for German citizenship and thereby submit to an ostensibly voluntary transfer to German territory.[3] Immediately after the Second World War, the

[1] Walter Adams, 'Extent and Nature of the World Refugee Problem', *Annals of the American Academy of Political and Social Science* 203 (1939), 26, at 33 ff.

[2] For suggestive, if heavy-handed, observations on the relation between Nazi views of sovereignty and Turkish and Chinese arguments about extraterritoriality, see Detlev F. Vagts, 'International Law in the Third Reich', *AJIL* 84 (1990), 661, at 688.

[3] On this see especially Joseph B. Schechtman, *European Population Transfers 1939–1945* (New York: Oxford University Press, 1946); Joseph B. Schechtman, 'The Option Clause in the Reich's Treaties on the Transfer of Population', *AJIL* 38 (1944), 356; and also Eugene M. Kulischer, *The Displacement of Population in Europe* (Montreal: International Labour Office, 1943). For a well-documented case study of how Nazi-affiliated states undertook population transfer, see further

Allied Powers made heavy use of compulsory transfer as a means of removing ethnic Germans from eastern Europe,[4] a process that overlapped with that of resettling displaced persons in occupied Germany, possibly the first true site of application for the budding post-war refugee rights regime.[5] The partition of British India in 1947, generating disputes about the management of population movements in addition to quandaries of state succession,[6] was followed in 1948 by the devastating exodus of Palestinian Arabs[7] and in 1972 by the expulsion of South Asians from Idi Amin's Uganda.[8] This, in turn, was trailed by forced migration in Cyprus in 1974–5[9] and throughout the former Yugoslavia, particularly Bosnia, during the 1990s.[10] The legal architecture of every such movement (and there were others) was different. Some took the form of unilateral transfers or bilateral exchanges inaugurated by law, while others were uncoordinated movements subject to *ex post* juridification. In certain cases law organized the movement from the outset; in others it completed a task that

Vladimir Solonari, *Purifying the Nation: Population Exchange and Ethnic Cleansing in Nazi-Allied Romania* (Washington: Woodrow Wilson Center Press/Baltimore: Johns Hopkins University Press, 2010).

[4] Alfred-Maurice de Zayas, *Nemesis at Potsdam: The Anglo-Americans and the Expulsion of the Germans—Background, Execution, Consequences* (London: Routledge & Kegan Paul, 1977); Alfred-Maurice de Zayas, *A Terrible Revenge: The Ethnic Cleansing of the East European Germans*, 2nd ed. (New York: Palgrave Macmillan, 2006); Matthew Frank, *Expelling the Germans: British Opinion and Post-1945 Population Transfer in Context* (Oxford: Oxford University Press, 2007); R. M. Douglas, *Orderly and Humane: The Expulsion of the Germans after the Second World War* (New Haven: Yale University Press, 2012). See also the official documents in Theodor Schieder, ed., *Documents on the Expulsion of the Germans from Eastern-Central-Europe*, 4 vols. (Bonn: Federal Ministry for Expellees, Refugees, and War Victims, n. d.).

[5] G. Daniel Cohen, 'The "Human Rights Revolution" at Work: Displaced Persons in Postwar Europe', in *Human Rights in the Twentieth Century*, ed. Stefan-Ludwig Hoffmann (New York: Cambridge University Press, 2011), 45, esp. at 50, 54. See also E. Reut-Nicolussi, 'Displaced Persons and International Law', *RCADI* 73 (1948-II), 1, at 31.

[6] Yasmin Khan, *The Great Partition: The Making of India and Pakistan* (New Haven: Yale University Press, 2007); Haimanti Roy, *Partitioned Lives: Migrants, Refugees, Citizens in India and Pakistan, 1947–1965* (New Delhi: Oxford University Press, 2013).

[7] See especially Ilan Pappe, *The Ethnic Cleansing of Palestine* (Oxford: Oneworld, 2006); and Victor Kattan, *From Coexistence to Conquest: International Law and the Origins of the Arab–Israeli Conflict, 1891–1949* (London: Pluto Press, 2009), esp. chs. 7–9.

[8] R. C. Chhangani, 'Expulsion of Uganda Asians and International Law', *Indian Journal of International Law* 12 (1972), 400; Frank Wooldridge and Vishnu D. Sharma, 'The Expulsion of the Ugandan Asians and Some Legal Questions Arising Therefrom', *Comparative and International Law Journal of Southern Africa* 7 (1974), 1.

[9] Christa Meindersma, 'Population Exchanges: International Law and State Practice', *International Journal of Refugee Law* 9 (1997), 335 and 613 (in two parts), at 351–64; *Legal Issues Arising from Certain Population Transfers and Displacements on the Territory of the Republic of Cyprus in the Period since 20 July 1974*, legal opinion prepared for the Republic of Cyprus by a committee of jurists (Georges Abi-Saab, Dieter Blumenwitz, James Crawford, John Dugard, Christopher Greenwood, Gerhard Hafner, Francisco Orrego Vicuña, Alain Pellet, Henry G. Schermers, and Christian Tomuschat) (30 June 1999), <http://www.cyprus.gov.cy/moi/pio/pio.nsf/All/A87E0AFB149260C3C2256D740028F4A2/$file/Opinion.pdf>.

[10] Christopher M. Goebel, 'Population Transfer, Humanitarian Law, and the Use of Ground Force in U.N. Peacemaking: Bosnia and Herzegovina in the Wake of Iraq', *New York University Journal of International Law and Politics* 25 (1993), 627; Michael P. Roch, 'Forced Displacement in the Former Yugoslavia: A Crime Under International Law?', *Dickinson Journal of International Law* 14 (1995), 1.

was already underway. Yet the logic of legally formalized population transfer—and the nation-building techniques with which it was accompanied and which were frequently rolled into broader development agendas[11]—circulated with remarkable consistency. Indeed, in most cases, from Potsdam to Dayton, the Greek–Turkish population exchange was cited as a key precedent.[12] Shortly before his death in 1942, none other than Politis would recognize as much when he suggested that the wartime Nazi–Soviet transfer agreements, and the Reich's policy in regard to population movements more generally, derived in large part from Lausanne.[13] Once considered only in respect to the Near East, a region regarded as falling short of Western standards of 'civilization' and subject to manipulation by imperialist powers, population transfer had now entered into the general lexicon of statecraft, appropriated by the very states that had voiced discomfort at its precedential consequences.[14]

Today it is generally agreed that compulsory population transfers are illegal under international humanitarian law and international human rights law. Express prohibitions or language with roughly similar constructive effect can be found in the Universal Declaration of Human Rights,[15] the Genocide Convention,[16] the Fourth Geneva Convention,[17] the 1951 Refugee Convention,[18] the Rome Statute of the International Criminal Court,[19] the Draft Declaration on Population Transfer and the Implantation of Settlers,[20] the International Law Commission's Draft Code of Crimes against the Peace and Security of Mankind and its draft articles on the expulsion of aliens,[21]

[11] Cf. Peter Gatrell, *The Making of the Modern Refugee* (Oxford: Oxford University Press, 2013), 66.

[12] See, e.g., Norman M. Naimark, *Fires of Hatred: Ethnic Cleansing in Twentieth-Century Europe* (Cambridge: Harvard University Press, 2001), 108, 110, 171; Dzovinar Kévonian, *Réfugiés et diplomatie humanitaire: Les acteurs européens et la scène proche-orientale pendant l'entre-deux-guerres* (Paris: Publications de la Sorbonne, 2004), 126–9; Onur Yıldırım, *Diplomacy and Displacement: Reconsidering the Turco–Greek Exchange of Populations, 1922–1934* (New York: Routledge, 2006), 12–13 ff.

[13] Nicolas Politis, 'Le transfert des populations', *Politique étrangère* 5 (1940), 83.

[14] Cf. Donald Bloxham, 'The Great Unweaving: The Removal of Peoples in Europe, 1875–1949', in *Removing Peoples: Forced Removal in the Modern World*, ed. Richard Bessel and Claudia B. Haake (Oxford: Oxford University Press, 2009), 167, at 202.

[15] Universal Declaration of Human Rights, GA Res. 217A (III), UN Doc. A/810 at 71 (1948), Arts 9, 13, 15, at 73–4.

[16] Convention on the Prevention and Punishment of the Crime of Genocide, 9 December 1948, 78 UNTS 277, Art 2, at 280.

[17] Geneva Convention relative to the Protection of Civilian Persons in Time of War, 12 August 1949, 75 UNTS 287, Arts 49, 147, at 318, 388.

[18] Convention relating to the Status of Refugees, signed at Geneva, 28 July 1951, 189 UNTS 150, Arts 32–3, at 174–6.

[19] Rome Statute of the International Criminal Court, 17 July 1998, 2187 UNTS 90, Arts 6–8, at 93–8.

[20] Draft Declaration on Population Transfer and the Implantation of Settlers, annex to Awn Shawkat Al-Khasawneh, *Human Rights and Population Transfer: Final Report of the Special Rapporteur*, UN Doc. E/CN.4/Sub.2/1997/23 (1997), 26.

[21] Draft Code of Crimes against the Peace and Security of Mankind, 51 UN GAOR Supp. (No 10) at 14, UN Doc. A/CN.4/L.532, corr.1, corr.3 (1996), Arts 17–18, 20, at 6–9; International Law Commission, *Report of the International Law Commission on the Work of Its Sixty-Fourth Session* (7 May–1 June, 2 July–3 August 2012), UN Doc. A/67/10, ch. 4.

and a number of other instruments.[22] In addition, international legal scholars have long characterized mass expulsions as an anomaly, a throwback to a cruder and less sophisticated age.[23] Yet population transfer and broadly analogous forms of demographic engineering, both domestic and international, continue to be implemented or entertained in a significant number of states—among them China,[24] Turkey,[25] Israel–Palestine,[26] and, most recently, France and Ethiopia.[27] Legal legitimacy is nearly always sought for such exercises, particularly when couched in 'voluntary' terms. If a member of the Institut de droit international and eventual judge of the International Court of Justice could argue in 1952 that '[f]rom the point of view of international law, there exists, in this matter, absolute freedom of action on the part of states provided that the laws of humanity are not

[22] For useful tabulations see Jean-Marie Henckaerts, *Mass Expulsion in Modern International Law and Practice* (London: Nijhoff, 1995), 206–9; Alfred-Maurice de Zayas, 'Forced Population Transfer', in *Max Planck Encyclopedia of Public International Law*, <http://www.mpepil.com>. For good synthetic discussion see further Grant Dawson and Sonia Farber, *Forcible Displacement Throughout the Ages: Towards an International Convention for the Prevention and Punishment of the Crime of Forcible Displacement* (Leiden: Nijhoff, 2012), ch. 3; and also Maria Stavropoulou, 'The Right Not to be Displaced', *American University Journal of International Law and Policy* 9 (1994), 689.

[23] See, e.g., Georges Scelle's contribution to Giorgio Balladore Pallieri, 'Les transferts internationaux de populations', *AIDI* 44 (1952-II), 138, at 176 ('Every transfer of populations constitutes a negation of modern international ethics, based primarily upon international legal order'); Alfred-Maurice de Zayas, 'Collective Expulsions: Norms, Jurisprudence, Remedies', *Refugee Survey Quarterly* 16 (1997), 149, at 150 ('Collective expulsions . . . are an anachronism in the post-Second World War era . . . [and] constitute an aberration and a threat to the peace that ought to be met by appropriate United Nations sanctions pursuant to Chapter VII of the UN Charter').

[24] See Human Rights Watch, '"They Say We Should Be Grateful": Mass Rehousing and Relocation Programs in Tibetan Areas of China' (June 2013), <http://www.hrw.org/sites/default/files/reports/tibet0613webwcover_0.pdf> (detailing large-scale transfers in Tibet); and also Anders Hoejmark Anderson, Sarah Cooke, and Michael Wills, *New Majority: Chinese Population Transfer into Tibet* (London: Tibet Support Group, 1995) (discussing the state-sponsored transfers of Han Chinese into Tibet).

[25] See, e.g., Gündüz Aktan, 'Geleceğe Doğru (4)', *Radikal* (10 January 2006), <http://www.radikal.com.tr/haber.php?haberno=175378&tarih=10/01/2006> (a retired diplomat proposing an exchange of Turkish Kurds and Iraqi Turkmen).

[26] See, e.g., Barak Ravid, 'Lieberman Presents Plans for Population Exchange at UN', *Haaretz* (28 September 2010), <http://www.haaretz.com/news/diplomacy-defense/lieberman-presents-plans-for-population-exchange-at-un-1.316197> (discussing Israeli Foreign Minister Avigdor Lieberman's proposal that certain territories be exchanged as part of a final peace settlement). Note, though, that this proposal, which has been floated for some time, involves the exchange of territories rather than populations; see Timothy William Waters, 'The Blessing of Departure: Acceptable and Unacceptable State Support for Demographic Transformation: The Lieberman Plan to Exchange Populated Territories in Cisjordan', *Law and Ethics of Human Rights* 2 (2008), 221. See further a UN rapporteur's appraisal of recent expulsions from East Jerusalem: Richard Falk, *Report of the Special Rapporteur on the Situation of Human Rights in the Palestinian Territories Occupied Since 1967*, UN Doc. A/HRC/16/72 (2011), 10–11.

[27] See, e.g., Human Rights Watch, 'France: Renewed Crackdown on Roma—End Discriminatory Roma Camp Evictions and Renewals' (10 August 2012), <http://www.hrw.org/news/2012/08/10/france-renewed-crackdown-roma>; Human Rights Watch, 'Ethiopia: Forced Relocations Bring Hunger, Hardship—Donor Funds Should Not Facilitate Abuse of Indigenous Groups' (17 January 2012), <http://www.hrw.org/news/2012/01/16/ethiopia-forced-relocations-bring-hunger-hardship>.

violated',[28] so too could a UN rapporteur who was until recently a judge of the same court argue as late as 1997 that in certain contexts 'population transfers are lawful if they are non-discriminatory and are based upon the will of the people'.[29] It is difficult to imagine circumstances in which whole peoples would submit 'voluntarily' to community-wide displacement. And the tenability of a strict distinction between 'compulsory' and 'voluntary' transfers is complicated by the fact that high levels of persecution and intimidation have typically characterized the latter, making migration effectively 'compulsory' even when it is not explicitly characterized as such. But international law arguably continues to permit reliance upon population transfer when such willingness is (or is deemed to have been) expressed 'freely'.

On a certain level, one can appreciate, if not necessarily acquiesce to, the appeals of population transfer. Those entrusted with the task of administering territories home to significant conflict have frequently looked to population transfer as a necessary evil, the most humanitarian of logistically viable options. Unsurprisingly, as the classic illustration of this mode of conflict resolution, the Greek–Turkish exchange has enjoyed pride of place in most such cases. The Palestine Royal Commission, charged with offering recommendations for the administration of the British mandate over Palestine, lauded 'the courage of the Greek and Turkish statesmen' involved in the exchange, declaring that relations between Greece and Turkey were 'friendlier than they have ever been before' and suggesting that a similar exchange be undertaken as part of Palestine's partition.[30] Likewise, Churchill lavished praise on those responsible for the Greek–Turkish exchange when pressed on the merits of the proposed transfer of Germans out of central and eastern Europe: 'disentanglement' had 'in many ways [proven] a success', and had, at any rate, 'produced friendly relations between Greece and Turkey ever since'.[31]

There is something to be said for all this. Tensions between Greece and Turkey would remain at a high level through the 1920s, but proved to be manageable during the two decades that followed. In 1930 Venizelos travelled to Ankara to sign a landmark 'friendship' treaty, having already set aside outstanding claims to properties

[28] Jean Spiropoulos' contribution to Balladore Pallieri, 'Les transferts internationaux de populations' (n 23), 186. The sentiment was shared by many members of the Institut, including Balladore Pallieri himself.

[29] Al-Khasawneh, *Human Rights and Population Transfer* (n 20), 19. On the implications for relevant provisions in the Draft Declaration on Population Transfer and the Implantation of Settlers, see further Emily Haslam, 'Population, Expulsion and Transfer', in *Max Planck Encyclopedia of Public International Law*, <http://www.mpepil.com>, esp. paras 14–15; Emily Haslam, 'Unlawful Population Transfer and the Limits of International Criminal Law', *Cambridge Law Journal* 61 (2002), 66, at 68–9.

[30] Palestine Royal Commission, *Report* (Cmd 5479) (London: His Majesty's Stationery Office, 1937), 390. For discussion see Yossi Katz, 'Transfer of Population as a Solution to International Disputes: Population Exchanges between Greece and Turkey as a Model for Plans to Solve the Jewish–Arab Dispute in Palestine during the 1930s', *Political Geography* 11 (1992), 55; Gregory H. Fox, *Humanitarian Occupation* (Cambridge: Cambridge University Press, 2008), 137 ff.

[31] Quoted in de Zayas, *Nemesis at Potsdam* (n 4), 11. See also Naimark, *Fires of Hatred* (n 12), 110.

lost or abandoned during the exchange.[32] Relations between the two states improved to such a degree that Kemal felt comfortable bringing his long-awaited vision of a 'Balkan Pact' to a head. Intended to cement commitment to *uti possidetis* through mutual security guarantees, the pact was signed and ratified by four states—Greece, Romania, Turkey, and Yugoslavia—in 1934, the work, it was thought, of a more enlightened understanding of the region's needs and resources.[33] Less consequential, but even more dramatic, was Venizelos' recommendation of Kemal for the Nobel Peace Prize in 1934.[34]

Still, it must be emphasized that very little of this proved to be lasting. The Balkan Pact, and similar plans for security integration,[35] never bore fruit. By the early 1940s the pact had shown itself to be toothless, a paper alliance flouted by espionage, growing rivalry, and shifting geopolitical dynamics. During the Second World War, Turkish authorities introduced a 'wealth tax', partly to support a fledgling defence industry. Although short-lived and formally extended to all Turkish citizens, the tax was applied discriminatorily to non-Muslims, stoking economic nationalization and further diluting the commercial power of minority groups.[36] A second 'Balkan Pact' was concluded between Greece, Turkey, and Yugoslavia in 1953.[37] The pact's trans-ideological character was remarkable: Tito's Yugoslavia maintained a notoriously uneasy relationship with the Soviet Union, while Greece and Turkey buttressed NATO's eastern flank under the shadow of the Truman Doctrine,[38] premised upon what Truman himself called a general fear of 'confusion and disorder'.[39] But

[32] Convention regarding the Final Settlement of the Questions resulting from the Application of the Treaty of Lausanne and of the Agreement of Athens relating to the Exchange of Populations, signed at Ankara, 10 June 1930, 108 LNTS 233. For analysis see especially Damla Demirözü, 'The Greek–Turkish Rapprochement of 1930 and the Repercussions of the Ankara Convention in Turkey', *Journal of Islamic Studies* 19 (2008), 309; and also John A. Petropulos, 'The Compulsory Exchange of Populations: Greek–Turkish Peacemaking, 1922–1930', *Byzantine and Modern Greek Studies* 2 (1976), 135, at 138.

[33] Pact of Balkan Entente, and Protocol-Annex, signed at Athens, 9 February 1934, 153 LNTS 153, esp. Art 1, at 155. For prospective and retrospective commentary see M. A. Caloyanni, 'The Balkan Union, the Balkan Conferences, and the Balkan Pact', *TGS* 18 (1932), 97 and *TGS* 19 (1933), 89 (in two parts); Hans W. Hartmann, 'Les relations gréco–turques du traité de Lausanne au pacte d'Ankara, 1923–1933', *Les Balkans* 11 (1939), 333.

[34] For a record of the recommendation letter see <http://www.nobelprize.org/nomination/peace/nomination.php?action=show&showid=2046>.

[35] See, e.g., Theodore I. Geshkoff, *Balkan Union: A Road to Peace in Southeastern Europe* (New York: Columbia University Press, 1940).

[36] Alexis P. Alexandris, *The Greek Minority of Istanbul and Greek–Turkish Relations, 1918–1974* (Athens: Centre for Asia Minor Studies, 1992), ch. 7; Samim Akgönül, *Türkiye Rumları: Ulus-Devlet Çağından Küreselleşme Çağına Bir Azınlığın Yok Oluş Süreci*, trans. Ceylan Gürman (İstanbul: İletişim Yayınları, 2007), 114–49; Ayhan Aktar, 'Varlık Vergisi Nasıl Uygulandı?' and 'Varlık Vergisi Sırasında Gayri Menkul Satışları ile Servet Transferi: İstanbul Tapu Kayıtlarının Analizi', in Ayhan Aktar, *Varlık Vergisi ve 'Türkleştirme' Politikaları* (İstanbul: İletişim Yayınları, 2000), 135 and 215 respectively; Rıfat N. Bali, *The 'Varlık Vergisi' Affair: A Study on Its Legacy—Selected Documents* (Istanbul: Isis Press, 2005).

[37] Treaty of Friendship and Collaboration, signed at Ankara, 28 February 1953, 167 UNTS 21.

[38] Svetozar Rajak, 'The Cold War in the Balkans, 1945–1956', in *The Cambridge History of the Cold War*, ed. Melvyn P. Leffler and Odd Arne Westad, vol. 1 (Cambridge: Cambridge University Press, 2010), 198, at 208, 215.

[39] Quoted in Odd Arne Westad, *The Global Cold War: Third World Interventions and the Making of Our Times* (Cambridge: Cambridge University Press, 2005), 21.

it too revealed itself to be vulnerable to the Cold War's vagaries, and was terminated formally in 1960. Pogroms in Istanbul in 1955 accelerated the emigration of the *établis*.[40] The Cyprus conflict came to the fore in full force during the same decade. Before long, large segments of the island's Greek-Cypriot population began to agitate for *enosis*, or union, with Greece; Greek-Cypriot paramilitaries committed to securing this union targeted Turkish civilians and British soldiers alike; Turkish Cypriots reacted by pressing for the island's *taksim*, or partition, and also by supporting their own paramilitaries; the two communities subsequently struggled for years until a pro-*enosis* coup in Nicosia and support from an Athenian *junta* brought the issue to a head in 1974, with Turkey intervening militarily to occupy the northern third of the island. As is well-known, numerous legal disputes have arisen from the mass expulsion of Greeks from Turkish-occupied territory, the ensuing flight of many Turkish Cypriots to the north, the contested status of the 'Turkish Republic of Northern Cyprus' declared unilaterally in 1983, and the difficulties engendered by Cyprus' accession to the European Union in 2004.[41] Equally challenging has been complex legal wrangling regarding maritime and airspace rights in the Aegean Sea.[42] Only rarely have international lawyers in Greece and Turkey sought to challenge such developments. More often than not they have simply affirmed the validity of official policy, a tendency encapsulated perhaps most crudely in Yılmaz Altuğ's statement that '[t]he minority is subordinate to the sovereignty of the state and it must respect the juridical order on which its rights depend'.[43]

Examined in the light of these later developments, the Greek–Turkish exchange seems considerably less 'successful' than has often been assumed. The exchange may have smoothed inter-state relations in the Near East to some degree. If nothing else, it cannot be denied that Greece and Turkey were now possessed of a much greater degree of ethno-religious homogeneity, and that this was more than likely an important factor in minimizing the risk of a recurrence of war. But it would clearly be reckless to risk stronger, more sweeping conclusions regarding the normative value, or even functional viability, of population transfer. As though the chequered history of Greek–Turkish relations during the remainder of the twentieth century were not enough to discredit such conclusions, the fact that much of the scholarship relating to the exchange has been dominated by misleading representations of the historical record, and that this continues to be the case despite efforts by critical historians,[44]

[40] See, e.g., Alexandris, *Greek Minority* (n 36), 256–66; Akgönül, *Türkiye Rumları* (n 36), 175–224; Alfred-Maurice de Zayas, 'The Istanbul Pogrom of 6–7 September 1955 in the Light of International Law', *Genocide Studies and Prevention* 2 (2007), 137.

[41] See, e.g., Marios L. Evriviades, 'The Legal Dimension of the Cyprus Conflict', *Texas International Law Journal* 10 (1975), 227; Zaim M. Necatigil, *The Cyprus Question and the Turkish Position in International Law*, 2nd ed. (Oxford: Oxford University Press, 1993).

[42] Haralambos Athanasopulos, *Greece, Turkey and the Aegean Sea: A Case Study in International Law* (Jefferson: McFarland & Co., 2001); Yücel Acer, *The Aegean Maritime Disputes and International Law* (Aldershot: Ashgate, 2003). Such wrangling has taken on additional importance with recent moves by Cyprus to exploit gas fields off its coast.

[43] Yılmaz M. Altuğ, *Turkey and Some Problems of International Law* (İstanbul: Yenilik Basımevi, 1958), 153.

[44] For commendably honest critique, see, e.g., Georgios Nakracas, *Anadolu ve Rum Göçmenlerin Kökeni: 1922 Emperyalist Yunan Politikasi ve Anadolu Felaketi*, trans. İbram Onsunoğlu

testifies to the resilience of entrenched rivalries. Indeed, it is arguable that while ameliorative of conflict in the short term, the Greek–Turkish exchange actually exacerbated such rivalry over the medium- to long-term: in the place of two states with 'mixed' populations and institutions equipped to regulate such heterogeneity, there were now two nation-states forged through conflict and expulsion, each with a citizenry that much more conscious and resentful of the other.

Given the need for scepticism in respect to the Greek–Turkish precedent, the popularity of population transfer and roughly analogous forms of mass expulsion seems stranger still. From a comparatively marginal response to conflict, thought to be legal but limited in application to a specific region, to a more or less 'universal' mechanism, deemed applicable to all manner of contexts even as its legality came under question, the international legal history of population transfer is a tale both of growing fascination and of growing opprobrium. After 1945 leading jurists and policymakers often regarded transfer as a legitimate competitor to group rights and individualistic human rights. Raphael Lemkin, lawyer and celebrated advocate of the Genocide Convention, may, for instance, have clung steadfast to minority protection, but the influential activist and demographer Joseph Schechtman considered transfer to be the only truly viable solution to ethno-nationalist violence.[45] Rather than delegitimizing their usage, Nazi and Allied transfers seemed to convince some that 'eliminating minorities was simply a necessary part of modern nationalism and modern internationalism alike'.[46] Although compulsory transfers have since attracted international legal sanction, lawyers employed by states seeking to gain acceptance of forced displacements work regularly to persuade their audiences that such endeavours accord with 'popular will'. Apart from the fact that the distinction between compulsory and voluntary movements is difficult to sustain in practice (it is almost perverse to speak of 'options' when a community is subject to pervasive and systematic persecution), the fact that the Greek–Turkish exchange—the chief precedent—was not nearly as effective at constraining ethno-nationalism as is generally believed should give us pause when evaluating such efforts.

If we are to understand the ongoing allure of population transfer, we must also understand its emergence in a region with unique customs and dynamics, not to mention grievances and aspirations. Regardless of where this or that group of interwar jurists may have stood on the question of legality, the feeling that violence

(İstanbul: Belge, 2003); Lambros Baltsiotis, 'Yunanistan ve Türkiye'de Muhacirlik ve Nüfus Mübadeleleri: İki Farklı Anlatım ve Yorumun Oluşma Şartları ve Sonuçları', trans. Halil Mustafa, in *Yeniden Kurulan Yaşamlar: 1923 Türk–Yunan Zorunlu Nüfus Mübadelesi*, ed. Müfide Pekin (İstanbul: İstanbul Bilgi Üniversitesi Yayınları, 2005), 401; Yıldırım, *Diplomacy and Displacement* (n 12), esp. 9–22; Onur Yıldırım, 'The 1923 Population Exchange, Refugees and National Historiographies in Greece and Turkey', *East European Quarterly* 40 (2006), 45; Ayhan Aktar and Damla Demirözü, 'Yunan Tarihyazımında Mübadele ve Göç', *Kebikeç* 22 (2006), 85.

[45] On the relation between the approaches outlined by Schechtman and Lemkin, see Mark Mazower, *No Enchanted Palace: The End of Empire and the Ideological Origins of the United Nations* (Princeton: Princeton University Press, 2009), ch. 3.

[46] Mazower, *No Enchanted Palace* (n 45), 107.

in Greece and Turkey called for measures distinct from the kind of minority protection that had become routine in Europe after 1919 but not as heavy-handed as a Mandate System-style regime was widely shared. We have grown accustomed in recent years to hearing that the states of south-east Europe and the Middle East have come to serve as a kind of 'laboratory' for state-building, humanitarian intervention, and international territorial administration.[47] Perhaps it should come as no surprise that one of the most ambitious and far-reaching techniques of nation-building should have had its origins in the Ottoman Empire's final dissolution.

[47] See, e.g., Mariella Pandolfi, 'From Paradox to Paradigm: The Permanent State of Emergency in the Balkans', in *Contemporary States of Emergency: The Politics of Military and Humanitarian Interventions*, ed. Didier Fassin and Mariella Pandolfi (New York: Zone Books, 2010), 153, at 168; David Chandler, *International Statebuilding: The Rise of Post-Liberal Governance* (Abingdon: Routledge, 2010), ch. 5.

Bibliography

I. DIPLOMATIC MEMORANDA AND CORRESPONDENCE

[Armenia] *The Armenian Question Before the Peace Conference: A Memorandum Presented Officially by the Representatives of Armenia to the Peace Conference at Versailles, on February 26th, 1919* (Paris: Imprimerie P. Dumont, 1919).

[Ecumenical Patriarchate] 'Note to the Great Powers', in Greek Patriarchate, *Persecution of the Greeks in Turkey, 1914–1918* (Constantinople, London: The Hesperia Press, 1919), 147.

[Greece] Eleutherios Venizelos, *La Grèce devant le Congrès de la Paix* (Paris: Imprimerie Chaix, 1919).

[Paris Peace Conference] 'Letter Addressed to M. Paderewski by the President of the Conference Transmitting to Him the Treaty to be Signed by Poland under Article 93 of the Treaty of Peace with Germany', reproduced in *A History of the Peace Conference of Paris*, ed. H. W. V. Temperley, vol. 5 (London: Henry Frowde and Hodder & Stoughton, 1921), 432.

[United States] Sharp, US Ambassador to France, to Bryan, US Secretary of State, 28 May 1915, reproduced in *Papers Relating to the Foreign Relations of the United States: 1915 Supplement* (Washington: United States Government Printing Office, 1928), 981.

II. REPORTS OF GOVERNMENTS AND INTERNATIONAL COMMISSIONS

[Britain] Palestine Royal Commission, *Report* (Cmd 5479) (London: His Majesty's Stationery Office, 1937).

[Commission on the Responsibility of the Authors of the War and on Enforcement of Penalties] *Violation of the Laws and Customs of War: Reports of Majority and Dissenting Reports of American and Japanese Members of the Commission of Responsibilities, Conference of Paris 1919* (Oxford: Clarendon Press, 1919).

[International Commission to Inquire into the Causes and Conduct of the Balkan Wars] *Report of the International Commission to Inquire into the Causes and Conduct of the Balkan Wars* (Washington: Carnegie Endowment for International Peace, 1914).

[Mixed Commission for the Exchange of Greek and Turkish Populations] 'Rapport final', annex to *Actes, décisions, sentences arbitrales relatifs à l'échange des populations grecques et turques*, vol. 2 (n.p.: Imprimerie Tsitouris frères, n.d.), 1.

[United States] *Instructions for the Government of Armies of the United States, in the Field. Prepared by Francis Lieber, LL.D., and Revised by a Board of Officers* (New York: D. Van Nostrand, 1863).

[United States] 'Outline of Tentative Report and Recommendations Prepared by the Intelligence Section, in Accordance with Instructions, for the President and the Plenipotentiaries, January 21, 1919', reproduced in David Hunter Miller, *My Diary at the Conference of Paris, with Documents*, vol. 4 (New York: Appeal Printing Co., 1924), 209.

[United States] 'Report of the American Section of the International Commission on Mandates in Turkey', reproduced in *Papers Relating to the Foreign Relations of the United States: The Paris Peace Conference 1919*, vol. 12 (Washington: United States Government Printing Office, 1947), 751.

III. LEAGUE OF NATIONS PUBLISHED DOCUMENTS

'Expulsion of the Œcumenical Patriarch from Constantinople—Letter from the Turkish Government to the Secretary-General of the League', LN Doc. C.160.1925.VII, *LNOJ* 6 (1925), 579.

'League of Nations Guarantee in respect of the Provisions contained in Articles 1 to 15 of the Treaty of Sèvres between the Principal Allied Powers and Greece', *LNOJ* 5 (1924), 1343.

'League of Nations Guarantee in respect of the Provisions contained in Articles 37 to 43 of the Treaty of Peace between the Principal Allied Powers, Greece, Roumania and the Kingdom of the Serbs, Croats and Slovenes, of the One Part, and Turkey, of the Other Part', *LNOJ* 5 (1924), 1344.

Nansen, Fridtjof. 'Reciprocal Exchange of Racial Minorities between Greece and Turkey', LN Doc. C.736.M.447.1922, *LNOJ* 4 (1923), 126.

Nansen, Fridtjof. 'Report by Dr. Fridtjof Nansen of an Enquiry by a Committee of Experts Made in Armenia under the Auspices of the International Labour Office (July 1925)', in *Scheme for the Settlement of Armenian Refugees: General Survey and Principal Documents*, LN Doc. C.699.M.264.1926.IV (Geneva: League of Nations, 1927), 65.

Protection of Linguistic, Racial and Religious Minorities by the League of Nations: Provisions Contained in the Various International Instruments at Present in Force, LN Doc. C.L.110.1927.I (Geneva: League of Nations, 1927).

'Question of the Expulsion of the Œcumenical Patriarch—Letter and Memorandum from the Greek Government to the Secretary-General of the League', LN Doc. C.211.M.70.1925.VII, *LNOJ* 6 (1925), 637.

'Report of the International Committee of Jurists Entrusted by the Council of the League of Nations with the Task of Giving an Advisory Opinion upon the Legal Aspects of the Aaland Islands Question', *LNOJ* Spec. Sup. No 3 (1920), 3.

'Resolution Adopted by the Council on September 5th, 1923', reproduced in *Protection of Linguistic, Racial or Religious Minorities by the League of Nations: Resolutions and Extracts from the Minutes of the Council, Resolutions and Reports Adopted by the Assembly, Relating to the Procedure to be Followed in Questions Concerning the Protection of Minorities*, LN Doc. C.24.M.18.1929.I (Geneva: League of Nations, 1929), 7.

IV. UNITED NATIONS PUBLISHED DOCUMENTS

Al-Khasawneh, Awn Shawkat. *Human Rights and Population Transfer: Final Report of the Special Rapporteur*, UN Doc. E/CN.4/Sub.2/1997/23 (1997).

Capotorti, Francesco. *Study on the Rights of Persons Belonging to Ethnic, Religious and Linguistic Minorities*, UN Doc. E/CN.4/Sub.2/384/Rev.1 (1979).

Falk, Richard. *Report of the Special Rapporteur on the Situation of Human Rights in the Palestinian Territories Occupied Since 1967*, UN Doc. A/HRC/16/72 (2011).

International Law Commission. *Report of the International Law Commission on the Work of Its Sixty-Fourth Session* (7 May–1 June, 2 July–3 August 2012), UN Doc. A/67/10.

V. *TRAVAUX PRÉPARATOIRES*

[Britain] *Lausanne Conference on Near Eastern Affairs (1922–1923): Records of Proceedings and Draft Terms of Peace* (Cmd 1814) (London: His Majesty's Stationery Office, 1923).

[Britain] *Protocols of Conferences Held at Paris Relative to the General Treaty of Peace* (London: Harrison & Sons, 1856).

[France] *Conférence de Lausanne sur les affaires du Proche-Orient (1922–1923). Recueil des Actes de la Conférence*, 6 vols. (Paris: Imprimerie nationale, 1923).

VI. LEGAL OPINIONS

Legal Issues Arising from Certain Population Transfers and Displacements on the Territory of the Republic of Cyprus in the Period since 20 July 1974, legal opinion prepared for the Republic of Cyprus by a committee of jurists (Georges Abi-Saab, Dieter Blumenwitz, James Crawford, John Dugard, Christopher Greenwood, Gerhard Hafner, Francisco Orrego Vicuña, Alain Pellet, Henry G. Schermers, and Christian Tomuschat) (30 June 1999), <http://www.cyprus.gov.cy/moi/pio/pio.nsf/All/A87E0AFB149260C3C2256D740028F4A2/$file/Opinion.pdf>.

VII. DOCUMENTS RELATING TO JUDGMENTS AND ADVISORY OPINIONS

Exchange of Greek and Turkish Populations, PCIJ Rep. Series C No 7-I (1925).

Expulsion of the Œcumenical Patriarch, PCIJ Rep. Series C No 9-II (1925).

VIII. POPULAR PUBLICATIONS

Aktan, Gündüz. 'Geleceğe Doğru (4)', *Radikal* (10 January 2006), <http://www.radikal.com.tr/haber.php?haberno=175378&tarih=10/01/2006>.

Editorial, *The Times*, 20 February 1857, 7.

Human Rights Watch. 'Ethiopia: Forced Relocations Bring Hunger, Hardship—Donor Funds Should Not Facilitate Abuse of Indigenous Groups' (17 January 2012), <http://www.hrw.org/news/2012/01/16/ethiopia-forced-relocations-bring-hunger-hardship>.

Human Rights Watch. 'France: Renewed Crackdown on Roma—End Discriminatory Roma Camp Evictions and Renewals' (10 August 2012), <http://www.hrw.org/news/2012/08/10/france-renewed-crackdown-roma>.

Human Rights Watch. '"They Say We Should Be Grateful": Mass Rehousing and Relocation Programs in Tibetan Areas of China' (June 2013), <http://www.hrw.org/sites/default/files/reports/tibet0613webwcover_0.pdf>.

Lane, Winthrop D. 'Why Greeks and Turks Oppose Being "Exchanged"', *New York Times Current History* 18 (1923), 86.

Near East Foundation. 'Near East Foundation Celebrates 90th Year; First U.S. International Development Organization; Pioneer of American Philanthropy Abroad' (2005), <http://www.neareast.org/images/uploads/90thanniv1.pdf>.

Ravid, Barak. 'Lieberman Presents Plans for Population Exchange at UN', *Haaretz* (28 September 2010), <http://www.haaretz.com/news/diplomacy-defense/lieberman-presents-plans-for-population-exchange-at-un-1.316197>.

IX. SECONDARY LITERATURE

'"A Different Reading of the International": Pierre Bourdieu and International Studies' (symposium), *International Political Sociology* 5 (2011).

Abou-El-Haj, Rifa'at 'Ali. *Formation of the Modern State: The Ottoman Empire, Sixteenth to Eighteenth Centuries*, 2nd ed. (Syracuse: Syracuse University Press, 2005).

Acer, Yücel. *The Aegean Maritime Disputes and International Law* (Aldershot: Ashgate, 2003).

Adams, Walter. 'Extent and Nature of the World Refugee Problem', *Annals of the American Academy of Political and Social Science* 203 (1939), 26.

Adanır, Fikret and Hilmar Kaiser. 'Migration, Deportation, and Nation-Building: The Case of the Ottoman Empire', in *Migrations et migrants dans une perspective historique: Permanences et innovations*, ed. René Leboutte (Bruxelles: P. I. E.–Peter Lang, 2000), 273.

Adelman, Howard and Elazar Barkan. *No Return, No Refuge: Rites and Rights in Minority Repatriation* (New York: Columbia University Press, 2011).

Ahmad, Feroz. *The Young Turks: The Committee of Union and Progress in Turkish Politics, 1908–1914* (Oxford: Clarendon Press, 1969).

Akarlı, Engin Deniz. 'The Tangled Ends of an Empire and Its Sultan', in *Modernity and Culture: From the Mediterranean to the Indian Ocean*, ed. Leila Tarazi Fawaz and C. A. Bayly (New York: Columbia University Press, 2002), 261.

Akçam, Taner. *A Shameful Act: The Armenian Genocide and the Question of Turkish Responsibility*, trans. Paul Bessemer (New York: Metropolitan Books, 2006).

Akçam, Taner. 'The Young Turks and the Plans for the Ethnic Homogenization of Anatolia', in *Shatterzone of Empires: Coexistence and Violence in the German, Habsburg, Russian, and Ottoman Borderlands*, ed. Omer Bartov and Eric D. Weitz (Bloomington: Indiana University Press, 2013), 258.

Akçam, Taner. *The Young Turks' Crime Against Humanity: The Armenian Genocide and Ethnic Cleansing in the Ottoman Empire* (Princeton: Princeton University Press, 2012).

Akçura, Yusuf. *Üç Tarz-ı Siyaset* (Ankara: Türk Tarih Kurumu Basımevi, 1976 [1904]).

Akgönül, Samim. *Une communauté, deux États: la minorité turco-musulmane de Thrace occidentale* (Istanbul: Les éditions Isis, 1999).

Akgönül, Samim. 'Les vestiges du système ottoman dans le traitement des minorités en Grèce et en Turquie', in *La perception de l'héritage ottoman dans les Balkans*, ed. Sylvie Gangloff (Paris: L'Harmattan, 2005), 43.

Akgönül, Samim. *Türkiye Rumları: Ulus-Devlet Çağından Küreselleşme Çağına Bir Azınlığın Yok Oluş Süreci*, trans. Ceylan Gürman (İstanbul: İletişim Yayınları, 2007).

Aksakal, Mustafa. *The Ottoman Road to War in 1914: The Ottoman Empire and the First World War* (Cambridge: Cambridge University Press, 2008).

Aktar, Ayhan. 'Cumhuriyetin İlk Yıllarında Uygulanan "Türkleştirme" Politikaları', in Ayhan Aktar, *Varlık Vergisi ve 'Türkleştirme' Politikaları* (İstanbul: İletişim Yayınları, 2000), 101.

Aktar, Ayhan. 'Nüfusun Homojenleştirilmesi ve Ekonominin Türkleştirilmesi Sürecinde Bir Aşama: Türk–Yunan Nüfus Mübadelesi 1923–1924', in Ayhan Aktar, *Varlık Vergisi ve 'Türkleştirme' Politikaları* (İstanbul: İletişim Yayınları, 2000), 17.

Aktar, Ayhan. 'Türk–Yunan Nüfus Mübadelesi ve Diplomasi', in Ayhan Aktar, *Türk Milliyetçiliği, Gayrimüslimler ve Ekonomik Dönüşüm* (İstanbul: İletişim Yayınları, 2006), 99.

Aktar, Ayhan. 'Varlık Vergisi Nasıl Uygulandı?', in Ayhan Aktar, *Varlık Vergisi ve 'Türkleştirme' Politikaları* (İstanbul: İletişim Yayınları, 2000), 135.
Aktar, Ayhan. 'Varlık Vergisi Sırasında Gayri Menkul Satışları ile Servet Transferi: İstanbul Tapu Kayıtlarının Analizi', in Ayhan Aktar, *Varlık Vergisi ve 'Türkleştirme' Politikaları* (İstanbul: İletişim Yayınları, 2000), 215.
Aktar, Ayhan and Damla Demirözü. 'Yunan Tarihyazımında Mübadele ve Göç', *Kebikeç* 22 (2006), 85.
Albrecht-Carrié, René. *A Diplomatic History of Europe since the Congress of Vienna* (New York: Harper & Brothers, 1958).
Alexandris, Alexis P. 'The Expulsion of Constantine VI: The Ecumenical Patriarchate and Greek–Turkish Relations, 1924–1925', *Balkan Studies* 22 (1981), 333.
Alexandris, Alexis P. *The Greek Minority of Istanbul and Greek–Turkish Relations, 1918–1974* (Athens: Centre for Asia Minor Studies, 1992).
Altuğ, Yılmaz M. *Turkey and Some Problems of International Law* (İstanbul: Yenilik Basımevi, 1958).
Al-Zaibag, Abdul-Malik Salim. 'The Mosul Boundary Question' (MA thesis, Tufts College, 1948).
American Committee Opposed to the Lausanne Treaty. *The Lausanne Treaty, Turkey and Armenia* (New York: n. p., 1926).
Anderson, Anders Hoejmark, Sarah Cooke, and Michael Wills. *New Majority: Chinese Population Transfer into Tibet* (London: Tibet Support Group, 1995).
Anderson, M. S. *The Eastern Question 1774–1923: A Study in International Relations* (London: Macmillan, 1966).
Anderson, Perry. *Lineages of the Absolutist State* (London: Verso, 1979).
Anghie, Antony. *Imperialism, Sovereignty and the Making of International Law* (Cambridge: Cambridge University Press, 2005).
Arai, Masami. *Turkish Nationalism in the Young Turk Era* (Leiden: Brill, 1992).
Aral, Berdal. 'An Inquiry into the Turkish "School" of International Law', *EJIL* 16 (2005), 769.
Argyll, George Douglas Campbell. *The Eastern Question; From the Treaty of Paris 1856 to the Treaty of Berlin 1878, and to the Second Afghan War*, vol. 1 (London: Strahan & Co., 1879).
Arı, Kemal. *Büyük Mübadele: Türkiye'ye Zorunlu Göç (1923–1925)* (İstanbul: Tarih Vakfı Yurt Yayınları, 1995).
Armstrong, S. W. 'The Doctrine of the Equality of Nations in International Law and the Relation of the Doctrine to the Treaty of Versailles', *AJIL* 14 (1920), 540.
Arslan, Ali. *Darülfünun'dan Üniversite'ye* (İstanbul: Kitabevi Yayınları, 1995).
Artinian, Vartan H. 'The Formation of Catholic and Protestant Millets in the Ottoman Empire', *Armenian Review* 28 (1975), 3.
Athanasopulos, Haralambos. *Greece, Turkey and the Aegean Sea: A Case Study in International Law* (Jefferson: McFarland & Co., 2001).
Aydın, Cemil. *The Politics of Anti-Westernism in Asia: Visions of World Order in Pan-Islamic and Pan-Asian Thought* (New York: Columbia University Press, 2007).
Åkermark, Athanasia Spiliopoulou. *Justifications of Minority Protection in International Law* (The Hague: Kluwer, 1997).
Badem, Candan. *The Ottoman Crimean War (1853–1856)* (Leiden: Brill, 2010).
Baer, Marc David. *The Dönme: Jewish Converts, Muslim Revolutionaries, and Secular Turks* (Stanford: Stanford University Press, 2010).

Bağış, Ali İhsan. *Osmanlı Ticaretinde Gayrî Müslimler: Kapitülasyonlar—Avrupa Tüccarları—Beratlı Tüccarlar—Hayriye Tüccarları (1750–1839)* (Ankara: Turhan Kitabevi, 1983).

Bain, J. Arthur. *Life and Adventures of Nansen, the Great Arctic Explorer* (London: The Walter Scott Publishing Co., 1897).

Bali, Rıfat N. *Cumhuriyet Yıllarında Türkiye Yahudileri: Bir Türkleştirme Serüveni (1923–1945)* (İstanbul: İletişim Yayınları, 1999).

Bali, Rıfat N. *The 'Varlık Vergisi' Affair: A Study on Its Legacy—Selected Documents* (Istanbul: Isis Press, 2005).

Balladore Pallieri, Giorgio. 'Les transferts internationaux de populations', *AIDI* 44 (1952-II), 138.

Balogh, Elemér. 'World Peace and the Refugee Problem', *RCADI* 75 (1949-II), 363.

Baltsiotis, Lambros. 'Yunanistan ve Türkiye'de Muhacirlik ve Nüfus Mübadeleleri: İki Farklı Anlatım ve Yorumun Oluşma Şartları ve Sonuçları', trans. Halil Mustafa, in *Yeniden Kurulan Yaşamlar: 1923 Türk–Yunan Zorunlu Nüfus Mübadelesi*, ed. Müfide Pekin (İstanbul: İstanbul Bilgi Üniversitesi Yayınları, 2005), 401.

Barkan, Ömer L. 'Osmanlı İmparatorluğunda Bir İskan ve Kolonizasyon Metodu Olarak Sürgünler', *İstanbul Üniversitesi İktisat Fakültesi Mecmuası* 11, 13, and 15 (1949–50, 1951–2, and 1953–4), 524, 56, and 209 (in three parts).

Barkey, Karen. *Empire of Difference: The Ottomans in Comparative Perspective* (Cambridge: Cambridge University Press, 2008).

Barlas, Dilek. 'Friends or Foes? Diplomatic Relations between Italy and Turkey, 1923–36', *International Journal of Middle East Studies* 36 (2004), 231.

Barton, James L. 'A Program for the Near East', *Annals of the American Academy of Political and Social Science* 108 (1923), 153.

Barton, James L. *Story of Near East Relief (1915–1930): An Interpretation* (New York: Macmillan, 1930).

Barton, James L. 'The Effect of the War on Protestant Missions', *Harvard Theological Review* 12 (1919), 1.

Barutciski, Michael. 'Les transferts de populations quatre-vingts ans après la Convention de Lausanne', *Canadian Yearbook of International Law* 41 (2003), 271.

Basdevant, Jules. 'La conclusion et la rédaction des traités et des instruments diplomatiques autres que les traités', *RCADI* 15 (1926-V), 535.

Bassiouni, M. Cherif. *Crimes against Humanity in International Criminal Law*, 2nd ed. (The Hague: Kluwer, 1999).

Baty, Thomas. *International Law in Twilight* (Tokyo: Maruzen Co., 1954).

Bayır, Derya. *Minorities and Nationalism in Turkish Law* (Farnham: Ashgate, 2013).

Baykara, Tuncer. *Osmanlılar'da Medeniyet Kavramı ve Ondokuzuncu Yüzyıla Dair Araştırmalar* (İzmir: Akademi Kitabevi, 2000).

Becker Lorca, Arnulf. 'Universal International Law: Nineteenth-Century Histories of Imposition and Appropriation', *HILJ* 51 (2010), 475.

Bederman, David J. 'The 1871 London Declaration, Rebus Sic Stantibus and a Primitivist View of the Law of Nations', *AJIL* 82 (1988), 1.

Bell, Duncan and Casper Sylvest. 'International Society in Victorian Political Thought: T. H. Green, Herbert Spencer, and Henry Sidgwick', *Modern Intellectual History* 3 (2006), 207.

Belli, Mihri. *Türkiye–Yunanistan Nüfus Mübadelesi: Ekonomik Açıdan Bir Bakış*, trans. Müfide Pekin (İstanbul: Belge Yayınları, 2006).

Bennett, G. H. *British Foreign Policy during the Curzon Period, 1919–24* (London: St. Martin's Press, 1995).
Benton, Lauren. *A Search for Sovereignty: Law and Geography in European Empires, 1400–1900* (Cambridge: Cambridge University Press, 2010).
Benton, Lauren. *Law and Colonial Cultures: Legal Regimes in World History, 1400–1900* (Cambridge: Cambridge University Press, 2002).
Bentwich, Norman. 'Nationality in Mandated Territories Detached from Turkey', *BYIL* 7 (1926), 97.
Bentwich, Norman. 'The League of Nations and Refugees', *BYIL* 16 (1935), 114.
Berkes, Niyazi. *The Development of Secularism in Turkey* (Montreal: McGill University Press, 1964).
Berman, Nathaniel. '"But the Alternative is Despair": European Nationalism and the Modernist Renewal of International Law', *Harvard Law Review* 106 (1993), 1792.
Bernard, Mountague. *On the Principle of Non-Intervention: A Lecture Delivered in the Hall of All Souls' College* (Oxford: J. H. and Jas. Parker, 1860).
Berridge, G. R. *British Diplomacy in Turkey, 1583 to the Present: A Study in the Evolution of the Resident Embassy* (Leiden: Nijhoff, 2009).
Berridge, G. R. *Gerald Fitzmaurice (1865–1939), Chief Dragoman of the British Embassy in Turkey* (Leiden: Nijhoff, 2007).
Berriedale Keith, A. 'The League of Nations and Mosul', *Journal of Comparative Legislation and International Law* 8 (1926), 38.
Bessel, Richard and Claudia B. Haake, eds. *Removing Peoples: Forced Removal in the Modern World* (Oxford: Oxford University Press, 2009).
Beşikçi, İsmail. *Tunceli Kanunu (1935) ve Dersim Jenosidi* (İstanbul: Belge Yayınları, 1990).
[Bilsel,] M. Cemil. *Lozan*, 2 vols. (İstanbul: Ahmet İhsan Matbaası, 1933).
Bjørnlund, Matthias. 'The 1914 Cleansing of Aegean Greeks as a Case of Violent Turkification', *Journal of Genocide Research* 10 (2008), 41.
Blaisdell, Donald C. *European Financial Control in the Ottoman Empire: A Study of the Establishment, Activities, and Significance of the Administration of the Ottoman Public Debt* (New York: Columbia University Press, 1929).
Bloxham, Donald. *The Great Game of Genocide: Imperialism, Nationalism, and the Destruction of the Ottoman Armenians* (Oxford: Oxford University Press, 2005).
Bloxham, Donald. 'The Great Unweaving: The Removal of Peoples in Europe, 1875–1949', in *Removing Peoples: Forced Removal in the Modern World*, ed. Richard Bessel and Claudia B. Haake (Oxford: Oxford University Press, 2009), 167.
Blumi, Isa. 'Agents of Post-Ottoman States: The Precariousness of the Berlin Congress Boundaries of Montenegro and How to Define/Confine People', in *War and Diplomacy: The Russo–Turkish War of 1877–1878 and the Treaty of Berlin*, ed. M. Hakan Yavuz with Peter Sluglett (Salt Lake City: University of Utah Press, 2011), 226.
Blumi, Isa. *Reinstating the Ottomans: Alternative Balkan Modernities, 1800–1912* (New York: Palgrave Macmillan, 2011).
Boghitchévitch, M. *Halbsouveränität: Administrative und politische Autonomie seit dem Pariser Vertrage (1856)* (Berlin: Verlag von Julius Springer, 1903).
Bonfils, Henri. *Hukuk-i Umumiye-yi Düvel*, ed. Paul Fauchille, trans. Ahmet Selâhattin and Mehmet Cemil (İstanbul: Matbaa-i Jirayir-Keteon, 1325 [1907–8]).
Boratav, Korkut. *Türkiye'de Devletçilik*, 2nd ed. (Ankara: İmge Kitabevi Yayınları, 2006).
Borchard, Edwin M. 'Basic Elements of Diplomatic Protection of Citizens Abroad', *AJIL* 7 (1913), 497.

Bourdieu, Pierre. 'From the King's House to the Reason of State: A Model of the Genesis of the Bureaucratic Field', in *Pierre Bourdieu and Democratic Politics: The Mystery of Ministry*, ed. Loïc Wacquant (Cambridge: Polity, 2005), 29.

Bourdieu, Pierre. 'The Force of Law: Toward a Sociology of the Juridical Field', trans. Richard Terdiman, *Hastings Law Journal* 38 (1987), 805.

Bowen, Herbert Wolcott. *International Law: A Simple Statement of Its Principles* (New York: G. P. Putnam's Sons, 1896).

Bowman, Isaiah. 'Constantinople and the Balkans', in *What Really Happened at Paris: The Story of the Peace Conference, 1918–1919*, ed. Edward Mandell House and Charles Seymour (New York: Charles Scribner's Sons, 1921), 140.

Bozarslan, Hamit. 'Kurdish Nationalism in Turkey: From Tacit Contract to Rebellion (1919–1925)', in *Essays on the Origins of Kurdish Nationalism*, ed. Abbas Vali (Costa Mesa: Mazda, 2003), 163.

Bozarslan, Hamit. 'L'alévisme et l'impossible équation du nationalisme en Turquie', in *Nationalismes en mutation en Méditerranée orientale*, ed. Alain Dieckhoff and Riva Kastoryano (Paris: CNRS Éditions, 2002), 133.

Bozkurt, Gülnihâl. *Batı Hukukunun Türkiye'de Benimsenmesi: Osmanlı Devleti'nden Türkiye Cumhuriyeti'ne Resepsiyon Süreci (1839–1939)* (Ankara: Türk Tarih Kurumu Basımevi, 1996).

Bozkurt, Gülnihâl. 'Tanzimat and Law', in *Tanzimat'ın 150. Yıldönümü Uluslararası Sempozyumu: Ankara: 31 Ekim—3 Kasım 1989* (Ankara: Türk Tarih Kurumu Basımevi, 1994), 279.

Braude, Benjamin and Bernard Lewis, eds. *Christians and Jews in the Ottoman Empire: The Functioning of a Plural Society*, 2 vols. (New York: Holmes & Meier, 1982).

Bridge, F. R. and Roger Bullen. *The Great Powers and the European States System 1815–1914* (London: Longman, 1980).

Brierly, J. L. 'Matters of Domestic Jurisdiction', *BYIL* 6 (1925), 8.

Brierly, J. L. *The Outlook for International Law* (Oxford: Clarendon Press, 1944).

Brinton, Jasper Yeates. *The Mixed Courts of Egypt* (New Haven: Yale University Press, 1930).

Brown, Philip Marshall. *Foreigners in Turkey; Their Juridical Status* (Princeton: Princeton University Press, 1914).

Brown, Philip Marshall. 'From Sèvres to Lausanne', *AJIL* 18 (1924), 113.

Brown, Philip Marshall. *International Society: Its Nature and Interests* (New York: Macmillan, 1923).

Brown, Philip Marshall. 'The Capitulations', *Foreign Affairs* 1 (1922–3), 71.

Buell, Raymond Leslie. 'The Protection of Minorities', *International Conciliation* 11 (1926), 348.

Bullard, Reader. *Large and Loving Privileges: The Capitulations in the Middle East and North Africa* (Glasgow: Jackson, Son, & Co., 1960).

Burgwyn, H. James. *Italian Foreign Policy in the Interwar Period 1918–1940* (Westport: Greenwood, 1997).

Butler, Geoffrey. 'Sovereignty and the League of Nations', *BYIL* 1 (1920–1), 35.

Buxton, Noel and T. P. Conwil-Evans. *Oppressed Peoples and the League of Nations* (London: J. M. Dent & Sons, 1922).

Cabanes, Bruno. *The Great War and the Origins of Humanitarianism 1918–1924* (Cambridge: Cambridge University Press, 2014).

Calderwood, H. B. *The Protection of Minorities by the League of Nations* (Geneva: Geneva Research Information Committee, 1931).

Caloyanni, M. A. 'The Balkan Union, the Balkan Conferences, and the Balkan Pact', *TGS* 18 (1932), 97 and *TGS* 19 (1933), 89 (in two parts).

Carty, Anthony. '19th Century Textbooks and International Law' (PhD dissertation, University of Cambridge, 1972).

Carty, Anthony. 'Thomas Baty: An International Lawyer as Public Intellectual between Imperial Japan and the Republic of China', *Japanese Yearbook of International Law* 56 (2013), 70.

Cassel, Pär Kristoffer. *Grounds of Judgment: Extraterritoriality and Imperial Power in Nineteenth-Century China and Japan* (Oxford: Oxford University Press, 2012).

Cassese, Antonio. 'Crimes Against Humanity: Comments on Some Problematical Aspects', in Antonio Cassese, *The Human Dimension of International Law: Selected Papers* (Oxford: Oxford University Press, 2008), 457.

Cassese, Antonio. *Self-Determination of Peoples: A Legal Reappraisal* (Cambridge: Cambridge University Press, 1995).

Cassimatis, Louis P. *American Influence in Greece 1917–1929* (Kent: Kent State University Press, 1988).

Chandler, David. *International Statebuilding: The Rise of Post-Liberal Governance* (Abingdon: Routledge, 2010).

Chang, Yi-ting. *The Interpretation of Treaties by Judicial Tribunals* (New York: Columbia University Press, 1933).

Chatty, Dawn. *Displacement and Dispossession in the Modern Middle East* (Cambridge: Cambridge University Press, 2010).

Chhangani, R. C. 'Expulsion of Uganda Asians and International Law', *Indian Journal of International Law* 12 (1972), 400.

Chirol, Valentine. 'Our Imperial Interests in Nearer and Further Asia', in *The Empire and the Century: A Series of Essays on Imperial Problems and Possibilities by Various Writers* (London: John Murray, 1905), 728.

Christopher, Emma, Cassandra Pybus, and Marcus Rediker, eds. *Many Middle Passages: Forced Migration and the Making of the Modern World* (Berkeley: University of California Press, 2007).

Clark, Bruce. *Twice a Stranger: The Mass Expulsions That Forged Modern Greece and Turkey* (Cambridge: Harvard University Press, 2006).

Claude Jr, Inis L. *National Minorities: An International Problem* (Cambridge: Harvard University Press, 1955).

Claude Jr, Inis L. *Swords into Plowshares: The Problems and Progress of International Organization*, 3rd ed. (New York: Random House, 1964).

Clavin, Patricia. *Securing the World Economy: The Reinvention of the League of Nations, 1920–1946* (Oxford: Oxford University Press, 2013).

Clogg, Richard. *A Concise History of Greece*, 3rd ed. (Cambridge: Cambridge University Press, 2013).

Clogg, Richard. 'A Millet Within a Millet: The Karamanlides', in *Ottoman Greeks in the Age of Nationalism: Politics, Economy, and Society in the Nineteenth Century*, ed. Dimitri Gondicas and Charles Issawi (Princeton: Darwin Press, 1999), 115.

Cohen, G. Daniel. 'The "Human Rights Revolution" at Work: Displaced Persons in Postwar Europe', in *Human Rights in the Twentieth Century*, ed. Stefan-Ludwig Hoffmann (New York: Cambridge University Press, 2011), 45.

Cole, Juan. *Napoleon's Egypt: Invading the Middle East* (New York: Palgrave Macmillan, 2007).

Comstock, John L. *History of the Greek Revolution, Compiled from Official Documents of the Greek Government . . .* (New York: William W. Reed & Co., 1828).

Conolly, Violet. *Soviet Economic Policy in the East: Turkey, Persia, Afghanistan, Mongolia and Tana Tuva, Sin Kiang* (London: Oxford University Press, 1933).

Corbett, P. E. 'What is the League of Nations?', *BYIL* 5 (1924), 119.

Cowan, Jane K. 'The Success of Failure? Minority Supervision at the League of Nations', in *Paths to International Justice: Social and Legal Perspectives*, ed. Marie-Bénédicte Dembour and Tobias Kelly (Cambridge: Cambridge University Press, 2007), 29.

Cowan, Jane K. 'Who's Afraid of Violent Language? Honour, Sovereignty and Claims-Making in the League of Nations', *Anthropological Theory* 3 (2003), 271.

Crampton, R. J. *Bulgaria* (Oxford: Oxford University Press, 2007).

Crampton, R. J. 'The Turks in Bulgaria, 1878–1944', in *The Turks of Bulgaria: The History, Culture and Political Fate of a Minority*, ed. K. H. Karpat (Istanbul: Isis Press, 1990), 43.

Curzon, George Nathaniel. *Lord Curzon in India, Being a Selection from His Speeches as Viceroy and Governor-General of India 1898–1905* (London: Macmillan, 1906).

Cuthell, David. 'A Kemalist Gambit: A View of the Political Negotiations in the Determination of the Turkish–Iraqi Border', in *The Creation of Iraq, 1914–1921*, ed. Reeva Spector Simon and Eleanor H. Tejirian (New York: Columbia University Press, 2004), 80.

Cuthell, David. 'The Circassian Sürgün', *Ab Imperio* 2003 (2003-II), 139.

Çanlı, Mehmet. 'Yunanistan'daki Türklerin Anadolu'ya Nakledilmesi I', *Tarih ve Toplum* 129 (1994), 54.

Çoker, Fahri. '"Dârülfünûn-i Osmani" ve "Mekteb-i Hukuk"', *Tarih ve Toplum* 121 (1994), 26.

Dadrian, Vahakn N. 'Genocide as a Problem of National and International Law: The World War I Armenian Case and Its Contemporary Legal Ramifications', *Yale Journal of International Law* 14 (1989), 221.

Dadrian, Vahakn N. and Taner Akçam. *Judgment at Istanbul: The Armenian Genocide Trials* (New York: Berghahn, 2011).

Dakin, Douglas. 'The Importance of the Greek Army in Thrace during the Conference of Lausanne 1922–1923', in *Greece and Great Britain during World War I: First Symposium Organized in Thessaloniki (December 15–17, 1983) by the Institute for Balkan Studies in Thessaloniki and King's College in London* (Thessaloniki: Institute for Balkan Studies, 1985), 211.

Daniel, Robert L. *American Philanthropy in the Near East, 1820–1960* (Athens: Ohio University Press, 1970).

Davison, Roderic H. 'Ottoman Diplomacy at the Congress of Paris (1856) and the Question of Reforms', in *VII. Türk Tarih Kongresi (Ankara: 25–29 Eylül 1970)—Kongreye Sunulan Bildiriler*, vol. 2 (Ankara: Türk Tarih Kurumu Basımevi, 1973), 580.

Davison, Roderic H. *Reform in the Ottoman Empire, 1856–1876* (Princeton: Princeton University Press, 1963).

Davison, Roderic H. '"Russian Skill and Turkish Imbecility": The Treaty of Kuchuk Kainardji Reconsidered', *Slavic Review* 35 (1976), 463.

Davison, Roderic H. 'The Armenian Crisis, 1912–1914', *American Historical Review* 53 (1948), 481.

Davison, Roderic H. 'The Ottoman Empire and the Congress of Berlin', in *Der Berliner Kongress von 1878: Die Politik der Grossmächte und die Probleme der Modernisierung in Südosteuropa in der zweiten Hälfte des 19. Jahrhunderts*, ed. Ralph Melville and Hans-Jürgen Schröder (Wiesbaden: Franz Steiner Verlag, 1982), 205.

Dawisha, Adeed. *Arab Nationalism in the Twentieth Century: From Triumph to Despair* (Princeton: Princeton University Press, 2003).

Dawn, C. Ernest. 'The Quality of Arab Nationalism', in *Arab Nation, Arab Nationalism*, ed. Derek Hopwood (Houndmills: Macmillan, 2000), 41.

Dawn, C. Ernest. 'The Rise of Arabism in Syria', in C. Ernest Dawn, *From Ottomanism to Arabism: Essays on the Origins of Arab Nationalism* (Urbana: University of Illinois Press, 1973), 148.

Dawson, Grant and Sonia Farber. *Forcible Displacement Throughout the Ages: Towards an International Convention for the Prevention and Punishment of the Crime of Forcible Displacement* (Leiden: Nijhoff, 2012).

Demirözü, Damla. 'The Greek–Turkish Rapprochement of 1930 and the Repercussions of the Ankara Convention in Turkey', *Journal of Islamic Studies* 19 (2008), 309.

Deringil, Selim. *The Well-Protected Domains: Ideology and the Legitimation of Power in the Ottoman Empire 1876–1909* (London: Tauris, 1998).

Devedji, Alexandre. *L'échange obligatoire des minorités grecques et turques en vertu de la convention de Lausanne du 30 janvier 1923* (Paris: Imprimerie du Montparnasse et de Persan-Beaumont, 1929).

Dewey, John. 'Foreign Schools in Turkey', *The New Republic* 41 (1924), 40.

Dezalay, Yves. 'Les courtiers de l'international: héritiers cosmopolites, mercenaires de l'impérialisme et missionnaires de l'universel', *Actes de la recherche en sciences sociales* 151–2 (2004), 5.

Dezalay, Yves and Bryant G. Garth. *Asian Legal Revivals: Lawyers in the Shadow of Empire* (Chicago: University of Chicago Press, 2010).

Dezalay, Yves and Bryant G. Garth. *Dealing in Virtue: International Commercial Arbitration and the Construction of a Transnational Legal Order* (Chicago: University of Chicago Press, 1996).

Dezalay, Yves and Bryant G. Garth. *The Internationalization of Palace Wars: Lawyers, Economists, and the Contest to Transform Latin American States* (Chicago: University of Chicago Press, 2002).

de Azcárate, Pablo. *League of Nations and National Minorities: An Experiment* (Washington: Carnegie Endowment for International Peace, 1945).

de Jessen, M. F. 'Grèce et Turquie—protection des minorités—échange obligatoire des populations turques et grecques', *RGDIP* 30 (1923), 514.

de Vattel, Emer. *Le droit des gens, ou Principes de la loi naturelle, appliqués à la conduite et aux affaires des Nations et des Souverains*, vol. 1 (Londres: n.p., 1758).

de Visscher, Charles. 'Protection of Minorities', in Charles de Visscher, *The Stabilization of Europe: Lectures on the Harris Foundation, 1924* (Chicago: University of Chicago Press, 1924), 27.

de Zayas, Alfred-Maurice. *A Terrible Revenge: The Ethnic Cleansing of the East European Germans*, 2nd ed. (New York: Palgrave Macmillan, 2006).

de Zayas, Alfred-Maurice. 'Collective Expulsions: Norms, Jurisprudence, Remedies', *Refugee Survey Quarterly* 16 (1997), 149.

de Zayas, Alfred-Maurice. 'Forced Population Transfer', in *Max Planck Encyclopedia of Public International Law*, <http://www.mpepil.com>.

de Zayas, Alfred-Maurice. 'International Law and Mass Population Transfers', *HILJ* 16 (1975), 207.

de Zayas, Alfred-Maurice. *Nemesis at Potsdam: The Anglo-Americans and the Expulsion of the Germans—Background, Execution, Consequences* (London: Routledge & Kegan Paul, 1977).
de Zayas, Alfred-Maurice. 'The Istanbul Pogrom of 6–7 September 1955 in the Light of International Law', *Genocide Studies and Prevention* 2 (2007), 137.
Dickinson, Edwin DeWitt. *The Equality of States in International Law* (Cambridge: Harvard University Press, 1920).
Djordjević, Dimitrije. 'Migrations During the 1912–1913 Balkan Wars and World War One', in *Migrations in Balkan History*, ed. Ivan Ninić (Belgrade: Serbian Academy of Sciences and Arts, 1989), 115.
Djuvara, T. G. *Cent projets de partage de la Turquie (1281–1913)* (Paris: Librairie Félix Alcan, 1914).
Doğan, Mehmet Ali and Heather J. Sharkey, eds. *American Missionaries and the Middle East: Foundational Encounters* (Salt Lake City: University of Utah Press, 2011).
Douglas, R. M. *Orderly and Humane: The Expulsion of the Germans after the Second World War* (New Haven: Yale University Press, 2012).
Doumanis, Nicholas. *Before the Nation: Muslim-Christian Coexistence and Its Destruction in Late Ottoman Anatolia* (Oxford: Oxford University Press, 2013).
Dragostinova, Theodora. *Between Two Motherlands: Nationality and Emigration among the Greeks of Bulgaria, 1900–1949* (Ithaca: Cornell University Press, 2011).
Drandar, A. G. *Les événements politiques en Bulgarie depuis 1876 jusqu'à nos jours* (Bruxelles: T. Falk & Cie, 1896).
Drew, Catriona J. 'Population Transfer: The Untold Story of the International Law of Self-Determination' (PhD dissertation, University of London, 2005).
Duguit, Léon. *Le droit social, le droit individuel et la transformation de l'Etat*, 2nd ed. (Paris: Félix Alcan, 1911).
Dupuy, René-Jean. 'La Révolution française et le droit international actuel', *RCADI* 214 (1989-II), 9.
Durand, André. *From Sarajevo to Hiroshima: History of the International Committee of the Red Cross* (Geneva: Henry Dunant Institute, 1984).
Dündar, Fuat. *Modern Türkiye'nin Şifresi: İttihat ve Terakki'nin Etnisite Mühendisliği (1913–1918)* (İstanbul: İletişim Yayınları, 2008).
Earle, Edward Mead. 'The Secret Anglo–German Convention of 1914 Regarding Asiatic Turkey', *Political Science Quarterly* 38 (1923), 24.
Ehrlich, Ludwik. 'L'interprétation des traités', *RCADI* 24 (1928-IV), 1.
Ekrem, Reşat. *Osmanlı Muahedeleri ve Kapitülâsiyonlar, 1300–1920, ve Lozan Muahedesi, 24 Temmuz 1923* (İstanbul: Muallim Ahmet Halit Kitaphanesi, 1934).
Eldem, Edhem. 'Capitulations and Western Trade', in *The Cambridge History of Turkey*, vol. 3, ed. Suraiya N. Faroqhi (Cambridge: Cambridge University Press, 2006), 283.
Eldem, Edhem. 'Ottoman Financial Integration with Europe: Foreign Loans, the Ottoman Bank and the Ottoman Public Debt', *European Review* 13 (2005), 431.
Eltis, David, ed. *Coerced and Free Migration: Global Perspectives* (Stanford: Stanford University Press, 2002).
Eminov, Ali. *Turkish and Other Muslim Minorities in Bulgaria* (London: C. Hurst & Co., 1997).
Engelhardt, Ed. *La Turquie et le Tanzimat, ou Histoire des réformes dans l'Empire ottoman depuis 1826 jusqu'à nos jours*, 2 vols. (Paris: A. Cotillon & Cie, 1882–4).
Epstein, M. *The Early History of the Levant Company* (London: George Routledge & Sons, 1908).

Erozan, Hüseyin Boğaç. 'Producing Obedience: Law Professors and the Turkish State' (PhD dissertation, University of Minnesota, 2005).
Essad, Mahmoud. *Du régime des capitulations ottomanes: leur caractère juridique d'après l'histoire et les textes* (Stamboul: Fratelli Haim, 1928).
Evans, Malcolm D. *Religious Liberty and International Law in Europe* (Cambridge: Cambridge University Press, 1997).
Evriviades, Marios L. 'The Legal Dimension of the Cyprus Conflict', *Texas International Law Journal* 10 (1975), 227.
Fachiri, Alexander P. *The Permanent Court of International Justice: Its Constitution, Procedure and Work*, 2nd ed. (London: Oxford University Press, 1932).
Fahmy, Khaled. *All the Pasha's Men: Mehmed Ali, His Army and the Making of Modern Egypt* (Cambridge: Cambridge University Press, 1997).
Fairman, Charles. 'The Interpretation of Treaties', *TGS* 20 (1934), 123.
Feis, Herbert. *Europe the World's Banker 1870–1914: An Account of European Foreign Investment and the Connection of World Finance with Diplomacy before the War* (New Haven: Yale University Press, 1930).
Findley, Carter V. *Bureaucratic Reform in the Ottoman Empire: The Sublime Porte, 1789–1922* (Princeton: Princeton University Press, 1980).
Findley, Carter V. 'The Foundation of the Ottoman Foreign Ministry', *International Journal of Middle East Studies* 3 (1972), 388.
Findley, Carter V. 'The Legacy of Tradition to Reform: Origins of the Ottoman Foreign Ministry', *International Journal of Middle East Studies* 1 (1970), 334.
Fink, Carole. *Defending the Rights of Others: The Great Powers, the Jews, and International Minority Protection, 1878–1938* (Cambridge: Cambridge University Press, 2004).
Fink, Carole. 'The Minorities Question at the Paris Peace Conference: The Polish Minority Treaty, June 28, 1919', in *The Treaty of Versailles: A Reassessment After 75 Years*, ed. Manfred F. Boemeke, Gerald D. Feldman, and Elisabeth Glaser (Washington: German Historical Institute/Cambridge: Cambridge University Press, 1998), 249.
Fiore, Pasquale. *Nouveau droit international public, suivant les besoins de la civilisation moderne*, 2nd ed., trans. Charles Antoine, vol. 1 (Paris: A. Durand & Pedone-Lauriel, 1885).
Fischer-Tiné, Harald. 'Global Civil Society and the Forces of Empire: The Salvation Army, British Imperialism, and the "Prehistory" of NGOs (ca. 1880–1920)', in *Competing Visions of World Order: Global Moments and Movements, 1880s–1930s*, ed. Sebastian Conrad and Dominic Sachsenmaier (New York: Palgrave Macmillan, 2007), 29.
Fisher, John. 'The Interdepartmental Committee on Eastern Unrest and British Responses to Bolshevik and Other Intrigues against the Empire during the 1920s', *Journal of Asian History* 34 (2000), 1.
Fleet, Kate. *European and Islamic Trade in the Early Ottoman State: The Merchants of Genoa and Turkey* (Cambridge: Cambridge University Press, 1999).
Fockema Andreæ, J. P. *An Important Chapter from the History of Legal Interpretation: The Jurisdiction of the First Permanent Court of International Justice (1922–1940)* (Leyden: Sijthoff, 1948).
Forsythe, David P. *The Humanitarians: The International Committee of the Red Cross* (Cambridge: Cambridge University Press, 2005).
Fox, Gregory H. *Humanitarian Occupation* (Cambridge: Cambridge University Press, 2008).
Fragistas, Charalambos N. 'Le droit musulman en Grèce', *Annales de la Faculté de droit d'Istanbul* 4 (1954), 129.

Frank, Matthew. *Expelling the Germans: British Opinion and Post-1945 Population Transfer in Context* (Oxford: Oxford University Press, 2007).

Fuad, Ali. *La question des Détroits: ses origines, son évolution, sa solution à la Conférence de Lausanne* (Paris: Imprimerie du Montparnasse et de Persan-Beaumont, 1928).

Fuccaro, Nelida. 'Minorities and Ethnic Mobilisation: The Kurds in Northern Iraq and Syria', in *The British and French Mandates in Comparative Perspectives*, ed. Nadine Méouchy and Peter Sluglett (Leiden: Brill, 2004), 579.

Garibian, Sévane. 'From the 1915 Allied Joint Declaration to the 1920 Treaty of Sèvres: Back to an International Criminal Law in Progress', *Armenian Review* 52 (2010), 87.

Gatrell, Peter. *The Making of the Modern Refugee* (Oxford: Oxford University Press, 2013).

Geshkoff, Theodore I. *Balkan Union: A Road to Peace in Southeastern Europe* (New York: Columbia University Press, 1940).

Gingeras, Ryan. *Sorrowful Shores: Violence, Ethnicity, and the End of the Ottoman Empire, 1912–1923* (Oxford: Oxford University Press, 2009).

Ginio, Eyal. 'Paving the Way for Ethnic Cleansing: Eastern Thrace During the Balkan Wars (1912–1913) and Their Aftermath', in *Shatterzone of Empires: Coexistence and Violence in the German, Habsburg, Russian, and Ottoman Borderlands*, ed. Omer Bartov and Eric D. Weitz (Bloomington: Indiana University Press, 2013), 283.

Girard, André. *Les minorités nationales ethniques et religieuses en Bulgarie* (Paris: Marcel Giard, 1933).

Gladstone, W. E. *Bulgarian Horrors and the Question of the East* (London: John Murray, 1876).

Gladstone, W. E. *The Berlin Treaty and the Anglo–Turkish Convention* (London: Liberal Central Association, 1878).

Goebel, Christopher M. 'Population Transfer, Humanitarian Law, and the Use of Ground Force in U.N. Peacemaking: Bosnia and Herzegovina in the Wake of Iraq', *New York University Journal of International Law and Politics* 25 (1993), 627.

Gong, Gerrit W. *The Standard of 'Civilization' in International Society* (Oxford: Clarendon Press, 1984).

Gorman, Daniel. 'Liberal Internationalism, the League of Nations Union, and the Mandates System', *Canadian Journal of History* 40 (2005), 449.

Gorman, Daniel. *The Emergence of International Society in the 1920s* (Cambridge: Cambridge University Press, 2012).

Göçek, Fatma Müge. 'The Decline of the Ottoman Empire and the Emergence of Greek, Armenian, Turkish, and Arab Nationalisms', in *Social Constructions of Nationalism in the Middle East*, ed. Fatma Müge Göçek (Albany: State University of New York Press, 2002), 15.

Göçek, Fatma Müge. 'The Politics of History and Memory: A Multidimensional Analysis of the Lausanne Peace Conference, 1922–1923', in *Histories of the Modern Middle East: New Directions*, ed. Israel Gershoni, Hakan Erdem, and Ursula Woköck (Boulder: Lynne Rienner, 2002), 207.

Göçek, Fatma Müge and M. Şükrü Hanioğlu. 'Western Knowledge, Imperial Control, and the Use of Statistics in the Ottoman Empire', in *Cultural Horizons: A Festschrift in Honor of Talat S. Halman*, ed. Jayne L. Warner (Syracuse: Syracuse University Press/ İstanbul: Yapı Kredi Yayınları, 2001), 105.

Gökay, Bülent. *A Clash of Empires: Turkey between Russian Bolshevism and British Imperialism, 1918–1923* (London: Tauris, 1997).

Gökay, Bülent. 'The Kurdish Question in Turkey: Historical Roots, Domestic Concerns and International Law', in *Minorities, Peoples, and Self-Determination: Essays in Honour of Patrick Thornberry*, ed. Nazila Ghanea and Alexandra Xanthaki (Leiden: Nijhoff, 2005), 315.

Grabill, Joseph L. *Protestant Diplomacy and the Near East: Missionary Influence on American Policy, 1810–1927* (Minneapolis: University of Minnesota Press, 1971).

Grahl-Madsen, Atle. 'The League of Nations and the Refugees', in *The League of Nations in Retrospect: Proceedings of the Symposium Organized by the United Nations Library and the Graduate Institute of International Studies, Geneva, 6–9 November 1980* (Berlin: Walter de Gruyter, 1983), 358.

Grew, Joseph C. *Turbulent Era: A Diplomatic Record of Forty Years, 1904–1945*, ed. Walter Johnson, vol. 1 (Boston: Houghton, Mifflin, & Co., 1952).

Grigoriadis, Ioannis N. *Instilling Religion in Greek and Turkish Nationalism: A 'Sacred Synthesis'* (New York: Palgrave Macmillan, 2013).

Guieu, Jean-Michel. 'The Debate About a European Institutional Order among International Legal Scholars in the 1920s and Its Legacy', *Contemporary European History* 21 (2012), 319.

Guilhot, Nicolas. *The Democracy Makers: Human Rights and the Politics of Global Order* (New York: Columbia University Press, 2005).

Guizot, François. *Mémoires pour servir à l'histoire de mon temps*, vol. 7 (Paris: Michel Lévy frères, 1865).

Gülalp, Haldun. 'Capitalism and the Modern Nation-State: Rethinking the Creation of the Turkish Republic', *Journal of Historical Sociology* 7 (1994), 155.

Hanioğlu, M. Şükrü. *A Brief History of the Late Ottoman Empire* (Princeton: Princeton University Press, 2008).

Hanley, Will. 'When Did Egyptians Stop Being Ottomans? An Imperial Citizenship Case Study', in *Multilevel Citizenship*, ed. Willem Maas (Philadelphia: University of Pennsylvania Press, 2013), 89.

Haraszti, György. 'Treaties and the Fundamental Change of Circumstances', *RCADI* 146 (1975-III), 1.

Hartmann, Hans W. 'Les relations gréco–turques du traité de Lausanne au pacte d'Ankara, 1923–1933', *Les Balkans* 11 (1939), 333.

Harvard Research in International Law. 'Law of Treaties', *AJIL Sup.* 29 (1935), 653.

Haslam, Emily. 'Population, Expulsion and Transfer', in *Max Planck Encyclopedia of Public International Law*, <http://www.mpepil.com>.

Haslam, Emily. 'Unlawful Population Transfer and the Limits of International Criminal Law', *Cambridge Law Journal* 61 (2002), 66.

Hathaway, James C. *The Rights of Refugees under International Law* (Cambridge: Cambridge University Press, 2005).

Hell, Stefan. *Siam and the League of Nations: Modernisation, Sovereignty and Multilateral Diplomacy, 1920–1940* (Bangkok: River Books, 2010).

Henckaerts, Jean-Marie. *Mass Expulsion in Modern International Law and Practice* (The Hague: Nijhoff, 1995).

Hershey, Amos S. 'History of International Law since the Peace of Westphalia', *AJIL* 6 (1912), 30.

Heyking, Alphonse. 'The International Protection of Minorities—The Achilles' Heel of the League of Nations', *TGS* 13 (1927), 31.

Hicks, Frederick Charles. *The New World Order: International Organization, International Law, International Coöperation* (Garden City: Doubleday, Page, & Co., 1920).

Higgins, Rosalyn. 'The Role of National Courts in the International Legal Process', in Rosalyn Higgins, *Problems and Process: International Law and How We Use It* (Oxford: Clarendon, 1994), 205.

Hinckley, Frank E. *American Consular Jurisdiction in the Orient* (Washington: W. H. Lowdermilk & Co., 1906).

Hirschon, Renée, ed. *Crossing the Aegean: An Appraisal of the 1923 Compulsory Population Exchange between Greece and Turkey* (New York: Berghahn, 2003).

Hobsbawm, Eric. *The Age of Revolution: Europe, 1789–1848* (London: Weidenfeld and Nicolson, 1962).

Hobson, J. A. *Imperialism: A Study* (London: James Nisbet & Co., 1902).

Hodges, Henry G. *The Doctrine of Intervention* (Princeton: Banner Press, 1915).

Holborn, Louise W. 'The Legal Status of Political Refugees, 1920–1938', *AJIL* 32 (1938), 680.

Holland, Thomas Erskine. *Lectures on International Law*, ed. Thomas Alfred Walker and Wyndham Legh Walker (London: Sweet & Maxwell, 1933).

Holland, Thomas Erskine, ed. *The European Concert in the Eastern Question: A Collection of Treaties and Other Public Acts* (Oxford: Clarendon Press, 1885).

Holquist, Peter. '"In Accord with State Interests and the People's Wishes": The Technocratic Ideology of Imperial Russia's Resettlement Administration', *Slavic Review* 69 (2010), 151.

Holquist, Peter. 'The Politics and Practice of the Russian Occupation of Armenia, 1915–February 1917', in *A Question of Genocide: Armenians and Turks at the End of the Ottoman Empire*, ed. Ronald Grigor Suny, Fatma Müge Göçek, and Norman M. Naimark (Oxford: Oxford University Press, 2011), 151.

Holquist, Peter. 'The Russian Empire as a "Civilized State": International Law as Principle and Practice in Imperial Russia, 1874–1878', National Council for Eurasian and East European Research grant document (2004), <http://www.ucis.pitt.edu/nceeer/2004_818-06g_Holquist.pdf>.

Housden, Martyn. 'White Russians Crossing the Black Sea: Fridtjof Nansen, Constantinople and the First Modern Repatriation of Refugees Displaced by Civil Conflict, 1922–23', *Slavonic and East European Review* 88 (2010), 495.

Howard, Harry N. *The King-Crane Commission: An American Inquiry in the Middle East* (Beirut: Khayats, 1963).

Hudson, Manley O. 'Law Reform in Turkey', *American Bar Association Journal* 13 (1927), 5.

Hudson, Manley O. *Progress in International Organization* (Stanford: Stanford University Press, 1932).

Hudson, Manley O. *The World Court, 1921–1938: A Handbook of the Permanent Court of International Justice*, 5th ed. (Boston: World Peace Foundation, 1938).

Huntford, Roland. *Fridtjof Nansen and the Unmixing of Greeks and Turks in 1924* (Oslo: Norwegian Academy of Science and Letters, 1998).

Huntford, Roland. *Nansen: The Explorer as Hero* (London: Duckworth, 1997).

Hurewitz, J. C. 'Ottoman Diplomacy and the European State System', *Middle East Journal* 15 (1961), 141.

Hurewitz, J. C. 'The Europeanization of Ottoman Diplomacy: The Conversion from Unilateralism to Reciprocity in the Nineteenth Century', *Belleten* 25 (1961), 455.

Hyde, Charles Cheney. 'The Interpretation of Treaties by the Permanent Court of International Justice', *AJIL* 24 (1930), 1.

Innes, Kathleen E. *The Story of Nansen and the League of Nations* (London: Friends Peace Committee, 1931).
Ivanoff, J. *Les Bulgares devant le Congrès de la Paix: Documents historiques, ethnographiques et diplomatiques* (Berne: Paul Haupt. Librairie académique, 1919).
İnalcık, Halil. 'Imtiyāzāt', in *The Encyclopaedia of Islam: New Edition*, vol. 3, ed. Bernard Lewis et al. (Leiden: Brill, 1971), 1179.
İnalcık, Halil. 'Ottoman Methods of Conquest', *Studia Islamica* 2 (1954), 103.
İpek, Nedim. *Rumeli'den Anadolu'ya Türk Göçleri (1877–1890)* (Ankara: Türk Tarih Kurumu Basımevi, 1994).
Jackson Preece, Jennifer. *National Minorities and the European Nation-States System* (Oxford: Clarendon Press, 1998).
Jenks, C. Wilfred. *The Prospects of International Adjudication* (London: Stevens & Sons, 1964).
Johnston, W. Ross. *Sovereignty and Protection: A Study of British Jurisdictional Imperialism in the Late Nineteenth Century* (Durham: Duke University Press, 1973).
Jones, Francis C. *Extraterritoriality in Japan and the Diplomatic Relations Resulting in Its Abolition, 1853–1899* (New Haven: Yale University Press, 1931).
Jwaideh, Wadie. *The Kurdish National Movement: Its Origins and Development* (Syracuse: Syracuse University Press, 2006).
Kabbara, Samy. *Le régime des Détroits (Bosphore et Dardanelles) avant et depuis le traité de Lausanne* (Lyon: Imprimerie Bosc frères & Riou, 1929).
Kamouzis, Dimitris. 'Reciprocity or International Intervention? Greek and Turkish Minority Policy, 1923–1930', in *Reciprocity: Greek and Turkish Minorities—Law, Religion and Politics*, ed. Samim Akgönül (İstanbul: İstanbul Bilgi University Press, 2008), 49.
Kansu, Aykut. *The Revolution of 1908 in Turkey* (Leiden: Brill, 1997).
Karacan, Ali Naci. *Lozan Konferansı ve İsmet Paşa* (İstanbul: Maarif Matbaası, 1943).
Karaömerlioğlu, M. Asım. 'Helphand-Parvus and His Impact on Turkish Intellectual Life', *Middle Eastern Studies* 40 (2004), 145.
Karpat, Kemal H. *Ottoman Population, 1830–1914: Demographic and Social Characteristics* (Madison: University of Wisconsin Press, 1985).
Karpat, Kemal H. 'The Muslim Minority in the Balkans', in Kemal H. Karpat, *Studies on Turkish Politics and Society: Selected Articles and Essays* (Leiden: Brill, 2004), 523.
Karpat, Kemal H. 'The Ottoman Adoption of Statistics from the West in the 19th Century', in Kemal H. Karpat, *Studies on Ottoman Social and Political History: Selected Articles and Essays* (Leiden: Brill, 2002), 132.
Karpat, Kemal H. *The Politicization of Islam: Reconstructing Identity, State, Faith, and Community in the Late Ottoman State* (Oxford: Oxford University Press, 2001).
Karpat, Kemal H. 'The Transformation of the Ottoman State, 1789–1908', *International Journal of Middle East Studies* 3 (1972), 243.
Karvounarakis, Theo. 'End of an Empire: Great Britain, Turkey and Greece from the Treaty of Sevres to the Treaty of Lausanne', *Balkan Studies* 41 (2000), 171.
Kasaba, Reşat. *A Moveable Empire: Ottoman Nomads, Migrants, and Refugees* (Seattle: University of Washington Press, 2009).
Kasaba, Reşat. 'A Time and a Place for the Nonstate: Social Change in the Ottoman Empire during the "Long Nineteenth Century"', in *State Power and Social Forces: Domination and Transformation in the Third World*, ed. Joel S. Migdal, Atul Kohli, and Vivienne Shue (Cambridge: Cambridge University Press, 1994), 207.

Kasaba, Reşat. *The Ottoman Empire and the World Economy: The Nineteenth Century* (Albany: State University of New York Press, 1988).

Kasaba, Reşat. 'Was There a Compradore Bourgeoisie in Mid-Nineteenth-Century Western Anatolia?', *Review* 11 (1988), 215.

Kattan, Victor. *From Coexistence to Conquest: International Law and the Origins of the Arab–Israeli Conflict, 1891–1949* (London: Pluto Press, 2009).

Katz, Yossi. 'Transfer of Population as a Solution to International Disputes: Population Exchanges between Greece and Turkey as a Model for Plans to Solve the Jewish–Arab Dispute in Palestine during the 1930s', *Political Geography* 11 (1992), 55.

Kayalı, Hasan. *Arabs and Young Turks: Ottomanism, Arabism, and Islamism in the Ottoman Empire, 1908–1918* (Berkeley: University of California Press, 1997).

Kazgan, Gülten. 'Millî Türk Devletinin Kuruluşu ve Göçler', *İstanbul Üniversitesi İktisat Fakültesi Mecmuası* 30 (1970–1), 311.

Keene, Edward. *Beyond the Anarchical Society: Grotius, Colonialism and Order in World Politics* (Cambridge: Cambridge University Press, 2002).

Keeton, G. W. *The Development of Extraterritoriality in China*, 2 vols. (London: Longmans, Green, & Co., 1928).

Keitner, Chimène I. *The Paradoxes of Nationalism: The French Revolution and Its Meaning for Contemporary Nation Building* (Albany: State University of New York Press, 2007).

Kelsen, Hans. *Legal Technique in International Law: A Textual Critique of the League Covenant* (Geneva: Geneva Research Centre, 1939).

Kemal, Mustafa. 'Ankara Hukuk Fakültesinin Açılışında (5.XI.1925)', in *Türkiye'de Siyasal Kültürün Resmî Kaynakları*, ed. Taha Parla, vol. 3 (İstanbul: İletişim Yayınları, 1992), 292.

Kemal, Mustafa. 'Gazi Mustafa Kemal Paşa Hazretlerinin İlk Türkiye İktisat Kongresindeki İftitahī Nutukları', in *İzmir İktisat Kongresi (17 Şubat–4 Mart 1923)*, ed. A. Afetinan (Ankara: Türk Tarih Kurumu Basımevi, 1982), 57.

Kennedy, C. M. *The Influence of Christianity upon International Law* (Cambridge: Macmillan, 1856).

Kennedy, David. 'The Move to Institutions', *Cardozo Law Review* 8 (1987), 841.

Keyder, Çağlar. 'Bir Türk Milliyetçilik Tarihi ve Coğrafyası', in Çağlar Keyder, *Memâlik-i Osmaniye'den Avrupa Birliği'ne* (İstanbul: İletişim Yayınları, 2003), 73.

Keyder, Çağlar. 'The Consequences of the Exchange of Populations for Turkey', in *Crossing the Aegean: An Appraisal of the 1923 Compulsory Population Exchange between Greece and Turkey*, ed. Renée Hirschon (New York: Berghahn, 2003), 39.

Keyder, Çağlar. *The Definition of a Peripheral Economy: Turkey 1923–1929* (Cambridge: Cambridge University Press/Paris: Éditions de la Maison des sciences de l'homme, 1981).

Kévonian, Dzovinar. *Réfugiés et diplomatie humanitaire: Les acteurs européens et la scène proche-orientale pendant l'entre-deux-guerres* (Paris: Publications de la Sorbonne, 2004).

Khadduri, Majid. 'The Alexandretta Dispute', *AJIL* 39 (1945), 406.

Khalidi, Rashid. 'Ottomanism and Arabism in Syria Before 1914: A Reassessment', in *The Origins of Arab Nationalism*, ed. Rashid Khalidi et al. (New York: Columbia University Press, 1991), 50.

Khan, Yasmin. *The Great Partition: The Making of India and Pakistan* (New Haven: Yale University Press, 2007).

Kieser, Hans-Lukas. *Nearest East: American Millennialism and Mission to the Middle East* (Philadelphia: Temple University Press, 2010).

Kieser, Hans-Lukas. *Vorkämpfer der 'Neuen Türkei': Revolutionäre Bildungseliten am Genfersee (1870–1939)* (Zürich: Chronos, 2005).

Kieser, Hans-Lukas. 'World War and World Revolution: Alexander Helphand-Parvus in Germany and Turkey', *Kritika: Explorations in Russian and Eurasian History* 12 (2011), 387.

Kiosséoglou, Th. P. *L'échange forcé des minorités d'après le Traité de Lausanne* (Nancy: Imprimerie nancéienne, 1926).

Kırzıoğlu, M. Fahrettin. *Bütünüyle Erzurum Kongresi*, vol. 2 (Ankara: Kültür Ofset, 1993).

Knop, Karen. *Diversity and Self-Determination in International Law* (Cambridge: Cambridge University Press, 2002).

Kocabaşoğlu, Uygur. *Anadolu'daki Amerika: Kendi Belgeleriyle 19. Yüzyılda Osmanlı İmparatorluğu'ndaki Amerikan Misyoner Okulları* (Ankara: İmge Kitabevi Yayınları, 2000).

Kolodny, Emile. 'Primauté de l'identité religieuse sur la citoyenneté: le cas des échanges obligatoires de population entre la Grèce et la Turquie (1923)', in *Religion et identité. Actes du colloque d'Aix-en-Provence, octobre 1996*, ed. Gabriel Audisio (Aix-en-Provence: Publications de l'Université de Provence, 1998), 134.

Kontogiorgi, Elisabeth. 'Economic Consequences following Refugee Settlement in Greek Macedonia, 1923–1932', in *Crossing the Aegean: An Appraisal of the 1923 Compulsory Population Exchange between Greece and Turkey*, ed. Renée Hirschon (New York: Berghahn, 2003), 63.

Kontogiorgi, Elisabeth. *Population Exchange in Greek Macedonia: The Rural Settlement of Refugees 1922–1930* (Oxford: Clarendon Press, 2006).

Korhonen, Outi. 'The "State-Building Enterprise": Legal Doctrine, Progress Narratives and Managerial Governance', in *The Role of International Law in Rebuilding Societies after Conflict: Great Expectations*, ed. Brett Bowden, Hilary Charlesworth, and Jeremy Farrall (Cambridge: Cambridge University Press, 2009), 15.

Koskenniemi, Martti. 'Into Positivism: Georg Friedrich von Martens (1756–1821) and Modern International Law', *Constellations* 15 (2008), 189.

Koskenniemi, Martti. *The Gentle Civilizer of Nations: The Rise and Fall of International Law 1870–1960* (Cambridge: Cambridge University Press, 2001).

Koskenniemi, Martti. 'The Legacy of the Nineteenth Century', in *Routledge Handbook of International Law*, ed. David Armstrong (London: Routledge, 2009), 141.

Kostopoulou, Elektra. 'The Art of Being Replaced: The Last of the Cretan Muslims Between the Empire and the Nation-State', in *Religion, Ethnicity and Contested Nationhood in the Former Ottoman Space*, ed. Jørgen Nielsen (Leiden: Brill, 2012), 129.

Köksal, Yonca. 'Rethinking Nationalism: State Projects and Community Networks in 19th-Century Ottoman Empire', *American Behavioral Scientist* 51 (2008), 1498.

Köse, Yavuz. 'Nestlé in the Ottoman Empire: Global Marketing with Local Flavour 1870–1927', *Enterprise and Society* 9 (2008), 724.

Kövér, Gustave. *Histoire d'une trahison: le calvaire des minorités nationales et la Société des Nations* (Genève: Éditions du Bureau central des minorités, 1939).

Kövér, Gustave. *L'erreur initiale de la Société des Nations: Documents pour servir à l'histoire de la question minoritaire* (Genève: Éditions du Bureau central des minorités, 1940).

Kreiten, Irma. 'A Colonial Experiment in Cleansing: The Russian Conquest of Western Caucasus, 1856–65', *Journal of Genocide Research* 11 (2009), 213.

Kulischer, Eugene M. *The Displacement of Population in Europe* (Montreal: International Labour Office, 1943).

Kuneralp, Sinan and Emre Öktem, eds. *Chambre des conseillers légistes de la Sublime Porte: Rapports, avis et consultations sur la condition juridique des ressortissants étrangers, le statut des communautés non musulmanes et les relations internationales de l'Empire ottoman (1864–1912)* (Istanbul: Les éditions Isis, 2012).
Kunz, Josef L. 'L'option de nationalité', *RCADI* 31 (1930-I), 107.
Kunz, Josef L. 'The Law of Nations, Static and Dynamic', *AJIL* 27 (1933), 630.
Kurmuş, Orhan. 'The 1838 Treaty of Commerce Re-examined', in *Économie et sociétés dans l'Empire ottoman (fin du XVIIIe—début du XXe siècle). Actes du colloque de Strasbourg (1er–5 juillet 1980)*, ed. Jean-Louis Bacqué-Grammont and Paul Dumont (Paris: Éditions du Centre national de la recherche scientifique, 1983), 411.
Ladas, Stephen P. *The Exchange of Minorities: Bulgaria, Greece and Turkey* (New York: Macmillan, 1932).
Laski, Harold J. *Studies in the Problem of Sovereignty* (New Haven: Yale University Press, 1917).
Lauren, Paul Gordon. 'Human Rights in History: Diplomacy and Racial Equality at the Paris Peace Conference', *Diplomatic History* 2 (1978), 257.
Lauterpacht, Hersch. 'International Law and Colonial Questions, 1870–1914', in *International Law, Being the Collected Papers of Hersch Lauterpacht*, ed. Elihu Lauterpacht, vol. 2 (Cambridge: Cambridge University Press, 1975), 95.
Lauterpacht, Hersch. 'Restrictive Interpretation and the Principle of Effectiveness in the Interpretation of Treaties', *BYIL* 26 (1949), 48.
Lauterpacht, Hersch. *The Development of International Law by the International Court*, 2nd ed. (London: Stevens & Sons, 1958).
Lauterpacht, Hersch. 'The Pact of Paris and the Budapest Articles of Interpretation', *TGS* 20 (1934), 178.
Laven, David and Lucy Riall. 'Restoration Government and the Legacy of Napoleon', in *Napoleon's Legacy: Problems of Government in Restoration Europe*, ed. David Laven and Lucy Riall (Oxford: Berg, 2000), 1.
Lawrence, T. J. 'The Primacy of the Great Powers', in T. J. Lawrence, *Essays on Some Disputed Questions in Modern International Law*, 2nd ed. (Cambridge: Deighton, Bell, & Co., 1885), 208.
Lawrence, T. J. *The Principles of International Law* (London: Macmillan, 1895).
Lawrence, T. J. *The Principles of International Law*, 4th ed. (Boston: D. C. Heath & Co., 1910).
Leach, Henry Goddard. 'Fridtjof Nansen', *University of Kansas City Review* 14 (1948), 167.
Lenin, V. I. 'Imperialism, the Highest Stage of Capitalism' [1917], in V. I. Lenin, *Collected Works*, vol. 22, trans. Yuri Sdobnikov (Moscow: Progress Publishers, 1964), 185.
Leontiades, Leonidas. 'Der griechisch–türkische Bevölkerungsaustausch', *ZaöRV* 5 (1935), 546.
Lerner, Natan. 'The Evolution of Minority Rights in International Law', in *Peoples and Minorities in International Law*, ed. Catherine Brölmann, René Lefeber, and Marjoleine Zieck (Dordrecht: Nijhoff, 1993), 77.
'Les musulmans en Grèce', *Revue du monde musulman* 28 (1914), 323.
Levene, Mark. 'Creating a Modern "Zone of Genocide": The Impact of Nation- and State-Formation on Eastern Anatolia, 1878–1923', *Holocaust and Genocide Studies* 12 (1998), 393.
Liebich, André. 'Minority as Inferiority: Minority Rights in Historical Perspective', *Review of International Studies* 34 (2008), 243.

Lipsett, H. Caldwell. *Lord Curzon in India 1898–1903* (London: R. A. Everett & Co., 1903).

Liu, Shih Shun. *Extraterritoriality: Its Rise and Its Decline* (New York: Columbia University Press, 1925).

Llewellyn Smith, Michael. *Ionian Vision: Greece in Asia Minor 1919–1922*, 2nd ed. (London: C. Hurst & Co., 1998).

Llewellyn Smith, Michael. 'Venizelos' Diplomacy, 1910–23: From Balkan Alliance to Greek–Turkish Settlement', in *Eleftherios Venizelos: The Trials of Statesmanship*, ed. Paschalis M. Kitromilides (Edinburgh: Edinburgh University Press, 2008), 134.

Loewenfeld, Erwin. 'The Protection of Private Property under the Minorities Protection Treaties', *TGS* 16 (1930), 41.

Loizos, Peter. 'Ottoman Half-Lives: Long-Term Perspectives on Particular Forced Migrations', *Journal of Refugee Studies* 12 (1999), 237.

Lorimer, James. 'Does the Corân Supply an Ethical Basis on Which a Political Superstructure Can Be Raised?' [1877–8], in James Lorimer, *Studies National and International, Being Occasional Lectures Delivered in the University of Edinburgh 1864–1889* (Edinburgh: William Green & Sons, 1890), 132.

Lorimer, James. 'Of the Denationalisation of Constantinople and Its Devotion to International Purposes' [1876], in James Lorimer, *Studies National and International, Being Occasional Lectures Delivered in the University of Edinburgh 1864–1889* (Edinburgh: William Green & Sons, 1890), 121.

Lorimer, James. *The Institutes of the Law of Nations: A Treatise of the Jural Relations of Separate Political Communities*, vol. 1 (Edinburgh: William Blackwood & Sons, 1883).

Lutfi, K. Omer. *Die völkerrechtliche Stellung Bulgariens und Ostrumeliens* (Erlangen: E. Th. Jacob, 1903).

Lybyer, Albert H. 'The Balkan Situation', *Journal of International Relations* 10 (1920), 404.

Macar, Elçin. *Cumhuriyet Döneminde İstanbul Rum Patrikhanesi* (İstanbul: İletişim Yayınları, 2003).

Macar, Elçin. 'Lozan'dan Günümüze Onikiada Türklerinin Sorunları', *İstanbul Üniversitesi Siyasal Bilgiler Fakültesi Dergisi* 34 (2006), 35.

Macartney, C. A. *National States and National Minorities* (London: Oxford University Press, 1934).

MacMillan, Margaret. *Paris 1919: Six Months That Changed the World* (New York: Random House, 2001).

Mair, L. P. *The Protection of Minorities: The Working and Scope of the Minorities Treaties under the League of Nations* (London: Christophers, 1928).

Makdisi, Ussama. *Artillery of Heaven: American Missionaries and the Failed Conversion of the Middle East* (Ithaca: Cornell University Press, 2008).

Makdisi, Ussama. 'Ottoman Orientalism', *American Historical Review* 107 (2002), 768.

Mandelstam, André. 'La Déclaration des droits internationaux de l'homme adoptée par l'Institut de droit international', *Revue de droit international* 5 (1930), 59.

Mandelstam, André. *La justice ottomane dans ses rapports avec les puissances étrangères* (Paris: A. Pedone, 1908).

Mandelstam, André. 'La protection des minorités', *RCADI* 1 (1923-I), 363.

Mandelstam, André. *La Société des Nations et les puissances devant le problème arménien* (Paris: A. Pedone, 1926).

Mandelstam, André. *Le sort de l'Empire ottoman* (Paris: Librairie Payot & Cie, 1917).

Manela, Erez. *The Wilsonian Moment: Self-Determination and the International Origins of Anticolonial Nationalism* (New York: Oxford University Press, 2007).

Mardin, Şerif. *The Genesis of Young Ottoman Thought: A Study in the Modernization of Turkish Political Ideas* (Princeton: Princeton University Press, 1962).

Marrin, Albert. *The Last Crusade: The Church of England in the First World War* (Durham: Duke University Press, 1974).

Marriott, J. A. R. *The Eastern Question: An Historical Study in European Diplomacy* (Oxford: Clarendon Press, 1917).

Marrus, Michael R. *The Unwanted: European Refugees in the Twentieth Century* (Philadelphia: Temple University Press, 1985).

Martens, F. *Das Consularwesen und die Consularjurisdiction im Orient*, trans. H. Skerst (Berlin: Weidmannsche Buchhandlung, 1874).

Martinez, Jenny S. *The Slave Trade and the Origins of International Human Rights Law* (New York: Oxford University Press, 2012).

Marx, Karl and Friedrich Engels. 'For Poland' [1875], trans. Paul Jackson, in Karl Marx, *The First International and After*, ed. David Fernbach (Harmondsworth: Penguin/New Left Review, 1974), 388.

Masters, Bruce. 'The Sultan's Entrepreneurs: The *Avrupa Tüccarıs* and the *Hayriye Tüccarıs* in Syria', *International Journal of Middle East Studies* 24 (1992), 579.

Mayer, Arno J. *Wilson vs. Lenin: Political Origins of the New Diplomacy, 1917–1918* (Cleveland: World Publishing Co., 1964).

Mazard, Jean Albert. *Le régime des capitulations en Turquie pendant la guerre de 1914* (Alger: Imprimerie Jean Gaudet, 1923).

Mazower, Mark. *Governing the World: The History of an Idea* (New York: Penguin, 2012).

Mazower, Mark. *Greece and the Inter-war Economic Crisis* (Oxford: Clarendon Press, 1991).

Mazower, Mark. *No Enchanted Palace: The End of Empire and the Ideological Origins of the United Nations* (Princeton: Princeton University Press, 2009).

Mazzini, Giuseppe. 'On Nonintervention' [1851], in *A Cosmopolitanism of Nations: Giuseppe Mazzini's Writings on Democracy, Nation Building, and International Relations*, ed. Stefano Recchia and Nadia Urbinati (Princeton: Princeton University Press, 2009), 213.

Mazzini, Giuseppe. 'The European Question: Foreign Intervention and National Self-Determination' [1847], in *A Cosmopolitanism of Nations: Giuseppe Mazzini's Writings on Democracy, Nation Building, and International Relations*, ed. Stefano Recchia and Nadia Urbinati (Princeton: Princeton University Press, 2009), 193.

McCarthy, Justin. *Death and Exile: The Ethnic Cleansing of Ottoman Muslims, 1821–1922* (Princeton: Darwin Press, 1995).

McDowall, David. *A Modern History of the Kurds*, 3rd ed. (London: Tauris, 2004).

McGarry, John. '"Demographic Engineering": The State-Directed Movement of Ethnic Groups as a Technique of Conflict Regulation', *Ethnic and Racial Studies* 21 (1998), 613.

McKinnon Wood, Hugh. 'The Treaty of Paris and Turkey's Status in International Law', *AJIL* 37 (1943), 262.

McMeekin, Sean. *The Berlin–Baghdad Express: The Ottoman Empire and Germany's Bid for World Power* (Cambridge: Harvard University Press, 2012).

McNair, Arnold D. 'Equality in International Law', *Michigan Law Review* 26 (1927), 131.

McNair, Arnold D. 'The Functions and Differing Legal Character of Treaties', *BYIL* 11 (1930), 100.

Meijknecht, Anna. *Towards International Personality: The Position of Minorities and Indigenous Peoples in International Law* (Antwerp: Intersentia, 2001).

Meindersma, Christa. 'Population Exchanges: International Law and State Practice', *International Journal of Refugee Law* 9 (1997), 335 and 613 (in two parts).
Meray, Seha L. *Devletler Hukukuna Giriş*, vol. 1 (Ankara: Ajans-Türk Matbaası, 1959).
Mestre, Achille. *L'étranger en Turquie d'après le Traité de Lausanne* (Paris: Revue politique et parlementaire, 1923).
Meyer, James H. 'Immigration, Return, and the Politics of Citizenship: Russian Muslims in the Ottoman Empire, 1860–1914', *International Journal of Middle East Studies* 39 (2007), 15.
Miller, David Hunter. *The Drafting of the Covenant*, 2 vols. (New York: G. P. Putnam's Sons, 1928).
Mirkine-Guetzévitch, Boris. 'L'influence de la Révolution française sur le développement du droit international dans l'Europe orientale', *RCADI* 22 (1928-II), 295.
Mirkova, Anna M. '"Population Politics" at the End of Empire: Migration and Sovereignty in Ottoman Eastern Rumelia, 1877–1886', *Comparative Studies in Society and History* 55 (2013), 955.
Molony, William O'Sullivan. *Nationality and the Peace Treaties* (London: George Allen & Unwin, 1934).
Mourelos, Yannis G. 'The 1914 Persecutions and the First Attempt at an Exchange of Minorities between Greece and Turkey', *Balkan Studies* 26 (1985), 389.
Murphey, Rhoads. *Exploring Ottoman Sovereignty: Tradition, Image and Practice in the Ottoman Imperial Household, 1400–1800* (London: Continuum, 2008).
Musgrave, Thomas D. *Self-Determination and National Minorities* (Oxford: Oxford University Press, 1997).
Myles, Eric. '"Humanity", "Civilization" and the "International Community" in the Late Imperial Russian Mirror: Three Ideas "Topical for our Days"', *Journal of the History of International Law* 4 (2002), 310.
Naff, Thomas. 'The Ottoman Empire and the European States System', in *The Expansion of International Society*, ed. Hedley Bull and Adam Watson (Oxford: Clarendon Press, 1984), 143.
Naimark, Norman M. *Fires of Hatred: Ethnic Cleansing in Twentieth-Century Europe* (Cambridge: Harvard University Press, 2001).
Nakracas, Georgios. *Anadolu ve Rum Göçmenlerin Kökeni: 1922 Emperyalist Yunan Politikasi ve Anadolu Felaketi*, trans. İbram Onsunoğlu (İstanbul: Belge Yayınları, 2003).
Nansen, Fridtjof. *Armenia and the Near East* (London: George Allen & Unwin, 1928).
Nansen, Fridtjof. *In Northern Mists: Arctic Exploration in Early Times*, 2 vols., trans. Arthur G. Chater (London: William Heinemann, 1911).
Nansen, Fridtjof. *Norway and the Union with Sweden* (London: Macmillan, 1905).
Nansen, Fridtjof, ed. *The Norwegian North Polar Expedition, 1893–1896: Scientific Results*, 6 vols. (Christiania: Jacob Dybwad, 1900–5).
Nansen, Fridtjof. 'The Suffering People of Europe', in *Nobel Lectures: Peace*, ed. Frederick W. Haberman, vol. 1 (Amsterdam: Elsevier, 1972), 361.
Nansen, Fridtjof. *Through Siberia, the Land of the Future*, trans. Arthur G. Chater (London: William Heinemann, 1914).
Nansen, Fridtjof. *Vers le Pôle*, trans. Charles Rabot (Paris: Ernest Flammarion, 1897).
Near East Relief. *Report to Congress for 1923* (New York: Near East Relief, 1924).
Necatigil, Zaim M. *The Cyprus Question and the Turkish Position in International Law*, 2nd ed. (Oxford: Oxford University Press, 1993).

Neuburger, Mary. *The Orient Within: Muslim Minorities and the Negotiation of Nationhood in Modern Bulgaria* (Ithaca: Cornell University Press, 2004).

Nicolson, Harold. *Curzon: The Last Phase 1919–1925: A Study in Post-war Diplomacy* (London: Constable & Co., 1934).

Nicolson, Harold. *The Congress of Vienna: A Study in Allied Unity: 1812–1822* (London: Constable & Co., 1946).

Nijman, Janne E. 'Minorities and Majorities', in *The Oxford Handbook of the History of International Law*, ed. Anne Peters and Bardo Fassbender (Oxford: Oxford University Press, 2012), 95.

Noel Baker, P. J. 'Nansen and Norway', in *Nansen: A Book of Homage*, ed. J. Howard Whitehouse (London: Hodder and Stoughton, 1930), 83.

Nollkaemper, André. *National Courts and the International Rule of Law* (Oxford: Oxford University Press, 2011).

Noradounghian, Gabriel. 'Le traité turco–belge de 1838 et la compétence en matière pénale des autorités ottomanes envers les étrangers', *RDILC* 8 (1906), 119.

Nur, Rıza. *Hayat ve Hatıratım*, vol. 3 (İstanbul: Altındağ Yayınevi, 1968).

Ogier, Marcel. 'L'élaboration des clauses économiques du Traité de Lausanne', *Revue de droit international* 1 (1927), 301.

Olson, Robert. *The Emergence of Kurdish Nationalism and the Sheikh Said Rebellion, 1880–1925* (Austin: University of Texas Press, 1989).

'On Freedom of Commerce in the Ottoman Empire', *Moniteur ottoman* [n.d.], reproduced in *Opinions of the European Press on the Eastern Question, Translated and Extracted from Turkish, German, French, and English Papers and Reviews*, ed. David Ross (London: James Ridgway & Sons, 1836), 1.

Oppenheim, L. *International Law: A Treatise*, 2nd ed., vol. 1 (London: Longmans, Green, & Co., 1912).

Oppenheim, L. *International Law: A Treatise*, 3rd ed., ed. Ronald F. Roxburgh, vol. 1 (London: Longmans, Green, & Co., 1920).

Oppenheim, L. *The League of Nations and Its Problems: Three Lectures* (London: Longmans, Green, & Co., 1919).

Oran, Baskın. 'Lausanne Barış Antlaşması', in *Türk Dış Politikası: Kurtuluş Savaşından Bugüne Olgular, Belgeler, Yorumlar*, ed. Baskın Oran, vol. 1 (İstanbul: İletişim Yayınları, 2001), 215.

Oran, Baskın. 'The Minority Concept and Rights in Turkey: The Lausanne Peace Treaty and Current Issues', in *Human Rights in Turkey*, ed. Zehra F. Kabasakal Arat (Philadelphia: University of Pennsylvania Press, 2007), 35.

Oran, Baskın. 'The Story of Those Who Stayed: Lessons from Articles 1 and 2 of the 1923 Convention', in *Crossing the Aegean: An Appraisal of the 1923 Compulsory Population Exchange between Greece and Turkey*, ed. Renée Hirschon (New York: Berghahn, 2003), 97.

Oran, Baskın. *Türkiye'de Azınlıklar: Kavramlar, Teori, Lozan, İç Mevzuat, İçtihat, Uygulama* (İstanbul: İletişim Yayınları, 2004).

Orhonlu, Cengiz. *Osmanlı İmparatorluğunda Aşiretlerin İskânı* (İstanbul: Eren Yayıncılık ve Kitapçılık, 1987).

Ostroróg, Léon. *Pour la réforme de la justice ottomane* (Paris: Pedone, 1912).

Owen, Roger. *The Middle East in the World Economy 1800–1914* (London: Methuen, 1981).

Örücü, Esin. 'The Impact of European Law on the Ottoman Empire and Turkey', in *European Expansion and Law: The Encounter of European and Indigenous Law in*

19th- and 20th-Century Africa and Asia, ed. W. J. Mommsen and J. A. de Moor (Oxford: Berg, 1992), 39.

Özbek, Nadir. *Osmanlı İmparatorluğu'nda Sosyal Devlet: Siyaset, İktidar ve Meşruiyet 1876–1914* (İstanbul: İletişim Yayınları, 2002).

Özcan, Azmi. *Pan-Islamism: Indian Muslims, the Ottomans and Britain (1877–1924)* (Leiden: Brill, 1997).

Özdemir, Renk. 'Borders of Belonging in the "Exchanged" Generations of Karamanlis', in *Land of Diverse Migrations: Challenges of Emigration and Immigration in Turkey*, ed. Ahmet İçduygu and Kemal Kirişci (İstanbul: İstanbul Bilgi University Press, 2009), 29.

Özel, Oktay. 'Migration and Power Politics: The Settlement of Georgian Immigrants in Turkey (1878–1908)', *Middle Eastern Studies* 46 (2010), 477.

Özsu, Umut. 'Agency, Universality, and the Politics of International Legal History', *HILJ Online* 51 (2010), 58, <http://www.harvardilj.org/2010/10/online_52_ozsu/>.

'Pacifier et punir' (symposium), *Actes de la recherche en sciences sociales* 173–4 (2008).

Pallis, A. A. 'The Exchange of Populations in the Balkans', *The Nineteenth Century and After* 97 (1925), 376.

Pamuk, Şevket. 'Economic Change in Twentieth-Century Turkey: Is the Glass More Than Half Full?', in *The Cambridge History of Turkey*, vol. 4, ed. Reşat Kasaba (Cambridge: Cambridge University Press, 2008), 266.

Pamuk, Şevket. 'The Ottoman Economy in World War I', in *The Economics of World War I*, ed. Stephen Broadberry and Mark Harrison (Cambridge: Cambridge University Press, 2005), 112.

Pamuk, Şevket. *The Ottoman Empire and European Capitalism, 1820–1913: Trade, Investment and Production* (Cambridge: Cambridge University Press, 1987).

Panaite, Viorel. *The Ottoman Law of War and Peace: The Ottoman Empire and Tribute Payers* (Boulder: East European Monographs, 2000).

Pandolfi, Mariella. 'From Paradox to Paradigm: The Permanent State of Emergency in the Balkans', in *Contemporary States of Emergency: The Politics of Military and Humanitarian Interventions*, ed. Didier Fassin and Mariella Pandolfi (New York: Zone Books, 2010), 153.

Papadopoulos, Alexander. *Persecution of the Greeks in Turkey Before the European War* (New York: Oxford University Press, 1919).

Pappe, Ilan. *The Ethnic Cleansing of Palestine* (Oxford: Oneworld, 2006).

Parvus Efendi. *Türkiye'nin Malî Tutsaklığı*, ed. Muammer Sencer (İstanbul: May Yayınları, 1977).

Pedersen, Susan. 'Getting Out of Iraq—in 1932: The League of Nations and the Road to Normative Statehood', *American Historical Review* 115 (2010), 975.

Pedersen, Susan. 'The Meaning of the Mandates System: An Argument', *Geschichte und Gesellschaft* 32 (2006), 560.

Pekin, Müfide, ed. *Yeniden Kurulan Yaşamlar: 1923 Türk–Yunan Zorunlu Nüfus Mübadelesi* (İstanbul: İstanbul Bilgi Üniversitesi Yayınları, 2005).

Pekin, Müfide and Çimen Turan, eds. *Mübadele Bibliyografyası: Lozan Nüfus Mübadelesi İle İlgili Yayınlar ve Yayımlanmamış Çalışmalar* (İstanbul: Lozan Mübadilleri Vakfı, 2002).

Pentzopoulos, Dimitri. *The Balkan Exchange of Minorities and Its Impact upon Greece* (Paris: Mouton & Co., 1962).

Petropulos, John A. 'The Compulsory Exchange of Populations: Greek–Turkish Peacemaking, 1922–1930', *Byzantine and Modern Greek Studies* 2 (1976), 135.

Petrov, Milen V. 'Everyday Forms of Compliance: Subaltern Commentaries on Ottoman Reform, 1864–1868', *Comparative Studies in Society and History* 46 (2004), 730.

Petsalis-Diomidis, N. *Greece at the Paris Peace Conference (1919)* (Thessaloniki: Institute for Balkan Studies, 1978).

Pélissié du Rausas, G. *Le régime des capitulations dans l'Empire ottoman*, vol. 1 (Paris: Arthur Rousseau, 1902).

Phillimore, Robert. *Commentaries upon International Law*, vol. 1 (Philadelphia: T. & J. W. Johnson, 1854).

Piana, Francesca. 'L'humanitaire d'après-guerre: prisonniers de guerre et réfugiés russes dans la politique du Comité international de la Croix-Rouge et de la Société des Nations', *Relations internationales* 151 (2012), 63.

Pitts, Jennifer. 'Boundaries of Victorian International Law', in *Victorian Visions of Global Order: Empire and International Relations in Nineteenth-Century Political Thought*, ed. Duncan Bell (Cambridge: Cambridge University Press, 2007), 67.

Politis, Nicolas. *La guerre gréco–turque au point de vue du droit international: contribution à l'étude de la question d'Orient* (Paris: A. Pedone, 1898).

Politis, Nicolas. 'Le problème des limitations de la souveraineté et la théorie de l'abus des droits dans les rapports internationaux', *RCADI* 6 (1925-I), 1.

Politis, Nicolas. 'Le transfert des populations', *Politique étrangère* 5 (1940), 83.

Politis, Nicolas. 'Les capitulations et la justice répressive ottomane à propos de l'affaire Joris', *Revue de droit international privé et de droit pénal international* 2 (1906), 659.

Pollard, A. F. *The League of Nations: An Historical Argument* (Oxford: Clarendon Press, 1918).

Pomeroy, John Norton. *Lectures on International Law in Time of Peace*, ed. Theodore Salisbury Woolsey (Boston: Houghton, Mifflin, & Co., 1886).

Popplewell, Richard J. *Intelligence and Imperial Defence: British Intelligence and the Defence of the Indian Empire 1904–1924* (London: Frank Cass, 1995).

Psomiades, Harry J. *The Eastern Question: The Last Phase—A Study in Greek–Turkish Diplomacy*, 2nd ed. (New York: Pella, 2000).

Quataert, Donald. 'The Age of Reforms, 1812–1914', in *An Economic and Social History of the Ottoman Empire*, ed. Halil İnalcık and Donald Quataert, vol. 2 (Cambridge: Cambridge University Press, 1994), 759.

Raitz von Frentz, Christian. *A Lesson Forgotten: Minority Protection under the League of Nations—The Case of the Germany Minority in Poland, 1920–1934* (Münster: Lit Verlag/New York: St. Martin's Press, 1999).

Rajak, Svetozar. 'The Cold War in the Balkans, 1945–1956', in *The Cambridge History of the Cold War*, ed. Melvyn P. Leffler and Odd Arne Westad, vol. 1 (Cambridge: Cambridge University Press, 2010), 198.

Rappard, William E. *International Relations as Viewed from Geneva* (New Haven: Yale University Press, 1925).

Rechid, Ahmed. 'La condition des étrangers dans la République de Turquie', *RCADI* 46 (1933-IV), 165.

Redslob, Robert. *Le principe des nationalités: les origines, les fondements psychologiques, les forces adverses, les solutions possibles* (Paris: Recueil Sirey, 1930).

Renan, Ernest. *Qu'est-ce qu'une nation? Conférence faite en Sorbonne, le 11 mars 1882*, 2nd ed. (Paris: Ancienne maison Michel Lévy frères, 1882).

Reut-Nicolussi, E. 'Displaced Persons and International Law', *RCADI* 73 (1948-II), 1.

Reynolds, Michael A. *Shattering Empires: The Clash and Collapse of the Ottoman and Russian Empires, 1908–1918* (Cambridge: Cambridge University Press, 2011).

Richmond, Walter. *The Circassian Genocide* (New Brunswick: Rutgers University Press, 2013).

Riddell, John, ed. *Toward the United Front: Proceedings of the Fourth Congress of the Communist International, 1922* (Chicago: Haymarket, 2011).

Robinson, Jacob et al. *Were the Minorities Treaties a Failure?* (New York: Institute of Jewish Affairs, 1943).

Roch, Michael P. 'Forced Displacement in the Former Yugoslavia: A Crime Under International Law?', *Dickinson Journal of International Law* 14 (1995), 1.

Rodogno, Davide. *Against Massacre: Humanitarian Interventions in the Ottoman Empire 1815–1914* (Princeton: Princeton University Press, 2012).

Rodrigue, Aron. *French Jews, Turkish Jews: The Alliance Israélite Universelle and the Politics of Jewish Schooling in Turkey, 1860–1925* (Bloomington: Indiana University Press, 1990).

Rolin-Jaequemyns, Gustave. 'Le droit international et la phase actuelle de la question d'Orient', *RDILC* 8 (1876), 293.

Root, Elihu. 'The Basis of Protection to Citizens Residing Abroad', *ASIL Pd.* 4 (1910), 16.

Root, Elihu. 'The Permanent Court of International Justice', *ASIL Pd.* 17 (1923), 1.

Ross, Frank A., C. Luther Fry, and Elbridge Sibley. *The Near East and American Philanthropy: A Survey Conducted under the Guidance of the General Committee of the Near East Survey* (New York: Columbia University Press, 1929).

Rosting, Helmer. 'Protection of Minorities by the League of Nations', *AJIL* 17 (1923), 641.

Rougier, Antoine. 'La question des Détroits et la convention de Lausanne', *RGDIP* 31 (1924), 309.

Rougier, Antoine. 'La théorie de l'intervention d'humanité', *RGDIP* 17 (1910), 468.

Rousseau, Jean-Jacques. *The Social Contract and Other Later Political Writings*, ed. Victor Gourevitch (Cambridge: Cambridge University Press, 1997).

Roy, Haimanti. *Partitioned Lives: Migrants, Refugees, Citizens in India and Pakistan, 1947–1965* (New Delhi: Oxford University Press, 2013).

Ruskola, Teemu. *Legal Orientalism: China, the United States, and Modern Law* (Cambridge: Harvard University Press, 2013).

Rustem Bey, A. 'The Future of the Oecumenical Patriarchate', *Foreign Affairs* 3 (1925), 604.

Samson, Marika Giles and Douglas Guilfoyle. 'The Permanent Court of International Justice and the "Invention" of International Advisory Jurisdiction', in *Legacies of the Permanent Court of International Justice*, ed. Christian J. Tams and Malgosia Fitzmaurice (Leiden: Nijhoff, 2013), 41.

Saraçoğlu, M. Safa. 'Some Aspects of Ottoman Governmentality at the Local Level: The Judicio-Administrative Sphere of the Vidin County in the 1860s and 1870s', *Ab Imperio* 2008 (2008-II), 223.

Sartiaux, Félix. 'Le sac de Phocée et l'expulsion des Grecs ottomans d'Asie-Mineure en juin 1914', *Revue des deux mondes* 24 (1914), 654.

Sauser-Hall, Georges. 'La réception des droits européens en Turquie', in *Recueil de travaux publié à l'occasion de l'Assemblée de la Société suisse des juristes à Genève, du 4 au 6 septembre 1938* (Genève: Imprimerie Albert Kundig, 1938), 323.

Schechtman, Joseph B. *European Population Transfers 1939–1945* (New York: Oxford University Press, 1946).

Schechtman, Joseph B. 'The Option Clause in the Reich's Treaties on the Transfer of Population', *AJIL* 38 (1944), 356.

Schenk, H. G. *The Aftermath of the Napoleonic Wars: The Concert of Europe—An Experiment* (London: Kegan Paul, 1947).

Scheuermann, Martin. *Minderheitenschutz contra Konfliktverhütung? Die Minderheitenpolitik des Völkerbundes in den zwanziger Jahren* (Marburg: Verlag Herder-Institut, 2000).

Schieder, Theodor, ed. *Documents on the Expulsion of the Germans from Eastern-Central-Europe*, 4 vols. (Bonn: Federal Ministry for Expellees, Refugees, and War Victims, n. d.).

Schmitt, Carl. *Constitutional Theory*, ed. and trans. Jeffrey Seitzer (Durham: Duke University Press, 2008 [1928]).

Schmitt, Carl. *The Crisis of Parliamentary Democracy*, trans. Ellen Kennedy (Cambridge: The MIT Press, 1988 [1923]).

Schmitt, Carl. *The* Nomos *of the Earth in the International Law of the* Jus Publicum Europaeum, trans. G. L. Ulmen (New York: Telos, 2003 [1950]).

Schroeder, Paul W. *The Transformation of European Politics 1763–1848* (Oxford: Clarendon Press, 1994).

Schulz, Matthias. '"Defenders of the Right"? Diplomatic Practice and International Law in the 19th Century: An Historian's Perspective', in *Constructing International Law: The Birth of a Discipline*, ed. Luigi Nuzzo and Miloš Vec (Frankfurt am Main: Klostermann, 2012), 251.

Schulz, Matthias. 'The Guarantees of Humanity: The Concert of Europe and the Origins of the Russo–Ottoman War of 1877', in *Humanitarian Intervention: A History*, ed. Brendan Simms and D. J. B. Trim (Cambridge: Cambridge University Press, 2011), 184.

Schwarzenberger, Georg. *The League of Nations and World Order: A Treatise on the Principle of Universality in the Theory and Practice of the League of Nations* (London: Constable & Co., 1936).

Schwarzenberger, Georg. 'The Standard of Civilisation in International Law', *Current Legal Problems* 8 (1955), 212.

Schwelb, Egon. 'Crimes against Humanity', *BYIL* 23 (1946), 178.

Scott, James Brown. 'La Déclaration internationale des droits de l'homme', *Revue de droit international* 5 (1930), 79.

Selâhattin Bey, Ahmet. 'Vekâlet ve Müzaheret' [1919], reproduced as 'Mandat ve Yardım', in *Lozan'ın 50. Yıl Armağanı* (İstanbul: Fakülteler Matbaası, 1978), 3.

Sezer, Ayten. *Atatürk Döneminde Yabancı Okullar (1923–1938)* (Ankara: Türk Tarih Kurumu Basımevi, 1999).

Séfériadès, Stelio. 'L'échange des populations', *RCADI* 24 (1928-IV), 307.

Shaw, Stanford J. *From Empire to Republic: The Turkish War of National Liberation 1918–1923: A Documentary Study*, vol. 2 (Ankara: Türk Tarih Kurumu Basımevi, 2000).

Shaw, Stanford J. 'Ottoman Population Movements during the Last Years of the Empire, 1885–1914: Some Preliminary Remarks', *Osmanlı Araştırmaları* 1 (1980), 191.

Shenfield, Stephen D. 'The Circassians: A Forgotten Genocide?', in *The Massacre in History*, ed. Mark Levene and Penny Roberts (Oxford: Berghahn, 1999), 149.

Shields, Sarah D. *Fezzes in the River: Identity Politics and European Diplomacy in the Middle East on the Eve of World War II* (New York: Oxford University Press, 2011).

Shimazu, Naoko. *Japan, Race and Equality: The Racial Equality Proposal of 1919* (London: Routledge, 1998).

Shupp, Paul F. *The European Powers and the Near Eastern Question 1806–1807* (New York: Columbia University Press, 1931).

Simpson, Gerry. *Great Powers and Outlaw States: Unequal Sovereigns in the International Legal Order* (Cambridge: Cambridge University Press, 2004).

Simpson, John Hope. *The Refugee Problem: Report of a Survey* (London: Oxford University Press, 1939).

Skouteris, Thomas. *The Notion of Progress in International Law Discourse* (The Hague: T. M. C. Asser Press, 2010).

Skran, Claudena M. *Refugees in Inter-war Europe: The Emergence of a Regime* (Oxford: Clarendon Press, 1995).

Smith, Leonard V. 'Wilsonian Sovereignty in the Middle East: The King-Crane Commission Report of 1919', in *The State of Sovereignty: Territories, Laws, Populations*, ed. Douglas Howland and Luise White (Bloomington: Indiana University Press, 2009), 56.

Smith, Neil. *American Empire: Roosevelt's Geographer and the Prelude to Globalization* (Berkeley: University of California Press, 2003).

Smuts, J. C. *The League of Nations: A Practical Suggestion* (London: Hodder and Stoughton, 1918).

Soguk, Nevzat. *States and Strangers: Refugees and Displacements of Statecraft* (Minneapolis: University of Minnesota Press, 1999).

Solonari, Vladimir. *Purifying the Nation: Population Exchange and Ethnic Cleansing in Nazi-Allied Romania* (Washington: Woodrow Wilson Center Press/Baltimore: Johns Hopkins University Press, 2010).

Soner, B. Ali. 'Citizenship and the Minority Question in Turkey', in *Citizenship in a Global World: European Questions and Turkish Experiences*, ed. E. Fuat Keyman and Ahmet İçduygu (London: Routledge, 2005), 289.

Sousa, Nasim. *The Capitulatory Régime of Turkey: Its History, Origin, and Nature* (Baltimore: The Johns Hopkins Press, 1933).

Soutou, Georges-Henri. 'Le Concert européen, de Vienne à Locarno', in *L'ordre européen du XVIe au XXe siècle. Actes du colloque de l'Institut des recherches sur les civilisations de l'Occident moderne, 15–16 mars 1996*, ed. Jean Bérenger and Georges-Henri Soutou (Paris: Presses de l'Université de Paris-Sorbonne, 1998), 117.

Spiermann, Ole. *International Legal Argument in the Permanent Court of International Justice: The Rise of the International Judiciary* (Cambridge: Cambridge University Press, 2005).

Spiermann, Ole. 'Judge Max Huber at the Permanent Court of International Justice', *EJIL* 18 (2007), 115.

Stahn, Carsten. *The Law and Practice of International Territorial Administration: Versailles to Iraq and Beyond* (Cambridge: Cambridge University Press, 2008).

Stavropoulou, Maria. 'The Right Not to be Displaced', *American University Journal of International Law and Policy* 9 (1994), 689.

Stone, Julius. *International Guarantees of Minority Rights: Procedure of the Council of the League of Nations in Theory and Practice* (London: Oxford University Press, 1932).

Stone, Julius. *Regional Guarantees of Minority Rights: A Study of Minorities Procedure in Upper Silesia* (New York: Macmillan, 1933).

Stone, Julius. 'The Legal Nature of the Minorities Petition', *BYIL* 12 (1931), 76.

Stouraiti, Anastasia and Alexander Kazamias. 'The Imaginary Topographies of the *Megali Idea*: National Territory as Utopia', in *Spatial Conceptions of the Nation: Modernizing Geographies in Greece and Turkey*, ed. P. Nikiforos Diamandouros, Thalia Dragonas, and Çağlar Keyder (London: Tauris, 2010), 11.

Stowell, Ellery C. *Intervention in International Law* (Washington: John Byrne & Co., 1921).

Stuart, John. 'Beyond Sovereignty?: Protestant Missions, Empire and Transnationalism, 1890–1950', in *Beyond Sovereignty: Britain, Empire and Transnationalism, c. 1880–1950*, ed. Kevin Grant, Philippa Levine, and Frank Trentmann (Houndmills: Palgrave Macmillan, 2007), 103.

Sultan Galiev. 'The Social Revolution and the East' [1919], reproduced in *Muslim National Communism in the Soviet Union: A Revolutionary Strategy for the Colonial World*, ed. Alexandre A. Bennigsen and S. Enders Wimbush (Chicago: University of Chicago Press, 1979), 131.

Sylvest, Casper. 'International Law in Nineteenth-Century Britain', *BYIL* 75 (2004), 9.

Symonds, Arthur G. 'The Balkan Committee 1905–1913', in *Memories of John Westlake* (London: Smith, Elder, & Co., 1914), 107.

Szporluk, Roman. *Communism and Nationalism: Karl Marx versus Friedrich List* (New York: Oxford University Press, 1988).

Şeker, Nesim. 'Demographic Engineering in the Late Ottoman Empire and the Armenians', *Middle Eastern Studies* 43 (2007), 461.

Şimşir, Bilâl N., ed. *Lozan Telgrafları: Türk Diplomatik Belgelerinde Lozan Barış Konferansı*, vol. 1 (Ankara: Türk Tarih Kurumu Basımevi, 1990).

Şimşir, Bilâl N., ed. *Rumeli'den Türk Göçleri*, 3 vols. (Ankara: Türk Tarih Kurumu Basımevi, 1989).

Tanör, Bülent. *Osmanlı-Türk Anayasal Gelişmeleri (1789–1980)* (İstanbul: Yapı Kredi Yayınları, 1998).

Tanzimat I. *Yüzüncü Yıldönümü Münasebetile* (İstanbul: Maarif Matbaası, 1940).

Taylor, A. J. P. *The Struggle for Mastery in Europe 1848–1918* (Oxford: Clarendon Press, 1954).

Tejirian, Eleanor H. and Reeva Spector Simon. *Conflict, Conquest, and Conversion: Two Thousand Years of Christian Missions in the Middle East* (New York: Columbia University Press, 2012).

Temperley, H. W. V. 'The Treaty of Paris of 1856 and Its Execution', *Journal of Modern History* 4 (1932), 387 and 523 (in two parts).

Teyssaire, Jean. 'Les concessions et le Traité de Lausanne', *RGDIP* 35 (1928), 447.

Ténékidès, C. G. 'Le statut des minorités et l'échange obligatoire des populations gréco–turques', *RGDIP* 31 (1924), 72.

'The Periphery Series: Alejandro Álvarez' (symposium), *Leiden Journal of International Law* 19 (2006).

Thompson, Joseph P. 'The Intercourse of Christian with Non-Christian Peoples' [1876], in Joseph P. Thompson, *American Comments on European Questions, International and Religious* (Boston: Houghton, Mifflin & Co., 1884), 104.

Thornberry, Patrick. *International Law and the Rights of Minorities* (Oxford: Clarendon Press, 1991).

Todorov, Nikolai. 'Sur quelques aspects du passage du féodalisme au capitalisme dans les territoires balkaniques de l'Empire ottoman', *Revue des études sud-est européennes* 1 (1963), 103.

Todorova, Maria. *Imagining the Balkans* (New York: Oxford University Press, 1997).

Toprak, Zafer. *Türkiye'de 'Milli İktisat' (1908–1918)* (Ankara: Yurt Yayınları, 1982).

Torpey, John. *The Invention of the Passport: Surveillance, Citizenship and the State* (Cambridge: Cambridge University Press, 2000).

Toumarkine, Alexandre. *Les migrations des populations musulmanes balkaniques en Anatolie (1876–1913)* (Istanbul: Les éditions Isis, 1995).

Toynbee, Arnold J. 'The East after Lausanne', *Foreign Affairs* 2 (1923), 84.

Toyoda, Tetsuya. 'L'aspect universaliste du droit international européen du 19ème siècle et le statut juridique de la Turquie avant 1856', *Journal of the History of International Law* 8 (2006), 19.

Trubek, David M., Yves Dezalay, Ruth Buchanan, and John R. Davis. 'Global Restructuring and the Law: Studies of the Internationalization of Legal Fields and the Creation of Transnational Arenas', *Case Western Reserve Law Review* 44 (1994), 407.

Tsitselikis, Konstantinos. *Old and New Islam in Greece: From Historical Minorities to Immigrant Newcomers* (Leiden: Nijhoff, 2012).

Tunaya, Tarık Zafer. *Türkiye'de Siyasal Partiler*, 2nd ed., vol. 2 (İstanbul: Hürriyet Vakfı Yayınları, 1986).

Turlington, Edgar. 'The Settlement of Lausanne', *AJIL* 18 (1924), 696.

Tusan, Michelle. '"Crimes Against Humanity": Human Rights, the British Empire, and the Origins of the Response to the Armenian Genocide', *American Historical Review* 119 (2014), 47.

Twiss, Travers. *On Consular Jurisdiction in the Levant, and the Status of Foreigners in the Ottoman Law Courts* (London: William Clowes & Sons, 1880).

Twiss, Travers. 'Rapport', *AIDI* 3–4 (1879–80), 301.

Ursinus, M. O. H. 'Millet', in *The Encyclopaedia of Islam: New Edition*, vol. 7, ed. C. E. Bosworth et al. (Leiden: Brill, 1990), 61.

Üngör, Uğur Ümit. *The Making of Modern Turkey: Nation and State in Eastern Anatolia, 1913–1950* (Oxford: Oxford University Press, 2011).

Üngör, Uğur Ümit. '"Turkey for the Turks": Demographic Engineering in Eastern Anatolia, 1914–1945', in *A Question of Genocide: Armenians and Turks at the End of the Ottoman Empire*, ed. Ronald Grigor Suny, Fatma Müge Göçek, and Norman M. Naimark (Oxford: Oxford University Press, 2011), 287.

Vagts, Detlev F. 'International Law in the Third Reich', *AJIL* 84 (1990), 661.

van den Boogert, Maurits H. *The Capitulations and the Ottoman Legal System: Qadis, Consuls, and* Beratlıs *in the 18th Century* (Leiden: Brill, 2005).

Venizelos, El. K. *Greece in Her True Light: Her Position in the World-Wide War*, trans. Socrates A. Xanthaky and Nicholas G. Sakellarios (New York: Socrates A. Xanthaky and Nicholas G. Sakellarios, 1916).

Verzijl, J. H. W. *The Jurisprudence of the World Court: A Case by Case Commentary*, vol. 1 (Leiden: Sijthoff, 1965).

Vinogradoff, Paul. 'Historical Types of International Law' [1923], in *The Collected Papers of Paul Vinogradoff, With a Memoir by The Right Hon. H. A. L. Fisher*, vol. 2 (Oxford: Clarendon Press, 1928), 248.

von Elbe, Joachim. 'Peacemaking in 1815', *AJIL* 36 (1942), 470.

von Jhering, Rudolph. *Der Zweck im Recht*, vol. 1 (Leipzig: Druck und Verlag von Breitkopf & Härtel, 1877).

von Liszt, Franz. *Das Völkerrecht, systematisch dargestellt* (Berlin: Verlag von O. Haering, 1898).

von Treitschke, Heinrich. *Politik: Vorlesungen, gehalten an der Universität zu Berlin*, vol. 1 (Leipzig: Verlag von S. Hirzel, 1899).

Voorhees, Dayton. 'The League of Nations: A Corporation, not a Superstate', *American Political Science Review* 20 (1926), 847.

Vucinich, Wayne S. 'The Nature of Balkan Society under Ottoman Rule', *Slavic Review* 21 (1962), 597.

Wallerstein, Immanuel. *The Modern World-System IV: Centrist Liberalism Triumphant, 1789–1914* (Berkeley: University of California Press, 2011).

Wallerstein, Immanuel, Hale Decdeli, and Reşat Kasaba. 'The Incorporation of the Ottoman Empire into the World-Economy', in *The Ottoman Empire and the World-Economy*, ed. Huri İslamoğlu-İnan (Cambridge: Cambridge University Press, 1987), 88.

Wambaugh, Sarah. *Plebiscites since the World War, with a Collection of Official Documents*, vol. 1 (Washington: Carnegie Endowment for International Peace, 1933).

Watenpaugh, Keith David. 'The League of Nations' Rescue of Armenian Genocide Survivors and the Making of Modern Humanitarianism, 1920–1927', *American Historical Review* 115 (2010), 1315.

Waters, Timothy William. 'The Blessing of Departure: Acceptable and Unacceptable State Support for Demographic Transformation: The Lieberman Plan to Exchange Populated Territories in Cisjordan', *Law and Ethics of Human Rights* 2 (2008), 221.

Webster, Donald E. 'State Control of Social Change in Republican Turkey', *American Sociological Review* 4 (1939), 247.

Weitz, Eric D. 'From the Vienna to the Paris System: International Politics and the Entangled Histories of Human Rights, Forced Deportations, and Civilizing Missions', *American Historical Review* 113 (2008), 1313.

Wertheim, Stephen. 'The League of Nations: A Retreat from International Law?', *Journal of Global History* 7 (2012), 210.

Westad, Odd Arne. *The Global Cold War: Third World Interventions and the Making of Our Times* (Cambridge: Cambridge University Press, 2005).

Westlake, John. *Chapters on the Principles of International Law* (Cambridge: Cambridge University Press, 1894).

Westlake, John. 'Territorial Sovereignty, Especially with Relation to Uncivilised Regions', in *The Collected Papers of John Westlake on Public International Law*, ed. Lassa Oppenheim (Cambridge: Cambridge University Press, 1914), 131.

Westlake, John. 'The Balkan Question and International Law', *The Nineteenth Century and After* 60 (1906), 889.

Wheaton, Henry. *Elements of International Law, With a Sketch of the History of the Science* (Philadelphia: Carey, Lea & Blanchard, 1836).

Wheeler-Bennett, J. W. and Maurice Fanshawe. *Information on the World Court, 1918–1928* (London: George Allen & Unwin, 1929).

White, Benjamin Thomas. *The Emergence of Minorities in the Middle East: The Politics of Community in French Mandate Syria* (Edinburgh: Edinburgh University Press, 2011).

White, Wilbur Wallace. 'The Status in International Law of the Fragments of the Ottoman Empire' (PhD dissertation, University of Chicago, 1935).

Williams, Brian Glyn. '*Hijra* and Forced Migration from Nineteenth-Century Russia to the Ottoman Empire: A Critical Analysis of the Great Crimean Tatar Emigration of 1860–1861', *Cahiers du monde russe* 41 (2000), 79.

Wilson, Robert R. 'Some Aspects of Treaty Interpretation', *AJIL* 33 (1939), 541.

Winfield, P. H. 'The Grounds of Intervention in International Law', *BYIL* 5 (1924), 149.

Wood, Alfred C. *A History of the Levant Company* (London: Oxford University Press, 1935).

Wooldridge, Frank and Vishnu D. Sharma. 'The Expulsion of the Ugandan Asians and Some Legal Questions Arising Therefrom', *Comparative and International Law Journal of Southern Africa* 7 (1974), 1.

Woolsey, L. H. 'The Unilateral Termination of Treaties', *AJIL* 20 (1926), 346.

Worringer, Renée. '"Sick Man of Europe" or "Japan of the Near East"?: Constructing Ottoman Modernity in the Hamidian and Young Turk Eras', *International Journal of Middle East Studies* 36 (2004), 207.
Wright, Quincy. 'The Interpretation of Multilateral Treaties', *AJIL* 23 (1929), 94.
Wright, Quincy. 'The Mosul Dispute', *AJIL* 20 (1926), 453.
Wurfbain, André. *L'échange gréco–bulgare des minorités ethniques* (Lausanne: Librairie Payot & Cie, 1930).
Yerasimos, Stefanos. *Türk–Sovyet İlişkileri: Ekim Devriminden 'Millî Mücadele'ye* (İstanbul: Gözlem Yayınları, 1979).
Yıldırım, Onur. *Diplomacy and Displacement: Reconsidering the Turco–Greek Exchange of Populations, 1922–1934* (New York: Routledge, 2006).
Yıldırım, Onur. 'The 1923 Population Exchange, Refugees and National Historiographies in Greece and Turkey', *East European Quarterly* 40 (2006), 45.
Yurdusev, A. Nuri. 'The Ottoman Attitude toward Diplomacy', in *Ottoman Diplomacy: Conventional or Unconventional?*, ed. A. Nuri Yurdusev (Houndmills: Palgrave Macmillan, 2004), 5.
Yü, Tsune-Chi. *The Interpretation of Treaties* (New York: Columbia University Press, 1927).
Zeman, Z. A. B. and W. B. Scharlau. *The Merchant of Revolution: The Life of Alexander Israel Helphand (Parvus) 1867–1924* (London: Oxford University Press, 1965).
Zimmern, Alfred. *The League of Nations and the Rule of Law, 1918–1935* (London: Macmillan, 1936).
Zürcher, Erik Jan. 'How Europeans Adopted Anatolia and Created Turkey', *European Review* 13 (2005), 379.
Zürcher, Erik Jan. 'The Late Ottoman Empire as Laboratory of Demographic Engineering', *Il mestiere di storico* 1 (2009), 7.
Zürcher, Erik Jan. *The Unionist Factor: The Rôle of the Committee of Union and Progress in the Turkish National Movement, 1905–1926* (Leiden: Brill, 1984).
Zürcher, Erik Jan. *The Young Turk Legacy and Nation Building: From the Ottoman Empire to Atatürk's Turkey* (London: I.B. Tauris, 2010).
Zürcher, Erik Jan. 'The Young Turks: Children of the Borderlands?', *International Journal of Turkish Studies* 9 (2003), 275.

Index